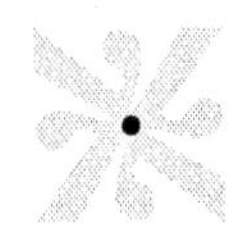

Keeping the Peace

Lasting Solutions to Ethnic Conflicts

Daniel L. Byman

The Johns Hopkins University Press
BALTIMORE AND LONDON

Printed in the United States of America on acid-free paper

9 8 7 6 5 4 3 2 1

The Johns Hopkins University Press
2715 North Charles Street
Baltimore, Maryland 21218-4363
www.press.jhu.edu

Library of Congress Cataloging-in-Publication Data
Byman, Daniel, 1967–
Keeping the peace : lasting solutions to ethnic conflicts / Daniel L. Byman.
p. cm.
Includes bibliographical references and index.
ISBN 0-8018-6804-1
1. Ethnic conflict—Political aspects. 2. World politics—1989– 3. Nationalism—Middle East. 4. Nationalism—Europe. 5. Middle East—Politics and government—20th century. 6. Europe—Ethnic relations. I. Title.
GN496 .B96 2002
305.8'009'05—dc21 2001001324

A catalog record for this book is available from the British Library.

CONTENTS

PREFACE

This is a book about ethnic conflict and how to prevent it. This study draws on past successes and failures of ethnic relations in order to shed light on how to stop ethnic conflict from recurring in the future. It focuses on what governments can do to prevent violence in the long term. Although the conclusions reached have implications for conflict in general, this effort devotes relatively little attention to the questions of how to stop conflict from occurring at all, what role non-government actors should play, how conflicts that are non-ethnic in nature should be handled, or how best to bring warring parties to the negotiating table.

The study of ethnic conflict is a once-minor but now-burgeoning field. The end of the Cold War and the subsequent surge in communal strife focused both public and scholarly attention on the problem and generated an explosion of empirical and theoretical work. When possible, I have tried to gather the insights of contemporary scholars, but I recognize that our knowledge of this field is growing beyond the capacity of any volume to capture. I hope, however, that the following chapters reflect many of the lessons learned by scholars in recent years and offer new insights, both theoretical and empirical.

Much of the data for my own work comes from studies of ethnic relations in the Middle East. In addition to my deep personal interest in the politics and peoples of the Middle East, the region is a fruitful place for the study of ethnic relations for several reasons. First, the Middle East contains a wide range of ethnic groups with strong ethnic identities. Arabs, Jews, Kurds, Persians, Berbers, and other communal groups have their own languages, political leaderships, and political cultures. In addition, the Middle East is home to both resolved and unresolved conflicts. This variance also allows us to learn from both successes and failures when studying strategies designed to prevent the recurrence of ethnic conflict. Another advantage for my purposes is that outside powers have played a major role in many Middle Eastern ethnic conflicts. Thus, a study of this region should produce insights into one of my key questions: how do outside powers affect attempts to keep the peace? Moreover, states in the Middle East have employed a wide variety of policies to manage ethnic relations, offering a wealth of information to the student of ethnic conflict. Furthermore, the range of regimes in the Middle East includes both strong and weak central governments, which some scholars posit as a key determinant of managing political turmoil. Finally, in elaborating my theories, I have drawn on both Western history and the studies of several scholars studying non-Arab and non-Muslim regions. I believe my work may add to their developed theories and benefit by employing ideas already tested in other parts of the world. (Of course, where the Middle East cases do not offer sufficient insights for the answers I seek, I freely borrow from the history of other regions.) This methodologically based focus on the Middle East, however, should not obscure my devotion to the region and my hope that peace and good government, both at home and between the region's countries, will come eventually.[1]

Interviews in both the United States and the Middle East supplemented my research. I would like to thank individuals at the Department of State, the Department of Defense, the Central Intelligence Agency, the Embassy of Israel, and the Center for Cross-Cultural Learning for their time and their assistance in helping me set up interviews. Given the highly sensitive nature of the subject, the majority of those interviewed asked not to be identified by name. Their anonymity should not diminish their importance to my work.

Many people helped in the research, writing, and final production of this book. First credit should go to the late Myron Weiner, who stimulated the idea for this project when it was a dissertation and who guided my imagination at every stage of my initial research. He will be fondly remembered by all lucky enough to have known him. Stephen Van Evera also deserves my warmest thanks. His rigor, and his personal commitment to his students, is a model for us all. Susan Gilson Miller gently directed me toward the most fruitful parts of my research, anticipating what was most exciting and rewarding to learn from the Middle East. Her enthusiasm and easy laugh made the effort far more enjoyable and more productive.

Several institutions provided financial and other forms of support. The MacArthur Foundation Transnational Security Issues program provided pre-doctoral support for work on this topic. A number of people at the RAND Corporation were invaluable in their assistance. Jerrold Green provided numerous insights and constant encouragement. Judy Lewis helped turn a fledgling product into a final project through her enthusiasm, editorial assistance, and willingness to publicize and promote my work. Rachel Fischer Alberts and Maria E. denBoer edited this book, tightening its conclusions and strengthening its writing. Henry Tom and Michael Lonegro of the Johns Hopkins University Press guided this book to its completion.

Several chapters in this book drew on previously published journal articles I wrote. These articles are: "The Logic of Ethnic Terrorism," *Studies in Conflict and Terrorism* 21, no. 2 (April–June 1998): 149–69; "Forever Enemies? The Manipulation of Ethnic Identities to End Ethnic Wars," *Security Studies* 9, no. 3 (Spring 2000): 149–90; "Rethinking Partition: Lessons from Iraq and Lebanon," *Security Studies* 7, no. 1 (Autumn 1997): 1–32; "Why They Fight: Hypotheses On the Causes of Contemporary Deadly Violence," *Security Studies* (Spring 1998): 1–50 (co-authored with Stephen Van Evera); and "Explaining Ethnic Peace in Morocco," *Harvard Middle East and Islamic Review* 4, nos. 1–2 (1997–98): 1–29. The journals have given permission to reprint selections from these essays.

The following people commented on various chapters at certain stages in their development or as academic articles: F. Gregory Gause III, Chaim Kaufmann, Kenneth Pollack, Bruce Pirnie, Daryl Press, Jeremy Shapiro, and Benjamin Valentino. Taylor Seybolt deserves particular credit for the material in Chapter 8, which he helped draft and research as part of an essay we co-authored. An anonymous reviewer for the Johns Hopkins University Press went above and beyond the duties of a press reviewer, offering many helpful suggestions. Needless to say, these individuals do not necessarily agree with the arguments in this book, and any mistakes are the author's alone despite their considerable help.

And for everything, but for her patience most of all, I would like to thank my wife Victoria.

Keeping the Peace

1 Ethnic Conflict in Today's World

In an era when different peoples seem perpetually at war, it is peace and harmony that demand explanation. Some scholars and statesmen argue that peace will almost never last after a bloody communal conflict. These pessimists note that the memory of conflict leaves communal groups highly sensitive to their security, making them likely to take up arms again. Furthermore, regimes often mistreat losers in communal conflicts. This mistreatment, combined with the memory of violence, keeps communal groups mistrustful of one another and reduces communal cooperation. Not surprisingly, ethnic wars are often seen as inevitable or impossible to resolve.

Pessimists, however, overstate their case. Communal conflict is a common event in history, but so too is lasting communal peace. Sectarian, tribal, and ethnic conflicts plagued Western Europe, and ancient texts from the *Iliad* to the Bible indicate the prevalence of communal warfare. Many of these conflicts, however, are resolved and forgotten. The ancestors of Visigoths no longer trample across Spain, and the sons of strong-greaved Achaeans do not endlessly besiege Phrygians at Troy. Peoples often have put the past behind them, learning to live together in peace and at times even in harmony.

This book explores how to prevent the recurrence of ethnic conflict, focusing specifically on the policies governments should use if they seek to prevent ethnic conflict from erupting repeatedly. It attempts to answer the following questions: What strategies can a government use to end violent ethnic conflict in the long term? Under what conditions do these strategies work best? What are the disadvantages of the various strategies? When can outside powers help foster peace?

The bloody and durable nature of ethnic conflict around the globe gives these questions special importance today. Internal conflict—ethnic and sectarian conflict in particular—is the dominant form of violence in the world, far bloodier than interstate wars.[1] In the 1990s, these conflicts claimed millions of lives, produced tens of millions of refugees, and caused billions of dollars in damage. Moreover, these wars tend to last longer and be more difficult to resolve through negotiation than interstate wars.[2] Ethnic divisions also threaten the growth of democracy. Trust, fairness, and a willingness to surrender power peacefully—all of which are necessary for democracy—are difficult to generate and preserve in the climate of fear that accompanies ethnic conflict.

Communal conflicts regularly recur. Since the end of World War II, conflicts in Angola, Burundi, Burma, Ethiopia, India, Iraq, Rwanda, Sudan, and Turkey all have recurred, with occasional years of peace broken by the renewal of war. Millions of people died when these conflicts flared anew. In many instances, the conflict has recurred with growing intensity. Conflict and pogroms in Rwanda killed tens of thousands in the 1950s, 1960s, and 1970s, and hundreds of thousands in the 1990s. Iraq exhibited a similarly alarming pattern of small-scale tribal revolts that became widespread unrest in the 1960s which, over time, led to truly genocidal levels of slaughter in the 1980s. Other wars, such as the long-standing civil wars in Sudan and Angola, appear endless. In both these disputes, numerous treaties were negotiated and power-sharing arrangements were considered, but in reality, any pause in fighting was simply a respite for the warring parties, which renewed the conflict later with equal or greater intensity.

Communal conflicts are particularly dangerous because they often spread and draw in outside powers. At the most basic (and most altruistic) level, outside powers become involved with the care and feeding of refugees, a task that is highly political when the refugees are also combatants in a communal war. Outside governments may also provide a haven or material assistance to warring parties. This aid may be motivated by sympathy toward one party due to bonds of kinship, an effort to increase regional influence, or a desire to weaken or overthrow a neighboring government that is unfriendly. Even when an outside government itself is not an active supporter of parties within a conflict, groups within that country may provide assistance that fuels a war.

As a result, conflict often spreads. Warring parties may even strike at enemy bases and supporters across state boundaries. At several times in the 1990s Turkey sent forces across Iraq's borders to crush Kurdish insurgents. At several points in the 1980s, the Soviet Union bombed Afghan refugee camps in Pakistan to intimidate Islamabad. During the 1994-96 conflict with Moscow, Chechen guerrillas struck deep into Russian territory to bring the war home to the Russian people. Sudan and Ethiopia regularly fostered ethnic insurgencies in each other's countries. Such intervention is the rule, not the exception, in communal conflict. Many disputes in a given country may also be carried on among ethnic kin living abroad. Fighting in refugee camps in Pakistan often occurred in response to tension among factions fighting in Afghanistan.

Indeed, ethnic conflicts can spread far beyond their initial locations, pulling in powers from around the world. The United States regularly took sides in communal wars during the Cold War, aiding belligerents in Afghanistan, Angola, Somalia, and elsewhere. In recent years, Washington has sent troops to Bosnia, Somalia, Iraq, and other lands home to ethnic struggles. Russia has supported groups in Afghanistan and throughout its former empire. France too has sent troops to many of its former colonies in Africa to prop up local allies, or, more rarely, to bring peace in a communal war.

Under the most troubling circumstances, groups or governments may try to foster an internal war in the supporting country itself, creating a new conflict that can grow and spread. Liberian rebels under Charles Taylor supported an insurgency in Sierra Leone to punish that government for supporting anti-Taylor forces in Liberia. The Rwandan government sought to crush remaining Hutu forces of the previous regime—one that had carried out a true genocide in 1994 against Rwanda's Tutsi population and Hutu moderates—by overthrowing the government in Congo (then Zaire) and installing a new regime that would ensure that Hutus there could not operate against Rwanda. Ethnicity does not respect national borders; ethnic wars do not either.

Policy Errors

The failure to understand how to prevent violent ethnic conflicts from recurring has contributed to disaster after disaster. Democratic institutions that might otherwise bring people together have instead helped to separate them. The freedom of speech that came to the former Soviet Union after it collapsed, for example, often allowed demagogues to inflame communal tension in several successor states. Government decrees of national unity typically have led to fears among minorities that their unique identities would be swallowed up by the nation-state. Various attempts by Burma's government to build a nation-state based on a Burmese identity led the Karen, the Kachin, and other communal groups to fear that their cultures would be obliterated. Efforts to promote local government institutions or otherwise employ federalism often worsened conflict by allowing communal groups to gain the resources necessary to fight a sustained and bloody conflict.

Foreign interventions can even inadvertently contribute to mass killings that far exceed the original problem. In 1994, for example, Western pressure on the Rwandan leaders compelled them to offer compromises to Tutsi rebels—compromises that alarmed Hutu extremists and led them to commit genocide rather than accept even limited power-sharing.[3] Similarly, the failure to recognize that ethnic conflict spreads leads outside powers to ignore conflict or even to exacerbate it unintentionally. Western humanitarian relief to Hutu refugees in what was then Zaire inadvertently aided Hutu fighters in their ongoing struggle with the Tutsi regime in Rwanda. Because the Hutus remained strong and dangerous in exile, the Tutsi regime intervened in Zaire and started a war there.[4] In short, even well-intentioned governments doing what they thought were purely humanitarian tasks have made grievous mistakes because their leaders have not understood what, if any, specific conditions were necessary for their policies to succeed.

Purpose of This Book

These policy errors occur in part because we do not know how to keep the peace. Local governments, humanitarian organizations, and intervening powers regularly repeat mistakes, leaving disaster in their wake. The intention of this book is to help educate scholars, students, journalists, soldiers, aid workers, and others concerned with the horrors of ethnic violence on ways to prevent ethnic conflict from recurring. This is accomplished by reviewing potential solutions—ideas presented by academic experts and drawn from the practices of governments—to the problem of recurring conflict and noting their advantages, disadvantages, and difficulties. A more successful record of intervention and prevention of course depends on many factors, but a better understanding of the potential solutions is one important step.

We lack a silver bullet for the problem of enduring ethnic strife. Many of the solutions presented in this book often work only under rare conditions or have serious drawbacks. Rather than gloss over these weaknesses, this book looks at the various possible strategies, warts and all. This lack of an ideal solution is frustrating, but it does reflect the complexity of the problem and the trade-offs inherent in all the solutions presented. I believe that the reader will find that, although there are no perfect solutions, there are better ones and better ways to implement them.

Key Definitions

Ethnic conflict is a widely used term that everyone understands. However, everyone understands it in a different way. This problem is exacerbated by the muddiness of the concept in question. Where an ethnicity begins and ends—and its relationship to other ambiguous group labels such as *tribe* and *nation*—is itself a question that has consumed scholarly attention for decades. Moreover, to the confusion of many, the term *conflict* is often used as a synonym for *tension*. And when a conflict "ends," a term so loaded with finality and certainty that any careful scholar shuns it, is also hard to discern. To avoid confusion, let me next define several important terms central to this book.

An *ethnic group* is a group of people bound together by a belief of common kinship and group distinctiveness, often reinforced by religion, language, and history.[5] Somewhat arbitrarily, I also define an ethnic group as one that numbers, or has numbered, over ten thousand people. Examples of ethnic groups are Russians (a common language, perceptions of a shared history) and Jews (belief in common ancestry reinforced by a common religion and history). Large tribal groups, such as the Aith Waryaghar tribal confederation in the Rif mountains in Morocco or the Bakhtiyari tribe of the Zagros area in Iran fall into this category as well.

The definition of an ethnic group is bound up in considerable controversy. Some scholars focus on language, others on kinship, and still others on a sense of shared boundaries. Although all these factors are important, I employ a broader definition that focuses on the beliefs of the actors involved, not on the reality of their ties. These ties, however weak or imaginary to outsiders, carry immense emotional weight. Thus, sophisticated European Jews at the birth of the Zionist movement in the late nineteenth century saw themselves as kin to worldwide Jewry, much of which neither spoke the same language, shared the same customs, nor identified with the Zionist cause. Nonetheless, they formed a community. In contrast, Somalia has a single dominant language, but Somali society is so divided by clan and kinship that most actors don't think of a Somali ethnicity.

Such ties are difficult to test empirically. For example, two Somalis who share a belief in a common ancestor and thus believe they are distinct from others who do not share that ancestor would be part of the same ethnic group even if this ancestor never existed. Two blood brothers, who for reasons of adoption do not consider themselves to be kin, would not be of the same ethnicity. Religion, language, and history also are imperfect fits. One can have Catholics who do not see themselves as having blood ties, or English speakers who do not see themselves as part of the same national family. Nevertheless, these ties can bind people together, leading them to die, and kill, in the name of their group.

An *ethnic conflict* is a violent conflict between ethnic groups or between an ethnic group and government forces that consist of one or more different ethnic groups. There are two main types of conflict: group versus group conflict, with the government acting as a third party of some kind (e.g., Hindu-Muslim riots in India) and group versus government conflict, where the government is an active party acting on behalf of one ethnic group (e.g., Tamil rebellions against the Sinhalese-dominated central government in Sri Lanka). Ethnic conflict, according to my definition, also embraces sectarian conflict, as long as the religious groups in question operate essentially as a community, as defined above. Maronite Christians and Druze in Lebanon, for example, fought along lines of religion that conveyed group distinctiveness. Given my definition of an ethnic group, intertribal warfare also falls into this category. This book examines all these types of conflict even though, as we shall see, their solutions are often quite different.[6]

I consider an ethnic conflict successfully terminated when deaths fall below a hundred per year for a minimum of twenty years. The deaths in question exclude murder done for personal or economic reasons not linked to ethnic sentiment. Deaths, of course, are only one measure of conflict. Rape, riots, and other forms of violence all are common to ethnic conflicts. Information on deaths in conflict, however, is often more reliable and easier to obtain than information on rape, rioting, or other forms of violence.[7] Thus, we should consider the death threshold a proximate measure for the overall level of conflict, recognizing that it is only one measure of conflict and that other forms of violence remain important to the phenomenon of ethnic conflict in general.

Values in Conflict

What constitutes success or failure when declaring that an ethnic conflict has been resolved? Ethnic harmony can be measured across a wide range of criteria, all of them estimable according to their own lights. Different answers to this question can result in vastly different policy prescriptions.

The most important measure of success, and the focus of this book, is human lives. Ethnic conflicts have a body count that can number in the millions, and regularly numbers in the hundreds of thousands. For any policy to plausibly claim to have ameliorated ethnic conflict, it must end the killing, or at least reduce it to low levels.

Self-determination is another value that is often at stake in ethnic conflicts. Many statesmen, scholars, and activists have long championed the right of peoples, a vague but real term, to govern themselves. The international community has shied away from declaring a right to self-determination, preferring instead to emphasize the sovereignty of existing states over the claims of the peoples within them. Yet increasingly international law is discussing the right of secession and increasing its focus on minority rights at the expense of state sovereignty.[8]

If sovereignty remains a supreme value, however, the right and duty of intervention itself comes into question. If governments are allowed to order their political affairs, determining when they have stepped over the line and merit intervention is difficult. Is it fair to say that governments should have the right to battle an ethnic insurgency demanding secession? If so, are there limits on the tactics it can use (i.e., no arbitrary detention or mass arrests)? Can it suppress free expression, if that expression is fueling a broader conflict? At what point do other nations have the right to intervene? And when does this right become a duty? Different leaders, different scholars, and different countries will have different policies as to when other concerns outweigh sovereignty and what their duties are in these cases.

Cultural diversity is often at issue. Promoting assimilation and adherence to a common identity is a frequent tactic to prevent ethnic divisions from spilling into conflict. In even the most benign countries, governments use education, national holidays, and other means to instill pride in the country as a whole that transcends rival identities. But these efforts often come at the price of cultural diversity. Although pluralism is not anathema to a unified state, it is often true that when individuals assimilate, groups lose their distinctiveness.[9] As Fernando Teson notes, "For ethnic identity as a political normative principle has a double face. In its kind face, the principle seems to stand for inclusion and vindication of some lofty cultural trait of which the members of the group are proud. But in its unkind face, the principle endorses ethnic homogeneity."[10] Turkey provides an example of this tension. The Turkish state seeks to standardize its citizenry, making them accept a Turkish nationality and language. This policy denies cultural diversity and involves the repression of alternative group identities.[11]

Ethnic claims also bring up a question of citizenship, the criteria for which vary widely by country. Citizenship is often defined in territorial terms: anyone who is a permanent resident in a country has a right to become a citizen there. Other countries use a civic judgment, demanding adherence to a common set of laws and institutions. Still others determine citizenship by when a person's ancestors arrived in a country, excluding more recent immigrants. In essence, the latter type of citizenship is linked to ethnicity (in its expression as a group with a perception of a shared heritage), while the first two types are open to individuals of all groups.[12] Social harmony may depend in part on a non-liberal definition of citizenship.

The coexistence of democracy and strong ethnic identities is often difficult. Majority rule is often considered essential to democracy, but in divided societies there may be no prospect of the minority ever becoming a political majority, confining it to political irrelevance.[13] Moreover, what if a minority has historical reasons for rejecting the legitimacy of the state? Grand compromises that bring all groups into the political equation, electoral systems that encourage intergroup cooperation, and limited ethnic democracies that favor one group but still include others (discussed in more detail in Chapter 6) all try to balance political participation and strong identities, but they all are imperfect solutions at best.

So too with human rights. As noted in Chapter 3, the use of force is often necessary to resolving conflict in the long term. Detention without trial, restrictions on organization, and other repressive measures can prevent violence. Although humanitarians would rightly consider these measures unacceptable, at times they have their benefits in preventing warring parties from resuming a conflict.

Several values are often in conflict, or at least in danger, when governments try to manage ethnic relations. For example, preserving sovereignty and endorsing broad claims to human rights and self-determination is at best a difficult balance and at worst impossible. An attempt at a consistent standard leads to the neglect of at least one widely recognized value; using ad hoc criteria, on the other hand, risks an uneven response to crises as they arise and broad confusion among communities and governments alike.

This book chooses to focus primarily on one value (preserving human life), but that should not blind us to other values or lead us to neglect the possible trade-offs that might result. Even if a particular strategy prevents any killing, it is narrow-minded to declare it a success if it devastates individual expression, cultural diversity, and other values. When various strategies for keeping the peace are evaluated in subsequent chapters, the primary criterion used to judge them is the strategy's success in preventing ethnic war. When appropriate, however, the costs of the strategy in terms of diversity, human rights, self-determination, and other values are also noted.

Methodology and Structure

Most of this book relies on historical case studies to assess the question of how governments can prevent ethnic conflicts from recurring.[14] As such, it uses historical evidence in two ways. First, it draws upon history to identify solutions to the problem of recurring ethnic conflict. That is, it looks to a range of cases to see what various governments have done when confronted with the problem of recurring conflict. Second, it uses various historical cases to test these solutions to see how well they work in practice and to judge limits to their effectiveness.[15]

The majority of this book is dedicated to the question of how governments can prevent ethnic conflict from recurring. The key to understanding conflict amelioration, however, often lies in understanding the root and proximate causes of conflict. Thus, this volume first briefly reviews leading causes of ethnic conflict. It does not pretend to offer a definitive description or testing of these causes, but rather to help organize leading explanations into a coherent framework that helps us better understand possible solutions.

This book contains nine chapters, each of which studies different facets of the question of how to keep the peace. Chapter 2 explores a range of potential causes of ethnic conflict, including security fears, a desire for hegemony, group status concerns, and political elite competition. Each cause is dissected, the conditions necessary for the cause to function are noted, and the characteristics of each type of conflict are identified. Because the focus of this book is on solutions to ethnic conflict rather than the causes of them, the various causes are presented to inform the remaining chapters of this book but are not tested rigorously.

With this background in mind, I present several strategies that governments can use to manage ethnic relations. Chapter 3 illustrates how governments can reduce conflict by providing security for citizens and otherwise controlling their actions. Security is often a necessary condition for peace, as even peaceful groups may take up arms if they feel threatened. In addition, aggressive police forces can hinder effective communal organization. However, even though active forms of control can keep communal groups weak and unable to use violence, such controls may leave a bitter legacy in the long term. Repressive governments may trade today's peace for tomorrow's conflict.

Providing security—and intimidating citizens—is not the only solution to ethnic conflict. Chapter 4 examines how governments can induce cooperation rather than compel it. By co-opting groups and their leaders, governments can reassure groups about their status in society and satisfy otherwise bellicose elites. Co-optation, while useful in keeping the peace, often has only a limited impact on belligerents and can become less effective over time.

Governments can also promote a national consciousness or otherwise try to manipulate ethnic identities, an idea discussed in Chapter 5. For centuries, governments have tried to forge different communities into a common nation, either defined as the culture of the dominant group or as a new identity linked to the state. Such strategies have often worked, leading to a common identity among former enemies. In the developing world, however, attempts at nation-building have often led to bitter conflict and have actually increased ethnic tensions.

Using elections or other forms of popular participation also can help improve ethnic relations. As Chapter 6 suggests, by giving individuals a voice in government, they are better able to resolve their differences peacefully through the political system. In deeply divided societies, however, elections often lead to tyrannies of the majority or to other undemocratic results.[16] In recent years, scholars have proposed better designed power-sharing systems that have kept the peace in once-divided countries like South Africa. If majoritarian participatory systems often fail, perhaps a better alternative is to devolve as much power as possible to the communities themselves. By moving issues from the national to the local level, communities will have less over which to fight. Such solutions, while highly effective in theory, actually work only in rare circumstances and often are not applicable to conflicts today.

Given the many difficulties in forging a lasting peace, it is perhaps better to divide communities into more homogeneous regions or countries. As Chapter 7 indicates, partition is difficult to implement and can lead the new titular majority to repress any remaining individuals from other ethnic groups. Perhaps most damningly, partition can foster interstate war. Yet despite these many perils, partition should be considered seriously for particularly intractable conflicts as it is often the only solution available.

Often governments do not seek peace or cannot implement the difficult changes necessary to stop the bloodshed. Chapter 8 looks at ways in which outside powers can bring lasting peace to bitter ethnic conflicts or alleviate some of the suffering. It reviews six distinct intervention strategies, noting their limits and how they affect the causes of conflict recounted in Chapter 2. The chapter also scrutinizes the difficulties faced by intervening powers and suggests conditions under which intervention is more or less effective.

The final chapter of this book, Chapter 9, assesses the challenges and trade-offs inherent in attempts to make peace. Increasing the policing of violent areas may risk civil rights violations. Attempts to nation-build can take a tremendous toll, whether deliberate or not, on cultural diversity. Failed interventions can lead to greater communal tension. This chapter spells out some of these difficult problems. It also observes the implications of this research for non-government actors, such as international organizations, human rights groups, and scholars, who affect ethnic dynamics. Often we are left with unpleasant choices: letting conflict continue, or endangering other values. Recognizing possible pitfalls, however, is preferable to the naive and short-sighted policies that are so common today.

The goal of this book is to explore a neglected subject: how governments can keep the peace over time. It focuses on a particularly difficult aspect of this topic, reviewing ways that governments can prevent the recurrence of ethnic conflict. This book does not pretend to offer definitive answers to this vexing question. Rather, it scrutinizes a range of strategies, demonstrating their value and when they are most effective. The strategies presented, of course, are not necessarily the only ones available to governments, although they are the most commonly used and most important in the opinion of the author. This book represents only a first step: each strategy deserves more comprehensive testing and its variants demand closer scrutiny. My hope is to begin this process by illustrating the various options and their drawbacks, not to provide a definitive test of their value and when they work best.

2 Causes of Ethnic Conflict

To learn how to prevent ethnic conflicts from recurring, we start by examining what causes conflict in the first place. By understanding the causes of ethnic conflict, we are better able to prevent, counter, or live with it. This chapter introduces four theories of the causes of ethnic conflict: the ethnic security dilemma, status concerns, hegemonic ambitions, and the aspirations of elites. The chapter presents each theory's arguments and the necessary conditions for the cause to function and the conflict to occur. These descriptions are followed with a section identifying the characteristics of this type of ethnic conflict. These conditions and characteristics are presented with an eye toward the discussion in subsequent chapters on how to solve, prevent, or disrupt these causes.

These theories are taken from the works of experts in the field or developed from commonsense explanations of conflict. This chapter does not attempt to rigorously test these four theories of ethnic conflict, although the additional evidence presented here should add to their overall validity. The cases presented as the causes are reviewed are intended primarily as an heuristic device, enabling the reader to better understand important causes of conflict as a prelude to the focus of this book: strategies for resolving conflict in the long term.

Selected Causes of Ethnic Conflict

Ethnic groups fight for many reasons, ranging from financial motives to cultural values that glorify war and feuding. Four causes of conflict stand out, however, both for their frequency and for their virulence. One cause is the ethnic security dilemma, a concept borrowed from international relations, which posits that groups war when no sovereign authority can ensure a group's security. Although this concept is particularly important when explaining conflicts where governments are absent or weak, it has explanatory power for all cases where groups feel threatened. The second cause is a group's status concerns. According to this theory, ethnic conflict occurs as an outgrowth of group fears of being dominated, in both material and cultural ways, by other groups. The specific concern with regard to status is cultural, not physical, survival. Groups fighting over status issues worry that their way of life and institutions will be overwhelmed, or made subordinate, to that of their neighbors. The third cause is a desire of one or several groups for hegemony. A hegemonic group is not satisfied with the survival of its own way of life and institutions: it seeks to have these become dominant. Hegemonic groups often seek state sanction for their superiority (i.e., having their language become the official language, their religion the official religion, and so on) and the subjugation of rival groups, forcing them to accept a lesser economic, political, and social position. A fourth cause of conflict is the ambitions of ethnic elites, who play on ethnic fears, hatreds, and ambitions to gain or to maintain power. These four causes often reinforce one another, and all are usually found in the bloodiest and most enduring of conflicts.

The Ethnic Security Dilemma

The security dilemma approach to ethnic conflict draws its insights from the often self-defeating nature of groups' attempts to ensure their security. If there is no central government to enforce order, social groups must rely on their own resources for survival. Afghanistan, Liberia, and Lebanon are but a few recent examples of states whose governments existed in name only. In these countries no sovereign authority exercised control and local militias enforced what little order there was. As long as groups care about survival and have no strong government to protect them from rivals, they will mobilize and arm to preserve themselves. This quest to ensure security, however, often continues to the point that it threatens other groups, which in turn mobilize and arm themselves. Hence the dilemma: seeking to enhance one's own security causes reactions that, in the end, can make one less secure.[1]

A simple example illustrates the security dilemma concept. Suppose I do not like the looks of my new neighbor. If I am confident of police protection, then I am likely to grimace and bear it since I have no reason to fear for my life. However, if the police are ineffectual (or worse, if they are non-existent or, worse still, related to my neighbor), then I may buy a gun to protect myself. Better safe than sorry, after all. My new neighbor, however, sees me with a gun and buys one to defend himself against his obviously paranoid neighbor. Thus, rather than two unarmed neighbors glaring at each other through the blinds, we are now two armed neighbors, fidgeting with our pistols while nervously eyeing each other. My quest for security has made me less secure.

Stretching this example to cases of ethnic conflict is relatively simple. Again, suppose members of my ethnic group do not trust members of a neighboring ethnic group. This lack of trust could stem from simple prejudice, previous cooperation with a colonizing outsider, or past warfare. If there is no government to prevent a small band of gunmen from a rival ethnic group from terrorizing my ethnic group, simple prudence might dictate arming and training in self-defense. Small bands of thugs can kill dozens even if the vast majority of a group is not violent. Arming and training, however, can easily provoke a spiral as the neighboring ethnic group arms and trains in response. Thus, both ethnic groups are less secure. In fact, both groups' suspicions of the other may have been confirmed by the mobilization, which suggests aggressive intentions.

Dynamics similar to a security dilemma can also come into play where sovereign authority is weak, where the central government is a party to conflict, or in situations of sudden change. Such conditions are not anarchy, the defining characteristic of the international relations–based concept, but they represent situations where groups fear others and believe they have no protection. When sovereign authority is weak—as it was in many traditional monarchies before colonialism—groups on the periphery could not rely on the central government for their security. Indeed, tribal leaders or private officials traditionally conducted many functions of modern government, such as tax collecting and law enforcement. Throughout much of the Middle East, governments relied on local officials for armies and revenues rather than the other way around. When this is the case, groups have had to rely on their own resources for self-defense. Male members of the tribe typically were proficient in warfare, and an almost constant low-level conflict kept fear strong.

Another situation in which the security dilemma concept plays a role occurs when the government is a party to ethnic conflict. Under these circumstances, one group not only cannot rely on the government to prevent violence but rather must immediately defend itself or risk defeat and slaughter. In Ba'athist Iraq, Kurds in the north rightly considered the government to be dominated by Arab nationalists, intent on using the power of the state to Arabize the country, forcing the Kurds to use Arabic and embrace an Arab identity. Under these circumstances, the Kurds perceived the army and the police as part of a hostile ethnic camp rather than an impartial arbiter. Again, the group's effort to defend itself, however justifiable, can create a spiral of hostility. Chauvinists within the Iraqi government saw Kurdish attempts to defend their traditional rights as a direct challenge to their rule rather than as an understandable response to harsh government policies. If the government seeks to assure its monopoly on violence, it may try to crush any ethnic dissent, leading ethnic groups to take up arms in defense, thus prompting an even harsher government crackdown.

Finally, situations of sudden change regarding government strength, group resources, or other factors that affect the balance between state and ethnic groups can inspire fear, and thus trigger the dynamics of a security dilemma. International relations specialist Barbara Walter notes five such circumstances: the breakdown of a government; the isolation of a minority group within a larger community; a shift in the political balance among groups; a change in groups' economic resources; and the demobilization of group military forces.[2] All these situations alarm group members, which can prompt security fears.

Perceptions or Structure?

In recent years, scholars of ethnic conflict have developed several distinct variants of the security dilemma model. Perhaps the most important point of divergence is whether security dilemmas are structural or perceptual.[3] Structural security dilemmas are hard to avoid. A lethal mix of geography, weapons technology, and population dispersion can make a security dilemma inevitable, even when the intentions of the parties are entirely benign.[4] As Robert Jervis noted in his classic description of how the security dilemma can spark interstate wars, "If technology and strategy are such that each side believes that the state that strikes first will have a decisive advantage, even a state that is fully satisfied with the status quo may start a war out of fear that the alternative to doing so is not peace, but an attack by its adversary. And, of course, if each side knows the other side is aware of the advantages of striking first, even mild crises are likely to end in war."[5]

Perceptual security dilemmas, on the other hand, emphasize the role that malleable factors such as group norms about the use of force, the degree of ethnic chauvinism, and elite manipulation of information play in leading to a security dilemma.[6] Even when the structure might foster violence, a security dilemma may not occur if groups are not chauvinistic, if they favor peaceful means of resolving conflict, and if leaders see it in their interest to avoid, rather than to encourage, violence.

Certain institutional structures can make it easier for elites to foster the perceptions necessary to trigger a security dilemma. Chauvinistic attitudes and false imputations of a rival group's hostile intent are easier to nurture when participatory institutions are weak. That is, in a mature democracy (such as the United States), norms of conflict resolution and bargaining are strong. In new democracies or semi-autocracies, however, the use of violence is often far more acceptable. In addition, the media in such states are often sources of extremism and false ideas rather than a check on the rhetoric of politicians.[7]

Of course, the distinction between perceptions and structure often blurs, and almost always becomes lost, as time goes on. As Stuart Kaufman argues, exaggerations about the dangers rival groups pose (a perceptual problem) can lead to actual violence, which may expose the bias or weakness of the police, the vulnerability of a rival group, or other structural problems, creating a self-sustaining conflict spiral.[8]

Necessary Conditions for the Security Dilemma to Function

A necessary condition for the security dilemma to operate among groups is that they must have a reason to fear one another or at least to be uncertain about another group's intentions. After all, in theory a group might welcome armed neighbors if they believed they would fight by their side against other unsavory elements. In Lebanon, for example, Sunni Muslim groups did not fear the increasingly armed Palestinian presence in the country, as they believed that the Palestinians would help them fight Christians, Druze, and other Lebanese rivals in the event of a conflict.

What is the source of this anxiety? One wellspring of fear is historical quarrels. Although scholars are quick to dismiss "ancient hatreds" as a source of conflict, it seems difficult to argue that the past is irrelevant. When groups have fought in recent memory, even the most well-intentioned and peaceful individuals must worry that they will do so again in the future. If past violence was widespread, as it was in the case of the Balkans, then groups will be quicker to arm. On the other hand, if groups see their neighbors as peaceful, they will be less likely to shoot first and ask questions later. Another source of fear is a group's concern about its status being degraded (see the status and hegemony sections in this chapter): a group may fear that another group will overwhelm it culturally or economically, thus leading to the possibility of a security dilemma situation. A third source of fear can develop when the same ethnic group lives in multiple states. In these circumstances, groups may worry that another government may support the ethnic group in their country. In such cases, a feedback cycle can develop. Simmering ethnic tension in one state can cause neighbors to threaten to intervene for nationalist reasons. These threats, in turn, raise the heat in the first state.[9] Finally, fear can come from deliberate distortions by group leaders, a factor further explored below under "elite competition."

When structural factors contribute to a security dilemma, it is far easier for a spiral to start. In such circumstances, it is relatively easier for would-be belligerents to spark a conflict. Even hazy memories of conflict can start a destructive cycle, creating fears that soon enough become realized as thugs and demagogues respond.

A weak or biased central government also is necessary for the security dilemma to function. When the government cannot, or will not, maintain order, violence is far more likely.[10] If the central government is strong and does not take the side of one particular ethnic group, then no group need fear for its security as the government will swiftly punish any violence. If the government is weak, however, or if it actively champions the cause of one ethnic group, then other ethnic groups must rely on themselves for their own security. In such cases, the government at best looks on passively while violence occurs or at worst joins in or encourages killing.

A third condition that contributes to a security dilemma is incomplete information. If groups are not certain of other groups' intentions and capabilities, they often assume the worst, particularly under conditions of anarchy.[11] However, if communication between the groups flows easily, this can prevent a spiral of fear and reaction from developing. Yet information is never perfect. For experts who believe that structural factors shape the security dilemma, incomplete information is a constant. You can never know what your neighbor thinks in his heart of hearts, and thus you must respond and defend yourself if only to be prudent.

Unfortunately, countries that experienced an ethnic conflict in the recent past are far more likely to have a security dilemma in the present. A necessary condition for the security dilemma to function—mutual fear—is almost invariably present if blood has flowed. A second necessary condition—a weak or biased government—also is common, as the recovery from civil strife often takes years if not decades. Learning how to overcome the security dilemma is thus almost always necessary if governments are to keep the peace.

Because fear or anxiety is a necessary condition for the security dilemma to function, this view of conflict works better as an explanation for the continuation of conflict or for escalation of existing tension to violence rather than as one for why peaceful societies suddenly become violent. Fear and anxiety often develop for reasons that have nothing to do with a security dilemma but then take on a far more deadly dimension when authority collapses or other conditions become ripe for conflict.

Characteristics of Ethnic Security Dilemma Behavior

Groups operating under the security dilemma exhibit certain distinguishing features. The military dynamics of ethnic conflict intensify the security dilemma, leading to conflict spirals. Offense dominance, a situation in which conquest is relatively easy, is common in ethnic conflict and it makes the security dilemma particularly intense. To return to our interpersonal example, if my neighbor and I live in fortresses and have only knives as weapons, we would not lie awake at night worrying about each other. First, the alarms in my fortress would give me plenty of warning time if my neighbor attacked, and for a knife wound to be deadly, the neighbor would need to be at close range. If my neighbor and I both live in tents on the prairie and are armed with machine guns, however, whoever shoots first has a good chance of killing the other with one spray of bullets. The latter situation, where offense is relatively easy, would be referred to as offense dominant while the former example would be better characterized as defense dominant.

Because of offensive dominance, strong groups usually strike first, either because they are threatened by a potential rival's mobilization or because they want to prevent such a mobilization from occurring at all. Better organized groups may see windows of opportunity to attack their rivals before they grow in power.[12] Other groups that have no desire for change are dragged in merely to protect themselves in an increasingly dangerous environment. A violent outrage committed by one group, or even a few individuals of that group, can trigger and rationalize a far worse outrage in response.

Killing large numbers of the enemy is relatively cheap and easy in ethnic conflict. Since the defenders in these cases often are unarmed civilians, including women, children, and the elderly, a few men with guns have a tremendous military advantage. Small bands of gunmen can easily create vast hordes of refugees. The military training required for such operations is minimal, and the weapons involved (usually small arms) are inexpensive and widely available. Because even small forces can wreak great havoc, groups have an incentive to go on the offensive and wipe out another group's forces before it can arm and train, encouraging preemptive strikes in the event of a crisis. Such windows of opportunity are especially likely if one group is better armed and better organized but fears that a numerically superior opponent will soon arm and organize itself.

International political dynamics also reward the offense. Traditionally, the United Nations and interested outside powers tend to intervene and arrange for a cease-fire after ethnic skirmishes have begun, thus rewarding aggression. Groups that can strike quickly are often given international assistance in consolidating their holdings.[13]

Because of offense dominance, ethnic groups must be highly sensitive to other ethnic groups' efforts to arm and mobilize. Even groups that do not seek to harm their neighbors have an incentive to mobilize and strike first before their opponent does the same to them. This is particularly so when sovereignty collapses, leaving all groups surprisingly vulnerable. Under offense-dominant conditions, negotiation is not likely to work. Groups are likely to shoot first and ask questions later as the risks of losing an offensive advantage are high. If defense were dominant, taking time to carefully evaluate situations would be less risky. Similarly, diplomatic agreements are more likely to be violated as groups have a tremendous incentive to strike first and fear for their survival if betrayed, leading to bad-faith situations. Finally, verification and compromise are both harder under offense dominance, since small changes can easily upset the military balance.

The security dilemma is even more intense when offensive and defensive military forces cannot be distinguished, reducing groups' ability to signal their defensive intent. Any buildup for defensive purposes could signal an offensive buildup. Again, using the interpersonal example, if I bought a whistle instead of a gun (a whistle would help me summon the police but would not physically harm my neighbor), my neighbor might not be alarmed, but I would feel more secure. This whistle would be a defensive weapon. A pistol, however, could be used for either offense or defense. With a pistol I could defend myself against a neighbor's attack or attack my neighbor—the nature of the weapon reveals nothing about my intentions.

On an intergroup level, more defense for one ethnic group in the form of guns and training can often look like more offense to a nervous ethnic rival, leading that rival to arm and mobilize in turn. Unfortunately, guns and mortars—the basic types of weapons used in ethnic conflict—can be used both to invade a neighbor's territory or to defend one's own home, making it difficult to distinguish offensive and defensive intentions. Moreover, whether the purpose of military training and popular mobilization, both of which are needed to form effective militias, is offensive or defensive also is impossible to distinguish. Finally, as Posen notes, the quantity and commitment of soldiers affect offensive military operations as much as any weapons system. People themselves are thus potentially offensive weapons, and efforts to mobilize one's group through propaganda and training can unwittingly signal offensive intent.

The existence of ethnic group members living outside the group's homeland makes the security dilemma even more intense. Such individuals are nightmares for defenders, who must worry about fifth columns within their ranks. Furthermore, concern about the well-being of ethnic compatriots in distant areas often is a major cause of aggression. Thus, there is an incentive both for offensive operations to liberate besieged compatriots and for ethnic cleansing to wipe out potentially hostile pockets before they have a chance to arm and strike.[14] To return to our (increasingly violent) neighborhood, if I am trying to protect my son, who lives a block away, as well as myself, it is not enough for me to have a secure home. I must have the ability to act a block away, which calls for offensive capabilities. Thus, self-defense requires potentially threatening offense. Similarly, if I suspect that a boarder in my home will help my neighbor get in the locked door, it might be best for me to expel the boarder. Thus, I must move simultaneously to purify my home while extending my reach to help my beleaguered kin.

When the security dilemma is active, noncombatants are quickly dragged into a general conflict as groups try to make captured areas ethnically homogeneous. The settlements of rival ethnic groups in another group's territory represent dangerous islands of potential traitors who, given arms and minimal training, will pose a serious military threat. "Cleansing" such areas, from a military point of view, is logical. Therefore, small bands of gunmen have an incentive to drive away or kill civilians in order to produce ethnically homogeneous areas. In the former Yugoslavia, almost all regions that experienced conflict, whether it be in Croatia or Kosovo, also witnessed the execution, or at least the expulsion, of young males who could bear arms.

Moderate voices are quickly shouted down when the security dilemma is active. Atrocities, real and exaggerated, discredit those advocating peaceful solutions. Even those who reject an exclusive ethnic identity and see themselves as cosmopolitan fear hostility both from their own people and from the enemy, which seldom distinguishes the assimilated from the non-assimilated. Indeed, much of the violence of an ethnic conflict often occurs within groups. In order to keep the group strong against outsiders (and to protect their own power), group leaders must prevent defections from within the group. Thus, leaders must coerce and cajole members of their own group to eschew compromise and to man the ramparts.[15]

Ethnic Status and Ethnic Strife

Fear of bloodshed and fear for survival are not the only elements that bring ethnic groups into conflict. A frequent cause of ethnic rivalry that leads to violence is the struggle over relative status and position in society. Which group's history is the nation's history? What language will be used for government and for schools? Who should administer a community: better-educated newcomers or members of the indigenous ethnic group? Although the answers to these status disputes—questions related to group demands for social and political recognition from the government and from other groups—seldom determine the life or death of an individual ethnic group member, they do touch on fundamental human issues of worth and belonging.

* Status causes conflict when one distinguishable group blocks another's quest for recognition or social legitimacy.[16] As Isaiah Berlin notes in reference to this type of dispute: "What they want, as often as not, is simply recognition (of their class or nation, or colour or race) as an independent source of human activity, as an entity with a will of its own, intending to act in accordance with it . . . and not to be ruled, educated or guided."[17] Such recognition, however, is not always accorded. Nationalists seek to glorify the dominant identity and play down rival claims to a state's history. Liberals note that individuals, not communities, deserve recognition. Ideologues of all stripes (Marxist, religious, fascist) exalt rival social categories. To ensure that group prerogatives are gained or respected, group members often must organize and act.

Questions of group worth easily become political. As groups struggle for legitimacy, recognition, and status, they often see other groups as rivals or as obstacles. Designating one group's language as official, for example, reduces the importance of other languages. Promises to include all groups in decision-making can result in struggles over the composition of a parliament or the civil service.

Group status concerns include, but go beyond, the classic formulation of politics as "who gets what." Indeed, individual economic well-being is usually considered a symbol of a group's social status in general rather than a commodity valued strictly for material reasons. Thus, perceived discrimination along economic or political lines can trigger conflict by inciting status concerns. At times even a relatively wealthy group may feel that its status in society is not sufficiently recognized. The Basques in Spain, for example, were wealthier than their Castilian neighbors but for many years resented their corresponding lack of social status. Similarly, in the former Yugoslavia the Slovenians seceded, in part because they felt that Serbia drained their wealth without granting them political prominence.

Status concerns differ from those of the security dilemma in that groups fear not only for their survival but also for their own cultural or social domination. Once a conflict begins, however, status concerns and security fears often become interwoven. Group fears of cultural extinction are reinforced by security fears that are often generated by actual violence. A great many traditional groups in particular fear extinction and subordination.[18]

Facilitating Conditions

For status to be a source of conflict, groups must be able to compare their relative positions in society. When groups are relatively self-contained, worth can be determined by different standards, which are particular to the group in question.[19] Inuits do not judge their worth by comparing themselves with Maori and vice versa. Both, however, compare themselves to neighbors who compete with them for power and recognition. It is competition that leads to conflict. As political scientist Myron Weiner notes: "Inequalities, real or perceived, are a necessary but not a sufficient condition for ethnic conflict; there must also be competition for control over or access to economic wealth, political power, or social status."[20] Although the reasons that group comparisons begin are myriad, five complementary (and often concurrent) events bring groups into positions where they can compare their status: migration, modernization, colonization, education, and the collapse of empire.

Migration often creates a "compulsion for change" among ethnic groups.[21] Migrants bring new skills, their own ethos, and a different attitude toward education that often gives them better access to high-paying, high-status positions. Migrants compete for leadership positions, which often are the essence of a group's status. As Myron Weiner notes, "nativism tends to be associated with a blockage to social mobility for the native population by a culturally distinguishable migrant population."[22] These attributes can bring previously peaceful ethnic groups into a violent rivalry with migrants.

Modernization is not a cause of ethnic conflict per se, but it often acts as a spur to status concerns. Like migration, modernization brings previously isolated groups in contact with each other. Modernization provides incentives for mobility and nurtures the growth of ethnic identification and cohesion. The development process also undermines the existing ethnic division of labor. Industrial expansion creates new job opportunities; irrigation changes the property and value of land; an expanded bureaucracy opens up the state as a forum for employment; and the political process at times permits competition for public office.[23] These processes, in turn, fuel increased political demands that many states are unable, or unwilling, to accommodate.[24]

Modernization also can cause other facilitating conditions such as education and migration, as opportunities open up due to new employment opportunities, easier transportation, and compulsory education. Thus, the composition of a region can change due to the migration fostered by modernization. Protecting one's traditional space and opportunities from migrants thus becomes a preoccupation of the local population.[25]

Colonial powers frequently redistribute political resources, often helping subordinate groups gain new influence, thus raising the potential for competition. Colonial powers often favored non-advanced ethnic groups either due to racial or religious stereotypes, perceived religious bonds, or a deliberate effort to undermine the traditional elite. Some groups became favored through chance proximity to the colonial capital or to religious missions, a key source of educational opportunities. Finally, colonial use of "indirect rule," an administrative approach in which traditional authorities acted as colonial proxies, often strengthened the idea that the ethnic group was a valid basis for administration.[26] Ethnic groups in Syria under the French mandate felt the impact of such favoritism. The French worked with the Alawite religious sect, for many years a backward and isolated community, giving them greater access to education and the military. This power led the Alawites to increase their share of economic and social power, angering other communities.

Colonialism often expanded the range of political, social, and economic activity of all groups while providing a common set of social aspirations. Thus, it often transformed an unranked system (where groups do not see themselves as part of the same social hierarchy as other groups) into a ranked one. The advances in communication and transportation under colonialism further increased ethnic group members' awareness of their cultural uniqueness.[27]

The post-colonial phase is particularly ripe for conflict. After the colonial power departs, a host of status-related questions arise regarding the official language, religion, and the composition of the government. Furthermore, as Weiner notes, "In the post-colonial phase those who come to exercise governmental authority often belong to the subordinate economic group in the economic division of labor, especially when power shifts to those who are the most numerous."[28]

The expansion of education creates a new class of individuals who claim a certain status in society that differs from that based on land, wealth, or parentage. These new elites upset the traditional social order. Middle-class nativism tends to emerge where the local population has produced its own educated class that seeks jobs held by migrants. This is particularly true when middle-class jobs are hard to find, which exacerbates competition.[29] Moreover, within an ethnic community, education can produce rival elites, thus creating competition that makes it harder to control the community and prevent conflict (see the discussion of co-optation in Chapter 4 for more on this problem).

Much post–Cold War violence has occurred in the successor states of former empires, especially the Soviet and Yugoslav empires. The reason lies in the powerful war-causing effects of imperial collapse. Before the end of the Cold War, the collapse of the British, French, Portuguese, and other colonial empires caused many conflicts in Asia and Africa, including some that continued into the 1980s and 1990s. Similarly, many of the successor governments that emerged after the fall of the Soviet Union and the collapse of Yugoslavia had little legitimacy and boundaries, which placed groups in direct competition with one another.[30]

This lack of legitimacy encouraged a violent scramble for power among leaders and interest groups and encouraged minorities to fear for their status in the successor state. Minorities that accept a subordinate status in a large, multiethnic empire often reject a minority status when an empire's collapse empowers an ethnic rival. In Georgia, for example, Georgian nationalists led by Zviad Gamsakhurdia took power as the Soviet Union collapsed, with widespread support among ethnic Georgians. However, two large minority communities in Georgia that had apparently accepted their minority status in the Soviet Union—the Abkhaz and the Ossetians—took up arms to prevent their incorporation into the Georgian-dominated state. Similarly, Moldova's nationalist movement alarmed residents in the Transnistria region, which is 60 percent ethnic Russian and Ukrainian. These Transnistrian Russians and Ukrainians proclaimed the formation of the Transnistrian Moldovan Soviet Socialist Republic and tried to remain attached to the Soviet Union. Only the dispatch of Soviet troops prevented widespread violence.[31] In all these cases, minorities in a multiethnic empire sought their own state after the empire collapsed in part because they feared that a successor government would not respect their status.

The problem of status is often compounded after an empire's collapse because successor states often inherit artificial borders that correspond poorly to natural boundaries or to local demography and have not been settled by agreements with neighbors. These borders often follow administrative boundaries that were imposed by the metropole without regard for local feelings. As a result, these borders bisect national groups and create ethnic-minority enclaves. It was in this way that the European powers partitioned Africa at the 1878 Congress of Berlin with little regard for the unity of African peoples, drawing lines that seldom followed geographic or communal boundaries.[32] Later, Stalin drew borders that split the Turkic and Muslim peoples of the Soviet empire into different administrative units in order to weaken their political strength. Cursed with such borders, several successor states to the Soviet and Yugoslav empires have fought bloody wars to resolve questions raised by maldesigned boundaries. What is the identity of the successor state, which often never had a historical precedent within its current boundaries? What are the rights of its various peoples? Answers to these questions, or the lack of them, often form the basis of an ethnic dispute.

Even when the boundary lines are sensible, empires foster national intermingling that can plague the politics of their successor states. During the imperial era, individuals can more easily move about within the empire, leaving their traditional homelands. Moreover, some empires deliberately mix national groups by inducing or compelling cross-migration among groups. As a result, the empire's successor states may have populations composed of mutually antagonistic peoples with no clear hierarchy among them. Stalin's forced marches of millions of subjects are perhaps the most infamous example of such enforced intermingling, and they sowed the seeds of current conflict. As long as the Russian empire remained, the status concerns of all peoples were held in check. When the Soviet Union collapsed, however, basic questions of status rose to the fore. Who among the various populations deserved to be there? Were they conniving interlopers, agents of a colonial power, or welcome neighbors? These questions, never openly raised during the days of the empire, are loudly heard after its end.

Characteristics of Status Conflict

Ethnic conflicts over status exhibit distinct characteristics. First, conflict is particularly likely between "advanced" and "backward" groups.[33] The advanced groups in general tend to be more tied to the modern sector of the economy. Backward groups will strive to ensure their fair share in society and government, and they fear being overwhelmed by the advanced group. Alternately (and less commonly), an advanced group will turn to violence because it believes it deserves a greater share of society's perks and status positions due to its advanced ranking—a phenomenon more typical of hegemonic conflict (discussed below).

Conflict is also likely when central authority collapses or another event occurs, such as migration and modernization, which brings groups into competition. As noted, just as the collapse of a colonial regime can raise security fears, so too can it bring up status concerns. Will a group's language remain inviolable? Will its cultural institutions be undermined in a new regime? The uncertainties inherent in a change of regime fuel group anxiety, raising the question of who will rule and creating fears that a ranked system will develop with one group subordinate and another dominant.[34] Similarly, modernization, migration, and education, while less sudden events, can promote even greater competition.

Symbols are particularly important in status conflicts. Citizenship, official languages, distinctive dress, and recognition of a group's "special position" in the state are issues of concern, and of conflict, for ethnic groups.[35] Education is a particularly important symbol. Education itself conveys symbolic benefits such as language, history, and group values. Furthermore, as education is often a source of new elites, particularly in a modernizing country, access to and control of the education system becomes an important issue for all groups. Thus, status conflict is often centered around nonmaterial issues, whereas material matters are often seen as symbols of broader social inclusion or status.

Teachers, writers, artists, historians, and other intellectuals who help form and transmit cultural identity play a vital role in status conflicts. These individuals can create a durable culture that demands recognition or helps meld the dominant and non-dominant cultures. A poem about a field of blackbirds, a remnant of an ancient temple in Jerusalem, a canvas with drawings of a majestic Western landscape, and other cultural artifacts become in essence sacred objects that inspire men and women, and indeed nations, to die and to kill.[36] Because of their importance, these elites are often targets of the hegemonic group and important leaders of resistance to it. Even if these intellectuals do not engage in overtly political behavior, their cultural activity makes them logical candidates for punishment.

A growth in ethnic status concerns can stem from rival nationalism, particularly if the nationalism in question is made up of a single rival ethnic group. Because a primary goal of nationalist movements is often control of the nation-state, the existence of one nationalist movement can spark status concerns of other aspirants for power, leading them to form their own nationalist movements. Thus, a status spiral often develops where, as one group strives for greater social recognition, other groups must also do the same, fearing their status will be jeopardized if they do nothing.

Hegemonic Ambitions and Ethnic Conflict

Conflicts stemming from the ethnic security dilemma and status concerns are primarily defensive in nature. That is, the fundamental sources of conflict behind these theories—personal insecurity and cultural defense—can be satisfied in harmony with other ethnic groups. An unarmed populace where people can speak their own language and worship as they please could conceivably satisfy all a country's ethnic groups if status concerns and the ethnic security dilemma were the only sources of ethnic conflict. But not all ethnic groups are satisfied with security and cultural survival—some prefer dominance. For members of hegemonic groups, their language must be the only official language; their religion must be followed by all citizens; and their institutions must be enshrined in government and society.[37] Hegemonic elites often believe that their narrow group is the legitimate ruler of the polity. To ensure their rule, they must promote the group's culture, language, demographic predominance, economic welfare, and political hegemony at the expense of other groups.[38] Hegemonic ambitions can be thought of as the shadowy mirror image of status and security fears: hegemonic groups want to ensure their status and security to a degree that subordinates that of other communities.

The quest for communal hegemony—and resistance to it—is a major source of conflict in the world today. Concerns about hegemony, both real and imagined, contributed to the post–Cold War conflicts that broke out in Georgia, Indonesia, Russia, and the former Yugoslavia. This problem also was widespread before the Cold War. Religious, tribal, or ethnic hegemonism fed communal violence in Angola, Burma, Burundi, Ethiopia, India, Iraq, Liberia, Pakistan, Rwanda, Somalia, South Africa, Sri Lanka, Sudan, and Turkey, among other places.

A range of factors can lead majorities to initiate violence-producing policies in the quest for communal hegemony. These include a hegemonistic ethos that brooks no compromise and adherence to a Jacobin, integrationist model of the state. At times, security fears (discussed above) may also become so extreme that a group seeks to dominate potential rivals. In addition, elite rivalries (discussed below) can lead to pressure for extreme policies.

The need for cultural validation through dominance has proven a potent cause of exclusive and violence-oriented policies. For example, Turkish and Hutu chauvinists have a self-image that requires a dominant role in the state and society. In the Turkish case, the need for cultural domination proved strong enough to lead the state to attempt a brutal assimilation campaign, destroying the Kurds by shattering their culture and integrating their numbers into the larger Turkish community. In Rwanda, cultural domination took the ultimate step and became a quest for the eradication of rival groups.[39]

A common motivation for the formation of nationalist movements is a desire for recognition. Human satisfaction depends in part on the Platonic *thymos:* open social acceptance of human dignity.[40] Communal hegemonists, however, go beyond the modest acknowledgment all communal groups demand. Hegemonists seek recognition as the supreme social group. As Isaiah Berlin notes, nationalism's pathological form "proclaims the supreme value of the nation's own culture, history, race, spirit, institutions, even of its physical attributes, and their superiority to those of others, usually of its neighbors."[41] The hegemonists' worldview depends on their domination of state and society. The very symbols and self-image of the group are intertwined with the symbols and realities of hegemony.

Often, the creation of these identities is reactive, stemming from nationalism elsewhere or from oppression and discrimination. Many nationalisms sprang simply from other, successful nationalisms.[42] The desire to redress their inferiority by creating a strong identity leads naturally to a hegemonic ethos. Chauvinistic identities may also be created to improve individual and group self-images vis-à-vis their neighbors.[43]

The importance of a hegemonic ethos suggests that the very identities created, rather than the circumstances in which an ethnic group and its leaders find themselves, influence ethnic conflict and violence. Often the change in identity leads to conflict by precipitating a change in the overall communal balance: the majority group, now self-aware, articulates greater demands that upset the current division of resources and status in order to satisfy its self-image.[44] But this is only part of the picture. With their conviction of superiority comes a conviction of their right to rule others.[45] At times, the majority simply denies minorities rights, thus inflaming their own nationalistic concerns. Often, the hegemonic group feels little need to engage in power-sharing, establish protections for minority rights, or otherwise reassure minorities that they will be protected and respected.

Minority groups, in essence, face an unpleasant choice when confronting a majority group with a hegemonic ethos. On the one hand, they could accept their subordinate status, suffering discrimination and second-class citizenship. Yet even subordination is no guarantee of survival. When chauvinism is extreme and magnified by security fears or elite competition, as in Rwanda, pogroms can happen despite a minority's passivity. On the other hand, they could protest and, if that failed, rebel. Either choice can produce violence.

In addition to an ethos of domination, hegemonism results because many leaders seek to build a strong state that forges together disparate peoples into a common union (a union often dominated by one group). Joining this nation requires abandoning characteristics that distinguish groups from the unified ideal. Groups must share a language, culture, and common historical symbols. Such an ideal unity inevitably comes into tension with the cultural and social mosaics of plural societies, laying the groundwork for later conflict.[46] Once again, minority groups face an unpleasant dilemma when the majority seeks a strong state that subsumes distinct groups. They can shed their distinct culture and assimilate, or resist and face conflict. Conflict does not break out when the minorities accept assimilation.

When the government is controlled by a hegemonistic majority, it creates a security threat to minorities. Under these circumstances, the minority not only cannot rely on the government to prevent violence but rather must immediately defend itself or risk defeat and slaughter. In contrast to the standard security dilemma dynamic, it is not state weakness that produces this but rather a strong state in the hands of a group's enemies. Thus, minorities are often caught in a bind when security fears are high. If they mobilize, they will alarm the majority, feeding its security fears. If they fail to do so, they will continue to be victims of limited depravations and violence.

Security fears can sustain hegemonism, although they often have had little to do with the origin of the conflict. Security fears do not explain why a majority that dominates the state would turn to violence out of fear. Rather, security violence is part of a cycle: oppression and discrimination stemming from a hegemonistic ethos or state-building create unrest, which in turn lays the foundation for subsequent security fears.

As discussed below, leaders often play on ethnic hegemonism to gain power from rival communities or to solidify power within their own communities. Elite competition can play on cultural validation concerns, an ideology of a strong state, or security fears. Minorities are often powerless to affect inter-elite competition. If they organize and mobilize to protect themselves, this may play into the hands of majority demagogues. Passivity, however, risks leaving the minority even more open to aggressive majority elites who seek to use violence to discredit moderates in their own community.

Communal hegemonism does not always produce violence. Minority groups frequently live side by side with a dominant group without bloodshed, accepting their inferior status as the price of communal peace. Non-Han Chinese, for example, were often treated as second-class citizens for much of the twentieth century, but they seldom rose up in protest. Nation-building also can lead subordinate groups to bypass violence. Ethnic, regional, and tribal minorities have often embraced national identities, welcoming the possibility of advancement as part of the new nation. Many Kurds in Turkey have attained positions of social, economic, and political prominence, but they have done so as Turks, not as Kurds.[47]

When are subordinate groups more likely to rebel? Minority resistance to attempted hegemony (resistance that in its essence bears many similarities to a group's quest for greater status) is made more likely by three factors: past bloodshed; a strong, established culture; and progress on minority rights elsewhere. Past bloodshed and a strong culture "harden" communal identity, thus increasing the likelihood that the group will take up arms to preserve its identity.[48] In addition to hardening communal identity, a bloody past also creates a sentiment of hostility toward the dominant group and makes security dilemma situations far more likely. Finally, the fate of minorities elsewhere can have a large impact abroad, leading them to resist subordination. The civil rights movement in the United States, for example, inspired Catholics in Northern Ireland to demonstrate for civil rights and equality.[49]

Hegemonic conflict is perhaps the most difficult type of conflict to solve. Either other groups must subordinate their own status and security concerns or the hegemonic group must change its ambitions—both of which are difficult undertakings. No solution that will satisfy all parties exists, yet hegemonic groups can coexist with other groups. During the Ottoman empire, for example, many non-Muslim communities accepted the second-class but protected status of *dhimmi* without repeated uprisings or violence. Furthermore, once-hegemonic groups can be changed—although the cost is often tremendous and the effort may take generations. Today, most Germans and Castilians now readily accept other ethnic groups as their equals even though for much of the twentieth century these peoples sought to dominate others in their countries.

Characteristics of Hegemonic Conflict

Like other forms of conflict, violence driven by hegemonic ambitions has its own set of distinct characteristics. For hegemonic conflict to occur, the hegemonic group must assert that it merits—and can achieve—political and social domination. In general, hegemonic conflict occurs when a group is numerically superior, considers itself more socially advanced, or both, although minorities have at times asserted their primacy. Groups without a plausible claim to domination, even when they have a feeling of superiority, generally do not assert their hegemonic claims. Throughout history Jews have accepted subordinate minority positions, despite a group perception of superiority. Hegemonic conflict is particularly likely when a once-dominant group has been displaced by former subordinates. In Ethiopia, many Amhara resent the loss of their dominance, which occurred when Tigrayan rebels took over the country in the early 1990s.

Hegemonic beliefs can inspire three varieties of attitudes, all of which can engender conflict. The first attitude is the right to rule. Even when hegemonic groups do not desire to kill or assimilate other groups, they do believe that decision-making power should be in their hands exclusively. Other groups may continue their lives with little change except for surrendering political power, a paternalism that often inspires resentment among the dominated groups and leads to conflict. The second attitude is the right to assimilate others and impose the dominant group's way of life. A certain language, set of laws, or way of life is proposed as an ideal that other ethnic groups must adopt. The French in Algeria, for example, expounded on their *mission civilisatrice* to justify transforming Algerians into Frenchmen. Language, national symbols, and perceptions of history are particularly important parts of such an assimilation effort. The third attitude is the right to kill or mistreat other groups on the grounds of their supposed inferiority. A hegemonic group may feel no compunction about slaughtering other groups, as they do not consider them on the same level of humanity. Such killings reflect contempt, not fear.

Whether stemming from a belief in a right to rule, the inferiority of others, or a civilizing mission, the hegemonic group actively seeks to subordinate rival cultures—a goal that is indicated in the policies it favors and the actions it takes toward rival groups. This is the distinction (often blurred in reality) between hegemonic conflict and conflict stemming from the security dilemma or status concerns. Even when a hegemonic group's security is ensured and it is free to practice its religion and speak its language, or is otherwise assured of its cultural survival, it will still engage in conflict with other groups if its superior position is not acknowledged. For example, after World War I ethnic Turks dominated Turkey's government and society, controlled the army and the police, and outnumbered other ethnic groups. Despite this security and social status, they used violence to subordinate minorities such as the Kurds.

For conflict to occur, rival groups must resist the hegemonic group. If subordinate groups will accept the loss of rights, land, and social prominence, then bloodshed can usually be avoided. Not surprisingly, among groups resisting hegemonic groups, resentment (usually inspired by status or security concerns) is common.

As noted, hegemonic conflict is akin to conflict stemming from the ethnic security dilemma or from status concerns. Thus, many of the characteristics of these conflicts—the importance of intellectuals, the key role of symbols, the discrediting of moderates, and the importance of group comparison—are also present in hegemonic conflict.

Elite Competition

The three causes of conflict discussed so far focus on group-level characteristics. A group's leaders, however, often have agendas of their own that lead to conflict or increase the scope and scale of existing tension. When elites compete for power, they often seek to outbid one another, promoting chauvinistic positions to gain popular support. Elites seek to make ethnicity—and, more important, their interpretation of what ethnicity means—the dominant political issue in order to increase their own power. They try to manipulate existing identities, making certain ones more politically salient and weakening national or other identities that might bring people together. Elites can do this to acquire political power for themselves, deriding the status quo's defenders as weak on core questions of ethnic status and security. Elites in power can also exploit ethnic tension, claiming that opposition figures will sell out to ethnic enemies.[50] Thus, ethnicity becomes a tremendously salient issue for political leaders: it can be used to gain power and to preserve it.

Struggles for group legitimacy are particularly important among elites or potential elites. It is they who are the standard bearers of ethnic politics, and it is they who will receive the positions that benefit from and display group worth.[51] Two distinct types of elites are important in cases of ethnic conflict: political and cultural elites. The former are leaders concerned with decision-making, whether they be tribal sheikhs or parliament representatives. The latter are intellectuals, poets, and other individuals who help create, sustain, and transmit a cultural identity. Political elites may or may not care about ethnic issues, while cultural elites invariably do. Both, however, often share an interest in promoting a group's status because it can enhance their position against ethnic rivals. Elites may promote conflict due to a genuine belief in the rightness of their cause (or the wrongness of their rivals) or to gain power from rivals. Ethnic elite authority and legitimacy, however, is bound up in the preservation and strength of their group's identity.[52]

Elite competition, in contrast to the other explanations of conflict above, is far more focused on within-group tension rather than intergroup problems. Elites often seek to whip up tension and convince individuals to identify themselves along ethnic, as opposed to class or national, lines. Alternatively, elites may try to depoliticize other issues by playing the "ethnic card" to attract supporters. For example, Serbian Communist Party members, Marxist intellectuals, nationalist writers, and parts of the Yugoslav army worked together to create a strong Serbian nationalist movement. They feared that, with an economic crisis looming, they would lose power unless they could divert attention to an identity (ethnicity) that increased the legitimacy of their leadership.[53]

At times the elite role in causing a conflict is minor. When mass sentiment is aroused, elites often simply ride the bandwagon rather than lead it: they cannot be said to cause the event in question, and perhaps contribute to it only in a limited way. Elites, however, can dampen conflict as well. Thus, the views of elites—whether for or against conflict—and their freedom to express these views can each potentially cause a peaceful situation to turn violent or defuse an otherwise tense situation.

Necessary Conditions and Characteristics

Outbidding requires both some degree of freedom to express opinions and a degree of communal antipathy to inflame. Elites exploit basic democratic freedoms, particularly freedom of expression but also freedom of assembly, to spread their message. Control over information is essential. As V. P. Gagnon notes, "The key is to make a particular identity, and a specific definition of that identity, the only relevant or legitimate one in political contexts."[54] When demogogues control the state, they exploit government propaganda resources, such as the education system. Newspapers and television spread messages of hate and amplify ethnic grievances. Chauvinistic elites can thus raise the specter of communal security, decry discrimination, or trumpet the group's rightful, but unfulfilled, place in the sun. Rival interpretations of events that do not support the elites' message are ignored. Ethnic antipathy can come from any of the three causes—the security dilemma, status concerns, or hegemonic beliefs—as well as other sources not addressed in this book.[55]

States in flux, particularly nascent democracies, are vulnerable to the spread of chauvinism and misperception. As Snyder notes, "democratizing states are likely to have highly imperfect political marketplaces where nationalist myths are fueled rather than refuted."[56] Moreover, information is often incomplete, allowing elites to exaggerate isolated incidents, play up sporadic violence, and otherwise manipulate what they have available on the intentions of other groups.

Indeed, elite competition can at times create a security dilemma. Elites can portray aggression as more likely to succeed, and other groups as more threatening, than a dispassionate analysis would suggest. The words and deeds of leaders often live on and are recalled when ethnic tension grows. Chauvinistic rhetoric and calls to violence often rightly alarm other groups, "proving" that the group in question is indeed hostile. Over time, groups come to see each other as threats, even when the rhetoric of elites was intended only for audiences of the same ethnic group.[57]

Elites often recruit their own mobs or thugs in their effort to whip up tension and protect themselves from rival demagogues. In Serbia, for example, Slobodan Milosevic and his cronies often offered mobs transportation, liquor, and food. The initial objective of such mobs is often theft and pillage rather than furthering an ethnic agenda. If these mobs are not stopped, however, they discredit moderates and alarm other communities. At times, small numbers of thugs or marauders are able to wreak havoc and escalate tensions, causing groups in general to become fearful of one another.[58]

When ethnic outbidding becomes intense, those who dare call for compromise are branded as traitors. Moderates are often threatened with violence, silenced, or even killed. Rival leaders use thugs and mobs to cow and intimidate those who oppose their efforts and question the use of violence.[59] In Sri Lanka, the Liberation Tigers of Tamil Eelam—one of the most violent ethnic movements in the world, which seeks a Tamil state in northern Sri Lanka—regularly assassinate more moderate Tamil leaders who are willing to compromise with the majority Sinhalese population there. Their campaign has silenced many Tamil voices opposed to violence.

Ethnicity also empowers a rival set of elites. In Yugoslavia during Tito's time, being a member of the elite required participation in the Communist Party and loyalty to Tito. For those excluded from this select group, ethnicity presented a new basis of legitimacy: ethnic loyalty. As this new type of legitimacy became accepted, would-be leaders gained power by showing loyalty to Serbian mastery or to Slovak rights, not to being a favored son of the Communist Party hierarchy. An entirely new set of elites, speaking different languages and having different qualifications for leadership, thus arose and became empowered.

Elite competition is more likely to occur when the status quo is in flux. When a country's political leadership's legitimacy is eroding, it is more likely to play the ethnic card to stay in power. Moreover, if the leadership appears vulnerable, its rivals also are more likely to seek to mobilize the populace, whether it be along ethnic lines or through some other method. In Yugoslavia, for example, Tito's death led to the slow unraveling of the federation structure that had kept a grim peace for forty years. As the structure unraveled, leaders and would-be leaders sought other bases of support, including calls for reform. Ethnicity, however, struck a chord among the populace at large, leading a number of leaders to successfully mobilize their followers along ethnic lines.

The dynamic of elite competition often leads to a competitive mobilization process. As one form of elite legitimacy (e.g., Communist Party service, participation in an anti-colonial movement, democratic elections) decays, all individuals in power suffer. Furthermore, when one group mobilizes along ethnic lines, security dilemma and status concerns grow. This combination of eroding legitimacy and new concerns makes playing the ethnic card attractive to leaders, who must shore up their declining power. As Yugoslavia decayed, for example, Serbian leader Slobodan Milosevic began to stress ethnic issues to keep and acquire more power for himself and his coterie in the face of a reformist challenge. He successfully advanced politically in the mid-1980s, despite opposition from the Communist Party leadership. By demonizing other groups, however, Milosevic in effect transformed the country's political dialogue. Croats, Slovaks, and others had to mobilize and organize for self-defense in the face of Milosevic's onslaught. As social groups armed and violence began, more moderate leaders, including many leaders at the federal level, who favored organizing the country around different concepts of power and identity, found themselves powerless.[60]

Elite competition assumes that identities are at least somewhat malleable (see Chapter 5). Competing elites try to make different identities salient, concentrating their energies on the ones that will reinforce the elites' positions. Ethnic leaders, for example, stress that an individual is a "Serb" rather than a "worker," a "Yugoslav," a "Banja Lukan," or another identity.

Identities, however, are not infinitely malleable. All individuals carry within them multiple identities, but bringing a specific identity to the fore is difficult. Circumstances often conspire to make individuals more aware of their regional, state, or economic bonds. Some identities are so weak that they have little political salience, despite the identity of would-be leaders. In theory, Americans could identify by hair color, football team preference, favorite soft drink, or some other marker. Although many Americans believe blondes have more fun, can identify Green Bay Packer "cheeseheads" by their distinctive headwear, and want to be "a Pepper," these superficial identities lack political meaning, and thus would have little resonance if politicians tried to mobilize people along these lines. In addition, individuals must receive outside validation for their identity to function.[61] Although I may claim to be an Inuit, for example, this claim has little political meaning unless others accept it and treat me accordingly.

Elite competition almost always masquerades as some other form of conflict and thus is difficult to distinguish. Competitive elites warn about security threats, the likelihood of discrimination, and the need to ensure group supremacy even when their goals are entirely self-serving and there is little reason for concern. Elite competition is often best seen as a catalyzing or facilitating factor for other, deeper causes of conflict although, as noted, it can at times trigger these causes with remarkably little effort.

The Need for Organization

All four causes previously discussed—the security dilemma, status concerns, hegemonic ambitions, and elite competition—have one similarity: all require at least some degree of successful organization for conflict to be sustained. Although disorganized groups can still run riot and kill thousands, a sustained campaign of violence is difficult if not impossible without at least a modicum of organization. A strong, well-organized movement is not necessary for ethnic conflict but, in general, it is essential for the most politically effective types of violence. Groups that cannot organize find it harder to confront other groups or press their governments.[62] To sustain an anti-government campaign, advance the cause of a communal group, or otherwise use violence as part of a long-term agenda, the group in question must have some established leaders, a modus operandi, an intelligence network, a recruitment arm, sources of money, and perhaps even links to outside supporters. Without organization, security and status fears often provoke little notice, and hegemonic goals are but the unvoiced ambitions of powerless peoples. Furthermore, for ethnic elites, successful organization is often far more important than actually achieving their avowed aims, for it is through organization that they gain power.

As discussed in subsequent chapters, many strategies to keep the peace do so by preventing autonomous political organization. Leaders who seek to rally their followers against the regime are often bribed, brutalized, or both, facing the choice of years in prison for continued opposition or a lucrative position if they desist. Their followers, to a lesser extent, face a similar choice between harassment or rewards. When inhibiting organization is successful, only the most dedicated activists continue. Over time, efforts to promote a new identity, remove the basis for status complaints, or reassure groups as to their security can sink in, reducing the salience of ethnicity as a means of political mobilization.

The Role of Outside Powers

The causes of conflict are not confined within a state's borders. Many ethnic groups live in more than one country, and a country's neighbors often intervene in communal politics for reasons of state. Outside powers have a tremendous impact on ethnic conflict. As noted in Chapter 8, they can at times help bring about a lasting peace. More commonly, outside powers can foster security fears, promote dissatisfaction with social status, make hegemony more plausible, and aid belligerent elites. Indeed, some scholars even argue that at least some measure of international sponsorship is necessary for an ethnic movement to become a successful national movement.[63]

Outside powers can trigger the security dilemma by threatening groups' future security. This is particularly likely if an outside power has historic ties to one group in particular. The growth of Shi'a radicalism in Iran and the subsequent Iranian revolution alarmed the Sunni Arab leadership in Iraq, who feared that the long-standing ties between Iraqi and Iranian Shi'a would lead to revolution in Iraq itself. To prevent any threat, the Sunni Arab–dominated government in Baghdad cracked down hard on Iraqi Shi'a, particularly on those individuals with any ties to Iran.

Outside support can make resistance a more plausible option, increasing an ethnic group's expectation that it will achieve its goals in spite of opposition from the state. In Iraq, the Kurds began receiving aid from Iran, the United States, and Israel in the 1960s. Since then, conflict has been almost constant. Outside support made the Kurds far more likely to rise up against the central government, simply because they were able to make a more credible attempt at gaining power. In Lebanon, a host of outside powers including Syria, Israel, Iran, Libya, Iraq, Palestinian groups, and Saudi Arabia provided money and weapons to their favored proxies. This enabled almost every communal group or faction to use violence.

Outside powers can also highlight the weakness of a central government, thus reducing its credibility regarding the enforcement of peace and the ability to protect one group from the hegemonic predations of another. The constant Israeli battering of Palestinians in Lebanon and the virtual autonomy attained by Palestinian militias within Lebanon discredited the central government and convinced ethnic groups that they would have to organize and arm to defend themselves since the government clearly was not up to the task. The Iraqi regime suffered a similar blow to its credibility after the Persian Gulf War, when its military was crushed and its boasts of vanquishing the United States were proven hollow. Iraq's Shi'a and Kurds rose up almost immediately.

In addition to increasing security concerns, outside powers and kinsmen abroad can foster disputes over a group's relative status. Like the stimuli of modernization, migration, education, and colonization already noted, outside powers can promote intergroup competition where none existed before. Comparison, after all, is the basis of status complaints. Events outside a country can highlight status deficiencies, and meddling outside governments can seize on status issues to generate unrest. The outside power can champion a downtrodden ethnic group, publicizing its misery and exhorting it to remedy its plight. For example, the Iranian government called on Shi'a around the world to rise up and establish a Shi'a-dominated society. The religious regime in Iran also organized and armed Shi'a in Lebanon. The result was a surge in Shi'a militancy around the world, particularly in Lebanon.

Outside powers can publicize claims of discrimination or subordination, thus heightening awareness of a potential slight. Such publicity need not be deliberate. Advances for a communal group in one country can trigger a demonstration effect, leading groups in other countries to demand the same privileges. The Iranian revolution galvanized the Shi'a community of Lebanon by its example as much as by its propaganda. The British grant of independence to Egypt, Syria, and Iraq in the 1930s heightened tension in the Palestine Mandate area by leading Palestinian Arabs to believe that they were excluded from this wave of freedom because of the Jewish presence. These examples of co-ethnic success abroad led the Lebanese Shi'a and Palestinian Arabs, respectively, to mobilize and demand greater recognition of their communal status. The outside influence, however, need not even be in a similar geographic area. The civil rights movement in the United States helped inspire a host of movements overseas, including those in Northern Ireland and South Africa.

Outside exhortations can alarm rival communities and heighten their status fears. The eager reception of Egyptian President Nasser's pan-Arabism by the world's Sunni Arab population heightened tensions with non-Sunni Arab communal groups in the Arab world. In different ways, Jews, Berbers, Kurds, and even Shi'a all feared Arab nationalism. In Iraq, Shi'a and Kurds came to oppose the pan-Arab cause for fear that it would subsume their identities. In Syria, minorities in the military and elsewhere became disillusioned with pan-Arabism when they realized it served as a tool for Sunni Arab dominance. Similarly, pan-Arab propaganda from foreign states increased tension between Lebanon's Christian communities and the Sunni Muslims, as the Christians feared that the Muslims sought to join Lebanon to the larger Arab world, thus greatly reducing the status of the Christians.

The same outside influences that inspire status and security concerns can also prompt hegemonic conflict. Foreign powers can change the ambitions of ethnic groups and increase fears of hegemony by rival social groups. The spread of Arab nationalism out of Egypt in the late 1950s inspired Arab nationalists throughout the Middle East, leading them to pursue a hegemonic agenda of Arabizing their countries. In Iraq and Syria, an Arab nationalist regime took power and sought to Arabize the country, despite the presence of many minority groups in the country. Outside powers can promote these changed attitudes by making hegemony more plausible through their example or by providing a group with material aid.

Finally, outside powers can also make elite competition more likely and more dangerous. Elites often use the public space provided by outside powers to promote their agendas. India supported Tibetan dissidents, including the Dalai Lama, in order to weaken China's hold on Tibet. Iraqi Kurdish leaders often operated out of Iran, keeping their cause alive even after the Ba'ath regime had destroyed Kurdish resistance within the country. More forcefully, outside powers can intervene to protect ethnic leaders, allowing them to mobilize their followers without interference. Indeed, in the Transnistr region of Moldova, Transnistrian politicians escalated their demands and violence after Moscow made its support for their cause clear. The Kremlin provided weapons, and members of the 14th Army, many of whom were from the Transnistr region, supported the rebels. This military support both encouraged the Transnistrian elites to, in effect, secede from Moldova and allowed them to succeed when Moldova tried to crush them.[64]

Conclusion

The theories presented in this chapter are not alternative explanations and often overlap in practice: groups that fear for their security, for example, often resent discrimination as well. Hegemonic groups often provoke status or security conflicts with subordinate groups. A particularly common cause of conflict that coexists with others is the presence of elite competition. Elites exploit broader mass grievances concerning security, status, or dominance. Outside powers play on all of these causes, exacerbating their influence. When various causes coexist, the potential for conflict grows.

The review of causes of conflict and their necessary conditions and characteristics is useful when delving into the broader question of how to keep the peace. If a government can prevent or disrupt the necessary conditions, then it will be better able to prevent that cause of conflict from functioning. If it can treat the characteristics, it might be able to mitigate the conflict. Or, in the worst case of all, outside governments can better recognize when little or nothing can be done and instead devote their resources to conflicts that can be solved. The remainder of this book draws on this base and addresses the possible means of overcoming these causes of conflict and of successfully keeping the peace.

3 Control Policies

No tool for keeping the peace is as controversial as the use of force. Humanitarians and civil libertarians are rightly suspicious of regimes that claim to use force to maintain social order because this is often a pretext for tyranny. Indeed, heavy-handed police and military forces, which see the truncheon and the jail cell as the best response to any dissent, regularly spark revolutions and social unrest. Nevertheless, force is perhaps the most widely used tool for preventing conflict. Even in the most benign democracies, certain types of behavior—assault, conspiracy to murder, and discrimination—are outlawed, with the threat of state-sponsored force to back the laws.

The necessity of force is well-established. Philosophers since the time of Thomas Hobbes have recognized that the threat of government punishment for the use of violence is at the core of a civilized society. The father of modern social science, Max Weber, argued that government can even be defined by its monopoly over the legitimate use of force. All governments use force at some time and when a government cannot use force to maintain order it is, in effect, no government at all. Given its importance and ubiquity, it is not surprising that the use of force is often at the heart of whether ethnic conflict begins, continues, or recurs. However unpleasant it is to admit, a variety of measures to "control" ethnic activism—a term used here to mean the use of force to shape political action—are necessary to keep the peace after ethnic conflict has occurred.[1]

What are the effective ways to control communal conflict? How does control affect the causes of ethnic conflict? What particular advantages does it offer to policymakers? What disadvantages are present when force is used? What are the conditions required for its successful implementation? These are the questions this chapter addresses.

Some form of control is required after ethnic conflict to dampen the security dilemma, restrain hegemonic ethnic groups, and deter potentially chauvinistic elites. Knowing that a strong government exists that will punish violence reassures ethnic groups, allowing them to avoid taking up arms purely for self-defense. For those individuals and groups that are hegemonic or seek to use violence to advance their own agendas, control creates a disincentive for ethnic unrest by threatening prison or worse. Hatred, fear, envy, or contempt between individuals of different ethnic groups may be strong, but the fear of punishment by the state prevents individuals from acting on their feelings. Control also can reassure dominant groups that they are secure in their dominant position: what more obvious sign of dominance is there than securing control over police and security forces?

Should such threats and reassurance fail, control can directly weaken a group by imprisoning its members, censoring its activities, or otherwise reducing its ability to organize and carry out violence. Effective police and security forces also prevent thugs and mobs from robbing and intimidating other groups and citizens in general. When potentially violent individuals cannot (or fear to) take up arms or organize because they are deterred by a strong government, peaceful citizens can sleep securely.

Control can also buy time for policymakers who seek to change their societies, allowing them to impose new institutions, or even new ways of life, on groups that otherwise would not freely accept them. Control in this sense acts as a complement to other policies discussed in this book, by helping governments to impose electoral systems, foster a new identity, or otherwise change ethnic and political dynamics.

Control, however, can also have many disadvantages. Most important (and least surprisingly), control generates resentment. Individuals do not like being restricted or harassed, and the level of resentment grows in direct proportion to the level of control. Thus, while control dampens the security dilemma, it often incites the status concerns of groups that feel they bear the brunt of government discrimination. More repressive governments risk trading today's peace for tomorrow's conflict.[2] Hegemonic groups are particularly resentful of control when they do not dominate the state. In such circumstances, control will be seen (rightly) as an obstacle to the group's ambitions.

Control policies are often difficult to implement. For control to succeed, the state must be stronger than the groups it seeks to dominate. Geography, leadership, demographics, social organization, and other factors all shape the implementation of control. Thus, policies that would strengthen groups at a local level (such as consociational democracy, discussed in Chapter 6) are often incompatible with control. Successful control requires excellent intelligence. It is not enough to repress, governments must repress well.

This chapter presents a typology of control and presents the putative effects of its variants. The actual effects of control are noted, drawing on two instances in the Middle East—Israeli Arab and Israeli Jewish relations following the creation of Israel and Arab-Kurd relations in Iraq under the Ba'ath since 1968—as examples. These effects then are related to the causes of ethnic conflict discussed in Chapter 2. The chapter concludes by presenting the advantages and disadvantages inherent to control and noting the ideal conditions for its implementation.

Variations of Control

The essence of control involves preventing political action through intimidation. Intimidation, however, takes many forms. As we shall see, the experiences of Israel and Iraq suggest four categories of control policies. The first type of control is police control, which involves providing groups with security by punishing the use of violence after the fact, similar to the role played by police forces in Western societies. The second type of control is selective control. Selective control is far more proactive than police control and involves repressing leaders and those seeking to organize along ethnic lines. The third type of control is brute force, which involves the systematic and widespread use of force to repress any expression of ethnic activity, violent or not. The fourth type of control is divide-and-rule. Unlike the first three types of control, divide-and-rule hinders organization by promoting internal divisions rather than by using punishment. Of course, these variations are ideal types, and governments often use elements of all four categories or shift their approach from one category to another.

Police control is the use of force to provide security from ethnic violence for all individuals. Police control is found to some degree in all functioning states, including all Western democracies. In the United States, for example, it is permissible to demonstrate for the rights of Italian-Americans or to march in a parade on Saint Patrick's Day. You will be arrested, however, if you try to use violence as part of any ethnic rights or solidarity campaign. In short, police control is distinguishable from other types of control by its widely accepted legitimate nature.

Police control is not just directed against minorities or weak groups; it also prevents the dominant group from attacking the minority group. Radicals within the majority group, for whatever reason, may seek to provoke or put down the rival minority group, and preventing such harassment is an important part of providing a secure overall environment.

When properly implemented, police control eases fears about other groups using force. If no group can use violence without suffering the consequences of being controlled, then no group need arm itself in self-defense. Thus, successful police control removes a necessary condition for the security dilemma to function. This relaxation in fear can foster social change in the long term. For example, if peace is widespread, individuals in the group can leave their tribe or home and pursue work elsewhere, a decision that in the past would have left the tribe vulnerable to military pressure from rival groups and left the individual vulnerable to attack away from the security of his home.

Selective control is the use of force against ethnic group leaders and those suspected of engaging in ethnic political activity, regardless of the degree of violence intended. This type of control is intended to prevent ethnic political organization that has the potential to produce violence. At low levels, such control might involve censorship, police harassment, or laws prohibiting organized ethnic political activity. With selective control, even a St. Patrick's Day parade might be out of the question if political intent was suspected. At higher levels, this type of control includes imprisonment, murder, or exile. Selective control does not include control against ethnic group members not involved (or suspected of being involved) in ethnic political activity.

Selective control is the most common way that Middle Eastern governments manage ethnic differences and attempt to prevent ethnic violence. Just to stay in power, most Middle Eastern governments have skilled intelligence, police, and security services. Human rights organizations' reports of bludgeoned Palestinians and imprisoned Bahraini Shi'a highlight a sad truth about the regularity of the use of force in the Middle East. Such visible violence is just the tip of the iceberg. Police harassment, press censorship, and limits on assembly also are used regularly to ensure that citizens, including potential ethnic dissidents, do not resist the government. Unlike police control, selective control is not accepted throughout the world as legitimate. Many elements of selective control violate civil liberties, such as the right to speak and assemble freely, that are taken for granted in the West.

Selective control tries to make a violent contest for power or gain unthinkable or unworkable through the use and threat of force. Group attempts to act collectively become more difficult as individuals within the group fear for their safety if they organize along ethnic lines. Selective control is directed at those individuals involved in politics as well as their immediate supporters; like police control, it dampens the security dilemma. Selective control is particularly effective at preventing any group mobilization along chauvinistic lines, thus hindering the efforts to would-be ethnic entrepreneurs and hegemonic groups that might seek to impose their will. Violence and rabble-rousing are often the essence of ethnic mobilization, enabling elites to gain power and intimidate rivals. Although this message may still be compelling, elites who act on it will face arrest and punishment. Selective control, when properly implemented, prevents mobilization as well as violence.

Brute force involves the use of force against ethnic group members regardless of ethnic political activity. Mere membership in the ethnic group is enough to impose the heavy hand of the state. Low levels of brute force might be limited to legal discrimination against all members of the group, while high levels would be characterized by widespread terror in the form of random extra-legal killings and torture. Unlike police control or selective control, those targeted are not necessarily involved directly in using violence or engaging in politics. For example, in Iraq in the late 1980s, the Ba'athist government systematically used collective punishment to discourage Kurds from supporting guerrilla forces. The intention was to discourage guerrilla activity by destroying potential havens and raising the costs in general for the Kurds of undertaking such activity.

Brute force can have a mixed effect on hegemonic groups and minorities, depending on the target of control policies. It can intimidate hegemonic groups and their leaders, reducing their incentives for any political action. When directed at minorities, brute force can satisfy hegemonic communities, helping assure them that they remain preeminent. Brute force, however, can easily produce a backlash. Brute force engenders status concerns among its victims and, if harsh enough, creates a security dilemma situation between the ethnic group and the government, which becomes a source of future violence.

A divide-and-rule strategy attempts to weaken an ethnic or national group by appealing to its component parts as corporate groups. Rather than use police or security forces, divide-and-rule exploits divisions within the group, whether based on religion, tribe, region, or an ascriptive feature. It uses a system of rewards to separate group members. This tactic of dividing a group to rule it is hardly new: since history began, rulers have tried to stay on top by playing one group against the other. In ethnic conflict, however, this tactic can be particularly effective, as it changes the number of groups and reduces their strength.

In Israel, members of the Druze sect of Islam live peacefully next to their Jewish neighbors. Arab (and Palestinian) nationalists both claim Israeli Druzes as part of "their" people, but the Israeli government has encouraged the Druze to maintain a separate identity, which in turn has limited Druze enthusiasm for Palestinian causes. The Druzes feel sympathy for Arab and Palestinian issues, but their political loyalty is to their sect. Thus, they cooperate more with the Jewish government than with Arab activists and rarely support violence. By helping make the level of ethnic identification more restrictive, the Israeli government has divided the ranks of potential opponents.

Divide-and-rule affects the components of the group and its propensity to organize. Divide-and-rule can include political, economic, or symbolic benefits that affect a subgroup's level of contentment with its position in society. For example, in Israel the Druze are granted control of their own religious establishment (a symbolic benefit), better access to government patronage, and disproportionate political representation. The intended effect of these benefits is to prevent the Druze from working with the broader Arab Muslim community, which is granted fewer benefits. Thus, if an individual Druze chooses to identify with the broader community, benefits gained from being considered a Druze rather than an Arab Muslim are jeopardized. Although Arabs in Israel often are treated poorly, Druzes on the whole are accorded a considerable measure of respect. Thus, individuals and elites among the Druze have less incentive to use violence.

Elites in particular are likely to be affected by divide-and-rule tactics. Such tactics turn the potential problem of elite competition into a government asset. If the elites of a smaller ethnic group (such as the Druze in Israel) were to join the larger community (Palestinian Arab Muslims), they may lose their elite positions. As a result, elites at a subethnic level have an incentive to rally supporters behind the government and to separate themselves from the ethnic group at large.

As this discussion makes clear, control policies often vary considerably in practice. Each variant targets different parts of society. Police control only affects those individuals engaging in violence; selective control focuses on preventing ethnic organization in general and thus pays particular attention to potential activists; and brute force targets all forms of ethnic activity. The distinction between police control and stronger variants can best be understood in terms of the difference between "denial" (weakening the target group to the point where it cannot cause problems) and "deterrence" (persuading the target group or individuals in it that the cost of making trouble is too high). Police control relies on deterrence, while selective force and brute force rely on both deterrence and denial. Divide-and-rule is somewhat distinct from other forms of control, since it focuses particular attention on cleavages and actors at the subethnic level. Tribe, sect, and region often become important as the government searches for possible sources of division that might prevent the group from acting as one corporate entity.

The means for each strategy vary as well. Police control jails or silences those involved in violence; selective control often involves censorship or limits on free assembly for activists of all stripes as well as more draconian punishments for those involved in violence; brute force often includes the killing of members of an ethnic group simply because they did not actively support the government. Divide-and-rule often involves administrative changes or other attempts to recognize and strengthen a component of a group.

In practice, control policies often are a mix of the above variants. The Israeli government used selective control to prevent Israeli Arab mobilization following the 1948 War of Independence, prohibiting autonomous political organization and censoring leaders. At the same time, the government used police control against Jews who might otherwise have harassed or killed their Arab neighbors. Finally, the government used divide-and-rule policies to separate Druze, Christians, and other minority groups from the broader Arab population. These combinations are common in the Middle East and in the world in general.

Table 1 provides an overview of the hypothesized effects of control policies, noting how different variants produce different effects. Various types of control affect group security concerns, the behavior of elites, the perceptions of hegemonic groups, and the abilities of groups to organize, among other key factors. The variants differ on how they affect leaders, whether they are targeted at active or passive individuals, and their impact on organization, among other factors.

Examples of Control

Given the efficacy of control, it is not surprising that governments throughout the world employ it. Levels of repression are particularly high in the Middle East, where the democratic revolution has yet to break. Indeed, perhaps more than in any other region of the world, Middle Eastern governments are skilled at blending many forms of repression to reduce communal violence and any form of political activism at all.

The degree, form, and scope of control policies differ considerably from country to country and from regime to regime. After independence in 1948, the Israeli government used selective control and divide-and-rule to prevent unrest among the Israeli Arab population, although this practice has declined considerably in recent years. In Iraq, the Ba'ath regime employed brute force to stop Kurdish activism. Neither of these regimes relied exclusively on control to keep order, but their experiences illustrate many of the fundamental questions about the efficacy and difficulty of employing control policies.

Israel: Arabs and Jews under the Military Government, 1948–1966

Why Arabs and Jews living within the Israeli state have not clashed since Israel's founding remains a mystery to many.[3] After the 1947–49 wars, most Palestinian Arabs left the new state of Israel. Those who remained were hostile to, and suspected by, their Jewish neighbors.[4] Although Jewish authorities admitted the so-called Israeli Arabs into the same state, the two groups did not form one Israeli community.[5] As Sammy Smooha and John Hofman note, "The two groups exhibit pervasive cultural differences. They differ in all basic values, such as ethnic origin, religion, language, nationality, and family structure."[6] Despite this gulf, violent con-

TABLE 1. Control Variants and Their Impact

Type of Control	*Deter Potentially Hostile Activists*	*Intimidate Entire Group*	*Hinder Ethnic Organization in General*	*Disrupt Militants Who Are Not Deterred*	*Alter Elite Incentives to Raising Ethnic Issues*	*Reassure Dominant Group*	*Buy Time for Regime to Impose New Institutions*	*Engender Status Concerns*	*Reassure Non-active Individuals as to Their Security*
Police control	x					x	x		x
Selective control	x		x	x	x	x	x	x	x
Brute force	x	x	x	x		x		x	
Divide-and-rule			x		x	x	x		

flict between Jews and Palestinians living within Israel's boundaries stopped after the wars of 1947–49. Israeli Arabs were not a fifth column during subsequent Arab-Israeli wars, nor did they support Palestinian terrorists. In fact, some Israeli Arabs participated in voluntary war work.

This mysterious passivity is especially surprising given the relationship between Israeli Arabs and Israeli Jews. After 1949, Israeli Arabs feared for their security and worried about their status—both potential sources of conflict. The violence during the period of British rule over the Palestine Mandate (which lasted from 1920 to 1948), the civil war preceding statehood, and even the early years of the military government led Israeli Arabs to fear for their security. Nor were Israeli Arabs well represented in elite positions or in government. The Jewish government had expropriated at least some of the land from over half of the Israeli Arab families. In general, the treatment of the Israeli Arabs by the Israeli government, when compared to the British government that ruled the area before Israeli independence, was far worse with regard to consulting with the community, allowing its members to organize, and respecting Arab culture. Conflict originating from the Jewish community also was possible. Israeli Jews had a hegemonic ideology, seeking a state for, and largely of, Jews. In addition, they feared that Israeli Arabs would prove loyal to the larger Arab community.

Events outside Israel and official ideology further strained relations and divided the communities. The strong irredentism of Israel's Arab neighbors exacerbated tension between the communities within Israel. Furthermore, Israeli Jews resented the Israeli Arabs' identification with the Palestinian cause and the broader Arab world, seeing it as proof that Israeli Arabs were not loyal to the Jewish state. Many Israeli Arabs, for their part, objected to Israel's raison d'être—the ingathering of Jews in a Jewish state—while Israeli slogans, such as the "redemption of the land" (*geulat haaretz*), similarly were considered exclusive by minorities.

Despite all these problems, violence did not break out. Given the level of communal division, the absence of violence following the establishment of the State of Israel is surprising. Although relations were hardly warm, they could easily have been far worse and led to widespread bloodshed. Control policies were important, indeed vital, to maintaining this peace.

RELATIONS AFTER INDEPENDENCE. In 1949, the Palestinians in the new State of Israel found themselves strangers in a familiar land. Perhaps as many as 750,000 Palestinian Arabs of a pre-war population of 900,000 had left or were driven out of Israel. Almost the entire Palestinian Arab elite were among those who had fled. Of those Palestinians who remained, one-sixth to one-half were internal refugees, separated from their homes and their land. Arab cities in particular were devastated. Jaffa's Mandate population of 70,000 Arabs shrank to fewer than 3,600; Haifa's went from 71,200 to 2,900; and the Arab communities of Tiberias and Safad disappeared completely. Israeli Arabs were (and remain) geographically concentrated in three areas. In 1948, approximately 90,000 lived in central or western Galilee; 31,000 lived in the "Little Triangle"; and 13,000, most of whom were bedouin, lived in the Negev.[7] The remaining 30,000 or so were scattered in mixed cities or in Jewish areas. Of those who remained, 71 percent were Arab Muslims; 21 percent were Christians; and 9 percent were Circassian and Druze. The change was enormous. By 1949, the new Israeli Arabs found themselves a much smaller, much weaker community.

Symbolic changes inherent in switching from a colonial state to a Jewish national home compounded these demographic and material losses for Israeli Arabs. The civic life of the new state—Independence Day, the Sabbath, Jewish festivals, and other official events—held little meaning for Israeli Arabs, or even reminded them of their loss of dominance. Furthermore, the Israeli stamp on their passports made them pariahs in the rest of the Arab world. As one Israeli Arab community leader noted, "It is difficult to explain the shock our community felt after the War. Overnight, it seemed, we had lost everything."[8]

For Israeli Jews, the new state came about at an enormous cost. Over six thousand Jews died in the fighting for independence. Even after the armistice, Arab infiltrators murdered dozens of Jews, and the neighboring Arab states never renounced their aggressive intentions. Not surprisingly, a siege mentality developed.

The practical problem of absorbing a flood of new citizens complicated this insecurity. Between 1948 and 1951, over 650,000 Jewish immigrants entered Israel, doubling the country's Jewish population. To absorb these returning kinsmen, the Jewish leadership sought to put Arab resources at the disposal of Jewish authorities and confiscated huge amounts of Palestinian land. As a result of various expropriations, Arab villages often lost more than two-thirds of their land, and much of the land that remained in their hands was of poor quality.

MANAGING ETHNIC RELATIONS. To manage the Palestinian Arab community, the Israeli government used a combination of selective control, co-optation, and divide-and-rule strategies. Co-optation, examined further in Chapter 4, helped make control policies more palatable and increased the benefits associated with divide-and-rule efforts. This combination of policies prevented Israeli Arabs from organizing independently of the government and reassured Israeli Jews of their security and status.

The new Israeli government immediately placed Arab areas under military rule. Although the use of military government had its origins in British laws enacted during times of unrest, the Israelis used these laws despite the lack of violence in the Israeli Arab population, justifying their decision as a preemptive security measure. Prime Minister Ben Gurion and other Israeli leaders cited internal subversion and aid to foreign infiltrators as possible dangers that might occur should military government be abolished.

The military government restrictions were an attempt to use selective control to prevent any hostile Israeli Arab political activity. Although they placed limits on the use of violence to terrorize a subject population, they allowed censorship, the restriction of free movement, and administrative detention. The military government also had the power to deprive individuals of their possessions, control contacts among suspected dissidents, require regular check-ins at a police station, and expel people. The government also maintained an active intelligence presence in Israeli Arab areas.

The military government sought to prevent Arabs from organizing and to weaken them as a community. The government appointed village headmen and used them as information sources, not as community representatives. Although Arab members of the Knesset existed, they were entirely creatures of the Mapai (which later became the Labor Party) government; for example, Arab members of the Knesset repeatedly voted against abolishing military government, which was widely loathed by Israeli Arabs. Israeli Arabs were under a strict curfew, and granting of work permits was often conditional on informing on those politically active in the village, particularly those who were considering violence.

Although the Israeli system promised nominal rights and equality for Arabs, the Mapai government did not enforce the laws protecting Israeli

Arab rights. Israeli courts were not willing to interfere on security matters, which by definition included almost anything concerned with the military government, and many of the laws passed to prevent discrimination were not enforced with regard to the Arabs.[9]

Over time, Israeli Arabs became increasingly dependent on the Jewish economy. Despite representing a substantial percentage of the total population, few Arabs, particularly Sunni Muslim Arabs, held white-collar jobs or academic positions, or were members of the professional classes. In part because government and Jewish institutions did not invest in Arab areas, infrastructure was lacking there, and Arab farmers and firms were at a competitive disadvantage. State regulations, administrative policies, and lack of action combined to prevent the development of an Arab economy. As a result, many Arabs became workers on Jewish concerns in agriculture or as urban wage-earners.

The extent of Jewish penetration of Arab society was far greater than that of the pre-independence, colonial government. As Sharif Kanaana notes:

> In this society the Jew, unlike the Britisher, is not only a soldier, he is the whole society, and he controls every aspect of the villager's everyday life. The Jew is the police officer, the tax collector, the nurse, the doctor, the lawyer, the taxi driver, the office clerk, the bank teller, the employer, the seller, the buyer of the crops, the political leader, the governor; he is everything, and always he is in a position of power and control, and he is hard to understand and to deal with, he is a stranger with strange ways.[10]

This penetration made it easier for the Israeli government to influence Israeli Arab behavior. Israeli Arabs had few economic or political resources independent of the government.

Israeli officials also tried to split off the Druze, Christian, and bedouin communities from the larger Arab one. The government gave Christians greater privileges to divide them from Muslims and allowed Druze and bedouin communities greater freedom of movement than other Arabs. Furthermore, the government permitted members of both the Druze and bedouin communities to join the army—a key concession because military service came with a host of economic benefits and was a symbol of civic inclusion. The government also fractured communities internally. The military government divided the bedouin into forty-one tribal factions and organized the Arab village population by clan.

The Druze in particular were culled from the Arab flock. In 1957, the government recognized the Druze as an independent Muslim religious community with their own religious courts and officials. The Druze were required to list "Druze" rather than "Arab" on their identity cards.[11] Druze villages were often given disproportionate financial assistance—three times as much as was spent on Muslim or Christian Arabs.[12] The Druze found it relatively easy to find work in Israel and hold high positions in the army, the Histadrut (the immensely powerful labor federation), and the Ministry of Education. Despite the traditional Druze culture of autonomy, they became increasingly dependent on the Israeli state. A Druze leadership developed that would not exist if the community were classed as part of the broader Muslim community.

The government also sought to assuage Jewish fears about security and to satisfy demands for Jewish hegemony. In general, Jewish institutions remained of and for Jews. Muslim and Christian Arabs, for example, were not allowed to join the army, which was a major source of material benefits (welfare assistance programs, jobs, among others) as well as a symbol of national identity and a guarantor of security. Jewish institutions originally founded to create a Jewish state—the Jewish Agency, the Jewish National Fund, and the World Zionist Organization—after 1948 worked to expand Jewish immigration and land ownership. These institutions often had budgets comparable to that of the Israeli government, and all of it was spent exclusively on Jews. Indeed, their internal constitutions pledged the organizations to work only for the welfare of Jews. Most government ministries had separate Arab departments, but these often operated without budgets or policies. Israeli leaders denied even token efforts to demonstrate binationalism. For example, in 1958, Prime Minister Ben Gurion refused to accept an identity card because it was also printed in Arabic.[13] The government employed a strong security presence in Israeli Arab areas to reassure the Jewish community as well as prevent subversion. As one Israeli expert noted: "Even then many people in government realized that the Arabs were peaceful. But no government could be seen as soft on this issue because most Jews still considered these Arabs to be enemies."[14]

POLITICAL PARTIES UNDER THE MILITARY GOVERNMENT. Political parties reinforced selective control (and to a lesser extent co-optation) by interfering with independent Israeli Arab political organization. Thus, political parties in Israel did not fulfill traditional functions of parties such as articulating community demands or helping interest groups be heard in decision-making. Although Israeli Arabs participated in the political process in large numbers, this did not provide them with tangible influence in decision-making.

The military government worked against the formation of independent Arab political movements, and Zionist political parties did not seek to create lasting institutions to keep Arabs politically active. The government discouraged independent political activity. Zionist political parties tacitly agreed not to bring parties that championed the Israeli Arab cause, such as the Communist Party, into governing coalitions. When Israeli Arabs tried to form their own political movement, Zionist political parties usually had separate Arab lists, which facilitated clientism rather than political mobilization. The fate of the Al-Ard (the Land) movement is instructive. Al-Ard, an Arab party that called for equal rights for Arabs and Jews and the return of expropriated land, held an Arab nationalist philosophy. Its rhetoric reflected sympathy for Nasser. In 1961, the group formed around a newspaper of the same name, which the military government quickly closed down. In 1964, the group registered in the Journalists League. The authorities then declared the group illegal on security grounds, jailed several leaders, placed others under house arrest, and made membership punishable by imprisonment.[15]

The Israeli government also prevented the formation of independent institutions (sport clubs, youth groups, writers' clubs, and so on) that might take on a political role. Often when such a group would arise, Israeli Jewish institutions such as the Histadrut would offer a rival to it while authorities would suppress the original independent group or harass group members. For example, attempts to form an Arab Sports Club to include youth from Galilee and the Little Triangle led the government to arrest its organizers and close the village where they tried to meet.[16] At the same time, the Histadrut began to form sports clubs for Israeli Arabs. Until 1967, *Al-Yawm* (the Day) was the only Arabic newspaper published, and it came out under the aegis of the Histadrut.

The Israeli elective system served to facilitate control, not representation, by intensifying clan rivalries. The government drew electoral lists from rival clans, and each clan was given different ballots, so the military authorities would know how they voted. Alarmed at the prospect of one clan forming an exclusive alliance with the military administration, elders of other clans sought their own connections with authorities. The military administration then based its patronage on which clan cooperated most, with cooperation being measured by the clans' willingness to inform on dissidents, sell land, and deliver votes.

Given that patronage was based on support for the government, it is not surprising that ruling parties, particularly the Mapai Party and the National Religious Party, gained most Israeli Arab votes during the military government period. These parties controlled the patronage gates and the levers of the military government. Without the approval of the Mapai Party, no Arab civil servant would be appointed and no help would be extended to an Arab area. The Ministry of Religion used its powers to appoint prayer leaders and religious court officials to reward government supporters. Because the Ministry was often controlled by religious parties, Arab villages at times voted to support Jewish religious parties.

The Israeli policy of undermining the Arab community proved successful. Throughout the duration of the military government, Israeli Arabs were not able to organize politically, even for peaceful purposes. In 1954, Moshe Karen, the Arab-affairs editor for *Ha'aretz,* wrote:

> [t]he Arabs who live in our State are almost the opposite of a pressure group; they constitute a group which has at its disposal almost no means of exerting pressure. Anyone who is aware of the decisive importance, in a system such as ours, of having access to means of exerting pressure in order to obtain some favor or satisfy some demand, will easily understand how not having access to such means of pressure influences the status of such a group and the likelihood that its needs will be met.[17]

LIMITED VIOLENCE BUT MUTUAL SUSPICION. Almost no violence against Jews by Israeli Arabs occurred during the time of the military government, and the few attempts at subversion were quickly discovered and prevented. At the same time, however, the military government's harsh hand engendered resentment among Israeli Arabs. The great majority of Israeli Arabs who actually became involved in violence were young men who were badly treated by the military government, which reaped the whirlwind of its policies. The vast majority of Israeli Arabs, however, became resigned to Israel's existence and even those who opposed it did not do so actively.

Despite the lack of violence, both communities remained hostile to the other. Although politically quiescent, Israeli Arabs did not support the established order. One survey taken at the end of military government indicated that over half of Israeli Arabs would prefer to live in an Arab state rather than in Israel. Press articles by Israeli Arabs suggested high levels of resentment over land expropriations, economic discrimination, and restrictions on education. Israeli Arab intellectuals and poets were particularly critical of the state.

Israeli Jews, for their part, remained highly suspicious of Israeli Arabs during the military government period. Declaring that these Arabs were now Israelis did not dispel this feeling immediately.[18] Uri Loubrani, the prime minister's adviser on Arab affairs, even declared that Israeli Arabs were the "sworn and everlasting enemies" of the state.[19] The chief of the North Command, who headed the military government, once called the Arabs of Galilee "a cancer in the heart of the nation."[20] Israeli Arabs were encouraged to accept Jewish dominance and learn Jewish ways, but this encouragement was not reciprocated. In Jewish schools, English was taught as the second language; Arabic or French was offered as a third.[21]

Secure in their dominant position under the military government, Jews did not use outright violence against Israeli Arabs, even though most Jews wanted them to remain subordinate or to leave Israel. Interviews conducted in 1996 indicate that many Jews considered the police and the army to belong to them: should the Arabs use violence, Jews, in a sense, have already armed and mobilized themselves.

The brutal exception to this peace was the Kafr Qasim killings. On the eve of the 1956 war, Israeli soldiers killed forty-seven Israeli Arabs returning to their village from work, who were violating a last-minute curfew that they did not know was imposed. Although the officers and soldiers involved were punished, the Israeli Arab population believed the penalties were too light. In general, however, violence against Israeli Arabs was rare despite the high level of Jewish suspicion of the community as a whole.[22]

Fears of violence, however, dominated Arab concerns. Fouzi el-Asmar, an Arab intellectual, writes of the pervasive atmosphere of violence and intimidation during his childhood. The Kafr Qasim massacre reinforced this fear and underscored the discord between the two communities. Similarly, the security services succeeded in convincing Israeli Arabs that they learned everything there was to know from a network of informers, thus dividing the Arab community.

Outside powers played a major role both in the imposition of military government and in the one instance of significant violence—the Kafr Qasim massacre of 1956. The hostility of Israel's Arab neighbors, and their active support for subversion within Israel, contributed to popular support for military government. Despite military government control, the prospect of war increased Israeli Jewish security fears. Indeed, the Kafr Qasim massacre, which occurred on the eve of the Suez War, cannot be understood without examining the international context. The Israeli government, fearing subversion, had hastily imposed draconian security restrictions on the Israeli Arab community. The haste brought about by the impending war led to sloppiness and exaggerated fear on the part of the Israeli Jews.

CONCLUSIONS ON THE ISRAELI MILITARY GOVERNMENT AND CONTROL POLICIES. Given the many obstacles to ethnic peace, the era of the military government in Israel should be considered an impressive success in communal relations. The military government did not end communal tension; indeed, its heavy-handed methods at times inflamed it. In general, however, the military government convinced both Arabs and Jews not to take up arms. Jews were satisfied in their dominant position, seeing the military government's strictures as necessary to preserve peace. Israeli Arabs, while hardly supportive of the military government, bowed to the power of the state. In both communities, leaders found that the communal card had limited value: for Arabs because it led to their arrest or to censorship; and for Jews because the community as a whole did not fear their Arab neighbors as long as the military government remained strong. This equilibrium remained steady, except when outside powers threatened to upset it, as they did in 1956. Even then, total deaths were limited, particularly when compared with the bloody periods before independence.

Ethnic Relations in Iraq

In contrast to Israel, Iraq represents an unmitigated failure of communal relations. Its recent experience is briefly described below to illustrate the perils of an excessive use of control in the form of brute force.[23]

Tribal and communal conflict has plagued Iraq since its inception and, if anything, it is far worse today than ever before in Iraq's history. Yet on the surface Iraq does not seem doomed to communal conflict. Oil wealth has enriched the country, allowing the regime to improve dramatically the standard of living for almost all of Iraq's inhabitants. Moreover, the country's many communities have at times cooperated against outsiders and lived together in harmony. Despite these advantages, Iraq today is home to some of the bloodiest communal conflicts in the Middle East. The Iraqi state has squandered its resources. Arab nationalist governments, particularly the Ba'ath regime that has dominated Iraq since 1968,[24] tried to subordinate Iraq's Shi'a and Kurdish communities and impose an unwanted identity on them—policies that led to repeated conflicts. After brute force was used to crush ethnic groups, once limited sectarian tension and tribal unrest became widespread, leading to hundreds of thousands of deaths. The result was a vicious security dilemma that led all communities to fear one another and the government.

Iraq had no formal existence until 1920, and its peoples shared few bonds. No Iraq existed during Ottoman rule: the area that is now Iraq consisted of the three Ottoman provinces of Basra, Baghdad, and Mosul. Ethnicity separated Iraq's Arabs, Kurds, Turkmen, and other groups, and religious differences among Muslims, Christians, and Jews created additional lines of division. Region and tribe further split Iraq's communities. Islam divided rather than unified Iraqis because the large Sunni and Shi'a communities seldom mixed and never intermarried.[25]

Beginning in the early 1960s, rebellions broke out in the Kurdish region, and agitation among Iraq's Shi'a population began in the 1970s. Although the Ba'ath temporarily quelled the Kurdish insurrection and destroyed any Shi'a opposition, in the 1980s renewed Kurdish fighting led Baghdad to carry out a mass slaughter of the Kurds—the Operation Anfal. When the Kurds and the Shi'a rose in 1991 after the Persian Gulf War, the Ba'ath killed tens of thousands from both communities and drove over a million Kurds and Shi'a into exile.

Much of the blame for these repeated insurgencies can be placed on the brutal and misguided policies of Iraq's ruling Ba'ath Party. The Ba'ath tried to impose an Arab identity on Iraq's Kurdish population and deny Iraqi Shi'a their own distinct culture and institutions. To back up its assimilation measures, the regime used a massive force, often literally annihilating those who dared to oppose their policies. These policies engendered tremendous resentment and led Kurds and Shi'a to take up arms. Arab Sunnis dominated the Ba'ath government. When the Ba'ath first came to power, almost the entire leadership consisted of Sunni Arabs from the triangle formed by Baghdad, Mosul, and the Syrian border. The Ba'ath also relied heavily on kinship and tribal networks. Three of the five members of the Revolution Command Council were from the village of Tikrit.

The blundering policy of brute force, exclusion, and assimilation created an additional security dilemma to be overcome—one between the government and the communal groups—that will prove almost impossible for any future regime to master. The Arab nationalist Ba'ath captured the Iraqi state, making it incapable of acting as an impartial third party. The sheer scale of the Ba'ath's killing and other crimes also reduces the likelihood that blandishments that might have created goodwill in the past will do so in the future.

THE BA'ATH AND THE KURDISH REVOLTS. In 1961, a Kurdish insurgency began that would last until 1975 and recur in the 1980s and 1990s. Led by tribes loyal to Mullah Mustafa Barzani, the Kurds initially strove for the right to use their language in schools, the control of local education, and a greater share of government revenue.

After taking power in 1968, the Ba'ath negotiated a short-lived peace agreement with the Kurds that soon ended in renewed fighting. In 1970, Ba'ath and Kurdish leaders agreed to a settlement granting the Kurds a high degree of autonomy. Almost immediately, the central government criticized the Kurds for seeking secession, not autonomy. The Ba'ath, however, openly flouted the accord. The regime did not implement the education or language agreements and gave Kurds almost no say in decision-making. The Ba'ath imposed Arab dominance by shutting down local schools, replacing Kurdish administrators and police, and otherwise not respecting Kurdish culture. The government often deported the leaders and engaged in mass arrests. The Kurds soon took up arms, and the region exploded into conflict. Thousands died in this conflict from the start, and it got bloodier over time. The government tried to contain the revolt by working with Barzani's Kurdish rivals. Soon tribal rivals and leftist groups began fighting against Barzani with government support.

Outside support enabled the Kurds to resist the Ba'ath initially, but eventually it proved their undoing. Israel began aiding the Kurds in 1966. More important, Iran also sent large amounts of arms and materiel to the Kurds and provided a haven to Kurdish fighters. In 1972, the United States began supporting the Kurds in cooperation with Iran. Tehran, however, was a fickle ally. The 1975 Algiers Accord granted Iran control over the Shaat al-Arab waterway and other concessions in exchange for Iran's abandonment of the Kurdish cause. The Iranian government sealed its border with Iraq and cut off supplies, leading to the end of the revolt. Kurdish cooperation with three of Iraq's declared enemies enraged the central government. Thus, many Arab nationalists came to see the Kurds as enemies of the state.

After 1975, the regime ruled with an iron hand in Iraqi Kurdistan. It resettled hundreds of thousands of Kurds outside Kurdistan in order to create a *cordon sanitaire* between Iran and Turkey and Iraq. The government destroyed over one thousand villages as part of this program. To break up concentrations of Kurds, the Ba'ath settled Arabs in their place. Torture, mass arrests, and executions ensured that everyone obeyed these brutal orders. The Ba'ath clamped down particularly hard on potential leaders. In 1975, the Ba'ath relocated the Barzani clan—traditional leaders of one of the dominant Kurdish factions—to southern Iraq, and in 1980 soldiers arrested up to eight thousand Barzani males, paraded them through the streets of Baghdad, and executed them.

The Kurds reacted to these measures with hostility, but divisions hindered effective resistance. The Kurds split into pro-Barzani forces of the Kurdish Democratic Party (KDP) and the nominally Marxist Patriotic Union of Kurdistan (PUK) of Jalal Talabani. By the late 1970s, these groups struggled far more with each other than with the central government. Dozens died in the late 1970s, as these two groups clashed, with the central government weeping crocodile tears while its opponents killed each other.

The Kurds rose again during the Iran-Iraq war, when the Ba'ath appeared threatened with defeat. Syria, Libya, and Iran armed the PUK in 1980, and Iran also worked with Barzani's Kurdish Democratic Party. Discord was so great, however, that several of the strongest factions regularly fought against one another. Not until 1986 did the Kurdish factions finally unite. Aided by Iranian advances that drained the Iraqi government's manpower, the Kurds steadily expanded their control over Kurdish areas, and the government's writ applied only during daylight hours.

The Ba'ath responded to Kurdish military successes with even more violence. They razed villages, tortured and executed families of fighters, and otherwise tried to intimidate the local population. Beginning in 1987, the regime began to use chemical weapons as part of its scorched-earth policies. Large swaths of territory were declared war zones, where anyone living would be killed on sight. In 1988, Iraq began the genocidal Operation Anfal to end the Kurdish problem. Aided by new troops who were available due to Iraqi victories in the war with Iran, the Ba'ath regional commander Ali Hasan al-Majid systematically killed Kurdish males who came into his hands. Perhaps two hundred thousand Kurds died in Operation Anfal, 1.5 million people were resettled, and several hundred thousand Kurds fled to Iran or Turkey.

But even the Anfal did not forever end Kurdish resistance to the central government. Once again, regime weakness led the Kurds to rebel—this time after the Persian Gulf War threatened the Ba'ath's hold on power. In March 1991, the Kurdish region exploded. Even Kurdish leaders such as Barzani admitted that the people took up arms spontaneously and that his group followed the people into the streets. Previous Ba'ath killings and discrimination had politicized the entire Iraqi Kurdish community. They considered the regime's weakness and the prospect of coalition assistance as an opportunity to gain their independence from the hated Ba'ath. As the regime recovered, it quickly clamped down on the Kurdish fighters. Tens of thousands of Kurds died as the central government reestablished itself. Over one million Kurds fled to Iran or Turkey.

THE SHI'A AND THE BA'ATH. The Kurds were not the only rebellious community. Iraqi Shi'a Muslims also opposed the Ba'ath. Shi'ism did not grow into a strong political movement until the 1970s. Before then, Shi'ism in Iraq was worn lightly by many adherents or considered a private affair, yet constant regime discrimination reinforced Shi'a identity and politicized it. Educated Shi'a resented the disproportionate Sunni influence in society, while religious Shi'a resented the regime's active suppression of their rites and observances. As with the Kurds, this widespread discrimination against even politically passive Shi'a engendered tremendous resentment.

The Ba'ath regime clamped down on any expressions of political Shi'ism. In 1977, during demonstrations at a religious procession, the regime arrested thousands of demonstrators and killed or imprisoned many of the procession's organizers. The Ba'ath also arrested large numbers of suspected Shi'a activists and executed Shi'a religious leaders.

The Iranian revolution led the Iraqi government to take symbolic steps toward placating Shi'ism while increasing its vigilance against any hint of Shi'a activism. The government lavished money on Shi'a shrines and gave public monies to the south. The government also appointed three Shi'a to positions on the ruling Revolutionary Command Council. Concurrent with these gestures, however, was further repression. The Ba'ath government feared that Iraqi Shi'a were working with Iran, which led it to increase surveillance. The Ba'ath also executed Shi'a leaders whom it considered threats. The Ba'ath's fears were not without foundation. During the Iran-Iraq war, Iran provided support for Iraqi Kurdish and Shi'a dissidents. In 1982, Iran formed the High Council of the Islamic Revolution to work with Iraqi Shi'a. In response, the Ba'ath regime executed hundreds of Iraqi Shi'a activists.

Like the Kurds, the Shi'a rose when the Iraqi regime appeared near collapse in 1991. And like it had done to the Kurds, the Ba'ath quickly crushed the rebellion and slaughtered many Shi'a. Although exact figures are scarce, the regime probably killed tens of thousands of Shi'a in putting down the revolt. Iran issued propaganda and provided a few weapons, but in general the revolt's sources were entirely indigenous.

CONCLUSIONS ON IRAQ AND CONTROL POLICIES. The Iraqi experience demonstrates how the excessive use of force can worsen ethnic relations. Rather than reduce the security dilemma, the regime created a new one: communal groups began to fear that the central government would repress and slaughter them rather than prevent violence in general. In contrast to the Israeli Arabs, however, the groups in Iraq had a greater ability to take up arms and were not content to accept a subordinate status. Support from Iran, and the greater numbers of the Kurds and the Shi'a, made them more willing to take up arms. Nor did the Ba'ath take steps to dampen the impact of control. In contrast to the Israeli military government, the Ba'ath did not work with local elites or consider steps to increase the status of local communities. Indeed, as discussed in Chapter 5, the Ba'ath's policy of forced assimilation worsened ethnic relations.

In Iraq, like Israel, outside meddling—or the fear of it—exacerbated ethnic tension. Iraq's problems were, if anything, more extreme. Iran's support for the Kurds and later for the Shi'a further polarized communal relations in Iraq, encouraging the various communal groups to rise up while leading the Ba'ath regime to take extremely harsh measures against both communities.

Control and the Causes of Ethnic Conflict

Table 2 summarizes the impact of control in the cases presented in this chapter. Control had a profound impact, often reducing individuals' desire, and ability, to organize for violence effectively. In Israel during the military government era, the government successfully used control to prevent Israeli Arabs from organizing against the Jewish state. Most Israeli Arabs were deterred from any violent activity, while those few who sought to use violence found themselves quickly arrested. Elites responded to control by cooperating with the state. Christian, Druze, and bedouin elites

TABLE 2. **Observed Impact of Control**

Effects of Control	*Israel, 1948–1966*	*Iraq*
Reassure non-active individuals	x	
Deter potentially hostile activists	x	
Intimidate entire group		
Hinder ethnic organization in general	x	x
Disrupt militants who are not deterred	x	x
Alter elite incentives to raising ethnic issues	x	x
Reassure dominant group	x	x
Buy time for regime to impose new institutions	x	
Engender status concerns	x	x

in particular found incentives to work against the Muslim Arab majority and cooperate with their Jewish neighbors.

These cases suggest that control policies have a strong effect on several causes of ethnic conflict. When properly implemented, control is particularly useful in reducing the ethnic security dilemma and stopping ethnic mobilization. It also can appease the ambitions of a hegemonic group. However, higher levels of control, which more effectively prevent many causes of conflict, often exacerbate status concerns and can create a new security dilemma between the state and the group.

Selective control and police control can effectively end or dampen the ethnic security dilemma. When no group can use violence without risking punishment, fears that another group will mobilize can be reduced. Thus, defensive measures to improve group security do not spiral out of control. Control also hinders organization. As groups' abilities to organize decrease, so too do neighbors' fears of harm or retaliation. As group confidence in its security reduces the group's perceived need to organize for violence, a self-sustaining cycle of confidence begins that further enhances security.

Ethnic relations after the creation of Israel indicate how dampening the security dilemma can lead to peace. Israeli police and security forces monitored, censored, and otherwise prevented Israeli Arabs from mobilizing and posing any threat to their Jewish neighbors. Over time, Israeli Jewish fears declined, despite a continued suspicion of their neighbors and of the Palestinians living in the West Bank and Gaza. Almost no violence has occurred between Israeli Jews and Israeli Arabs in the past fifty years: the few killings were small in number compared with the tragic bloodletting of the Mandate era.

Ba'athist Iraq illustrates an important caveat to the general point about control of the state. When one communal group controls the state, attempts to enforce order can be seen as a bid for hegemony, which often provokes greater violence. The Iraqi Ba'ath sought communal peace, but they also wanted to ensure that Arab nationalists dominated in Iraq. Thus, a strong police and army inflamed rather than dampened the security dilemma by convincing groups that their communal security was in jeopardy and required rebellion. In contrast to a hypothesized result of brute force, efforts to intimidate the entire group often failed. When the central government weakened, groups quickly rose up.

With the use of control, hegemonic conflict also can be reduced. In theory, control can impede mobilization and prevent expressions of superiority, as long as the government is willing to suppress the would-be hegemonic group. The Iraqi and Israeli cases, however, provide no evidence either way about whether control can be used to suppress the dominant group's mobilization and assembly. The Israeli case, however, reinforces the argument that control can reassure or even pacify otherwise violent dominant groups. Although this factor is often overlooked, violence by Jews against Israeli Arabs was quite limited, probably because the Jews felt secure that the police and army would protect them. In Israel, Jews have seldom engaged in violence against Israeli Arabs despite Jewish security fears, suspicions of Arab loyalty, and their desire to ensure that the country remain "Jewish" in character. This Jewish confidence is particularly remarkable given past violence between Arabs and Jews during the Mandate and the active attempts by neighboring states to invade and subvert Israel. The Kafr Qasim killings represent the exception that proves the rule: the worst instance of violence occurred on the eve of war, when outside powers threatened the Jewish monopoly on control.

Control plays an important role in preventing ambitious elites from stirring up conflict. Any Israeli Arab leader who advocated violence was quickly silenced by the government's police and security services. Not surprisingly, Israeli Arab elites constantly complained about control policies, primarily because these policies prevented them from exercising rights to free speech and free organization. Arab leaders were clear, however, that the imposition of even the threat of greater control also led them to carefully avoid violence. Effective control policies also bolstered moderates. When control was used, leaders who advocated compromise or even those who were little more than Israeli puppets not only kept their lives but also were able to exercise considerable power. For Israeli Jewish leaders, strong control policies removed a potential issue from the public agenda. Fear of an internal Arab threat was quashed by the obviously strong police forces. Thus, Jewish leaders could score few points with voters by raising concerns about a nonexistent Arab peril, effectively preventing outbidding by Jewish leaders.

Divide-and-rule tactics proved particularly effective in managing elite aspirations, transforming ethnic elites from potential foes into friends of the government. The Israeli government worked with Druze, bedouins, Christians, and other minorities to separate them from the larger Sunni Arab community. Leaders of these communities recognized that their leadership roles would be jeopardized if they were incorporated into the broader Arab community. As a result, these leaders became de facto allies.

Despite its many advantages, control must be used carefully since it incites the status concerns of communities. The Israeli Arabs resented military rule and the constant restrictions on their ability to assemble and express themselves, creating bitterness that hindered better relations between them and the Jewish majority. The Kurds and Shi'a of Iraq greatly resented the brutal levels of force used against them, repeatedly rising up in rebellion to demand more respect for their communities.

Even when control policies fail to deter leaders and followers from engaging in violence, they often effectively prevent conflict by weakening the combatants. The most effective way to weaken groups is to prevent them from organizing. All four variants of control—police control, selective control, brute force, and divide-and-rule—attempt to interfere with ethnic organization at some level. Interference can encourage ethnic peace in two ways. First, it raises the costs for individuals who would use violence to advance their ends: elites fear to lead, and the populace fears to follow. Second, the imposition of control measures disrupts organization. Even those few individuals who do not fear the regime are less able to communicate with one another and thus organize effectively.

Israel's experience neatly illustrates how control can inhibit effective political organization. For many years after independence, the Israeli government firmly suppressed all independent Israeli Arab political activity, and an active intelligence and police force monitored the community for dissent. The threat of expulsion, and the obvious precedent of the expelled 1948 Palestinians, made clear the serious nature of the Israeli threat. Press censorship, jailings, and limits to assembly also reinforced government control over the Israeli Arab population. Israeli political institutions, which the government was able to impose because it had pacified the Israeli Arab community, also hindered Israeli Arab organization. Political parties and the economic structure of Israeli society decreased the Arab community's resources and strengthened the government's position.

Brute force, however, can actually improve ethnic radicals' ability to organize. The Ba'ath regime's use of such force did at times hinder organization and disrupt elite efforts to foment violence. The Kurds found it difficult to organize politically, and the government successfully disrupted some attempts at rebellion. The suppression of an entire community, however, reduces incentives to remain passive. Although being a member of an armed faction carried with it certain death in Iraq, simply living in the wrong village or being part of the wrong community often led to deportation or other stiff penalties. Thus, communal leaders found ready recruits, especially since collaboration offered few rewards.

The line between when force inspires resistance and when it cows potential belligerents is blurry and shifts from location to location and era to era. The ideal level of force—from both a human rights point of view and one of efficacy—is the minimal level needed to deter, and if necessary deny, groups from organizing for violence effectively. The more force that is used, the more likely it is that status concerns will become an issue and that control itself will reduce incentives to remain passive by becoming non-discriminatory in its application. Ideally, governments will use other strategies to reduce the level of force needed, giving elites and individuals in general incentives not to engage in violence. If not, then the short-term benefits of control are likely to be overwhelmed over time.

Divide-and-rule strategies also prove highly effective in weakening the ability of an ethnic group to resist the central government. Once sown, identity is hard to uproot. Despite Arab propaganda to the contrary, Druzes and bedouins in Israel remain politically distinct from Israeli

Arabs as a whole. Both Jews and other Arabs perceive these two as distinct groups more allied with Jews than with Arab communities. As a result, political movements or activities that cut across these divisions are rare. Members of these groups have proven to be loyal Israeli soldiers, who seldom support violence and are more likely to believe the Israeli system works to their benefit.[26] It should be noted, however, that divide-and-rule policies often succeed incompletely, weakening the ability of an ethnic group to use violence but not preventing it altogether. The Kurds are divided, but they are still a potent force in Iraq.

Control and Social Change

Peace, however tentative, can lead to tremendous social change that makes lasting harmony more likely. Thus, even though control tactics generate immediate resentment, they may buy time for the government to implement policies that in the long term make conflict less likely. Solving the security dilemma can lead to tremendous social change. Because control makes intergroup and intragroup violence unlikely, individuals can disarm and change their way of life (such as emigrating to work abroad or settling down to farm) without fear of depriving their tribe or sect of needed manpower or of exposing themselves as individuals to the depredations of rival groups. Thus, although control's most obvious impact is that it changes individual and group calculations about the utility of violence and political action, it can also change the very dynamic of social interaction.[27]

Control also allows the government to build organizations that facilitate government power in the long term. The military government in Israel, for example, organized Israeli Arabs through Jewish political parties rather than through autonomous parties or organizations. The party structure made it easier for the government to control Arabs and prevented inter-Arab coordination. Measures to facilitate government power over the long term are particularly important when higher levels of control are used. In Ba'athist Iraq, the regime did not weaken Kurdish organization successfully, create an alternate identity, or otherwise change ethnic dynamics. The Kurds rose whenever brute force eased.

Successful control in the short term allows an easing of control in the long term by creating an expectation that violence will be punished. Israel today is peaceful even though the level of force used against Israeli Arabs has fallen dramatically since the days after Independence. Although Israeli Arabs by the 1990s enjoyed relative freedom to organize (see the discussion in Chapter 6), two factors have limited the potential for violence. The first and most important is the knowledge among both Jews and Arabs that any use of violence by Israeli Arabs will not only result in swift punishment but might even turn back many of the political gains made by the Israeli Arab community in recent years. Second, because of their small numbers and exclusion from security positions, Israeli Arabs recognize that they have no chance of controlling the state. Unlike Palestinian Arabs of the past, Israeli Arabs are not hegemonic in their aims. Jews are comfortable that their ultimate hegemony is secure, while Arabs moderate their demands by recognizing that extreme demands will be counterproductive.

Who Controls?

The composition and direction of a state's police and security forces have a tremendous impact on the efficacy of control. Whether police forces inspire confidence or fear, pride or resentment, depends in part on whether one group dominates these forces and whether they are used to arbitrate among groups or to enforce discriminatory and hegemonic state policies.

Ideally, police and security forces are composed proportionally of all groups and enforce an impartial government's policies. In the United States, for example, municipal police forces usually make great efforts to recruit and promote individuals from all parts of the municipality. Many groups that have suffered discrimination seek a greater role in policing, both to ensure that their communities' needs are respected and as a symbol of their status in society. Although these efforts seldom achieve complete success, in general they reduce sentiments that the police are alien oppressors.

Israel's experience, in contrast, is one where Jews dominate the security forces and police. The Israeli government still implemented selective control effectively because it did not try to crush the group's identity and coopt group leaders to assist in its efforts. Israeli Arabs found themselves too weak and disorganized to resist, leading them to accept the imbalance in the security forces. Military rule rankled, however, and led to growing Israeli Arab resentment. Thus, although control functioned efficiently, it did provoke a backlash that raised status concerns.

Iraq demonstrates how an extreme form of domination produces a serious backlash that can at times flare into war. Iraqi police and security forces acted to enforce Sunni Arab hegemony. This not only involved ensuring Sunni Arab security, but also crushing the leadership and culture of Kurds and Shi'a. The security forces threatened rather than reassured. As a result, when these oppressed communities have been able to rise up, they have done so. Control policies, in this instance, exacerbated security and status fears.

When one community controls security forces, many of the incentives for groups to initiate conflict are unchanged or even increase. Particularly if that group is an active party to a current conflict, then many of the dynamics of the security dilemma outlined in Chapter 2 are exacerbated rather than reduced.[28] Rather than being reassured by a government's provision of order, groups find it a threat to their identity and even their lives. Simple self-defense may necessitate arming and organizing to defend against a predatory government.

Indirectly, an exclusive police force raises status concerns. A visible symbol of a group's integration into society is its participation in the provision of order, one of the basic functions of government. Israel's refusal to allow Arab Muslims into the Israeli army, for example, demonstrates that this community remains distinct from other Israelis and does not enjoy an equal status in society. The more brutal and discriminatory the security forces, the more status concerns are raised.

Control's impact on a group's ability to organize and other "denial" aspects, however, are less affected by the issue of which group dominates the security forces. Security forces can still imprison individuals, prevent public gatherings, and otherwise impede anti-government organization regardless of whether they are composed of one group or many—as long as they have the strength and organization to do so. Yet even denial becomes harder when the security forces are exclusive. In such cases, nonrepresented groups may see the police and army as hostile and be reluctant to provide information on fellow group members, even when they do not approve of radicals' activities. Identifying the radicals, and hindering their activities, becomes far harder. Security forces in such cases will find selective control more difficult and may shift toward brute force, even though this is likely to engender increased resentment.

Exclusive control over security forces, however, may reassure a hegemonic group, reducing incentives for violence from that quarter. Dominance over the forces of law and order is a potent symbol of a group's predominant place in society, particularly if those forces ensure that one group remains superior to others. In such cases, hegemonic communities are likely to turn to the police and the army when they feel threatened rather than organize on their own at a substate level for violence. It is remarkable that Israeli Jews, despite the intense security threat they perceived from their Arab neighbors in times of crisis, did not conduct more than sporadic violence and harassment. In large part, this is because Jews recognized that the government would ensure their security if necessary.

What type of control is employed depends heavily on the composition of the security forces. Targeting one group, as is typical with selective control and brute force, is almost impossible when the security forces represent a broad spectrum of society. In such circumstances, individuals seldom join, or are loyal to, security forces that oppress their own people.[29] On the other hand, many of the benefits of police control stem from the perceived impartiality of the security forces. If this image is tarnished due to an exclusive composition of the forces, the benefits are less likely to accrue.

Implementing an impartial version of control is difficult, particularly when there is no broad and equitable power-sharing arrangement for government in general. A government must be able to trust all groups to the point of giving them guns and training them—no mean feat if groups fought each other openly only years before. Indeed, governments must make particular efforts to seek out individuals from groups that are excluded because these individuals often face hostility from their own community if they join the security forces.

The Disadvantages of Control Policies

Control is susceptible to several major problems that limit its effectiveness and require it to be used in conjunction with other tools. Foremost among these problems is that most forms of control lead to bitterness and complaints about a group's status in society. Brute force tactics often produce a backlash—creating security, status, and hegemonic fears, and worsening ethnic relations in the long term.

Control produces resentment. Not surprisingly, individuals generally do not like to be harassed, monitored, or even policed. When these activities are conducted by once-hostile groups or a suspect government, resentment is higher still. Israeli Arabs in the 1990s, for example, regularly complained about heavy-handed police and security forces, even though they suffered far less harassment than they did in the past. The 2000 shooting of Israeli Arab demonstrators supporting the "Al Aqsa" *intifada* enraged the Israeli Arab community, highlighting their second-class status. This resentment can spill over and create status concerns. In part because they are a regular target for harassment by police and security officials, Israeli Arabs took less pride in the Israeli state and considered themselves second-class citizens. The resulting bitterness continues to the present day. Divide-and-rule efforts also often anger the group, particularly its leaders, that is being weakened or divided. Leaders correctly see it as a way to denigrate their influence and to decrease the power of the group as a whole.

Brute force is particularly dangerous because it incites the status and security fears of a community simultaneously. Moreover, it creates a fear of the central government. Thus, when brute force lets up—as it did in Iraq when the Ba'ath faced military defeats from Iran and from the U.S.-led coalition—the groups that had been subjected to brute force take up arms. The Ba'ath regime actually created a security dilemma between the government and the Kurds and Shi'a of Iraq. These communal groups now fear not only Sunni Arabs but a strong government as well.

Control in general also involves the curtailment of civil liberties. In addition to being undesirable in and of itself, this generates further resentment among the affected communities. Indeed, by restraining civil liberties, control often increases other types of civil strife that are not motivated by ethnicity.

Circumstances That Affect Control's Viability

Control is often difficult to carry out. Some regimes cannot implement control measures, while others can capitalize on circumstances that increase the effectiveness of control. The resources of an ethnic group, the level of outside backing, its access to arms, its social structure, and the type of regime are among the many factors that affect control's influence on ethnic relations. Of course, an important point not to be overlooked is that governments with a high degree of popular support and skilled police and intelligence services are more likely to implement control policies more effectively.

The resources of the ethnic group in question affect how well control works. Poor groups and those dependent on the government cannot risk their livelihood by supporting resistance. Israeli Arabs for many years barely lived above subsistence levels. The *fellah* who might support violent resistance to Israeli rule under the military government, for example, would find his land as well as that of his family confiscated. Even tacit support might lead the government to cut off an individual from the land, which often meant the difference between economic prosperity and survival. As time went on and the Israeli Arab population became wealthier, however, the impact of economic punishments decreased.

The need for at least minimal wealth in order to resist authority is common for all forms of resistance, not just that which is ethnically based. As Eric Wolf notes, "A rebellion cannot start from a situation of complete impotence; the powerless are easy victims."[30] At the same time, greater levels of wealth are a disincentive for rebellion. Individuals have too much to lose from change, and thus are often reluctant to pursue it.

Civil society (social clubs, religious organizations, unions, sporting groups, and other associations that are independent of the state) define an important resource of a group, and control is more effective when civil society is weak. The communal organizations that make for a vibrant civil society also provide a ready base of organization for political action. Thus, many governments seek to shatter civil society. The Israeli military government tried to co-opt and repress civil society institutions, thus reducing potential rivals to government organizations.

A group's access to arms is another key resource. In part, this access depends on wealth: poor groups cannot buy heavy arms that are necessary to directly confront government forces. But even poor groups can acquire light machine guns, mortars, and other portable and cheap weapons that can prove exceptionally bloody. As the Carnegie Commission on Preventing Deadly Violence notes, "The worldwide accessibility of vast numbers of lethal conventional weapons and ammunition makes it possible for quite small groups to marshal formidable fire power."[31] Food and medicine are often far harder to find than weapons. Thus, controlling violence is far more difficult today than in the past, when governments generally outgunned potential rivals.

Control becomes far harder to implement when a group has outside support. Much of the success of control depends on expectations. Governments must convince individuals that ethnic organization for violence (or for political activity in general) is fruitless and possibly dangerous. When leaders and larger cadres have a haven outside a country's borders to gather, train, and organize with impunity, creating this expectation of defeat is far more difficult. Not surprisingly, groups like the Kurds that have repeatedly received support from neighboring governments have proven far harder to control.

Control is also more difficult to implement when the terrain makes movement difficult and aids concealment. If roads and other forms of transportation are well-established, governments can move their forces quickly and respond rapidly to any flare-up in violence. On the other hand, if the transportation grid is poor, as it is in much of Africa, government forces often arrive too late to have an impact. This problem becomes particularly acute if the ethnic groups in question live in jungles, mountains, swamps, or other inaccessible terrain, which makes it easy for them to act and organize with relative impunity.[32] Inaccessible terrain increases the plausibility of revolt and decreases the credibility of government promises of security.

In addition to group resources in general, a group's social structure has a tremendous impact on the success of control. Control is far more effective when there are divisions within the group to exploit, divisions that in turn depend in part on the strength of the ethnic identity in question. The Israeli government, for example, found it relatively easy to separate Israeli Arab Christians and bedouin from the mainstream Israeli Arab community, as preexisting tensions had prevented a strong overarching identity from jelling. In general, ethnic groups that are clan-based or rely only on a few established leaders prove easier to control because they have a readily identifiable organization structure that a government can target. When these individuals are controlled, the ethnic group as a whole generally follows. Thus, colonial governments, by co-opting and controlling tribal leaders, gained tremendous leverage over various tribal groups.

Subethnic divisions, of course, are not the only sources of separation. Class, region, religion, and ideology often present important cleavages that enable governments to divide groups and keep them weak. Not surprisingly, ethnic groups constantly strive to unite their potential followers. Much of their violence is often aimed at increasing internal support and eliminating alternate sources of political identity.[33]

As this discussion of social structure and group resources suggests, the effectiveness of control comes down to a contest of organization. Governments strive to disrupt, channel, or neuter hostile or potentially hostile ethnic organizations, while ethnic movements try to build organizations that will enable them to coordinate their actions and resist the state. Control was far easier for Israel to implement after 1948 because much of the Palestinian Arab elite had fled during the civil war and war of independence. Absent their natural leadership, the Israeli Arabs proved far more docile. Control, to succeed, must convince individuals that organization will not work. If organization can be disrupted, potentially disciplined ethnic cadres break down into disorganized groups. No longer can ethnic militants blend in among the population at large. Over time, they become mere bandits to sustain themselves and lose even a vestige of popular support.[34]

The ideal allies for a government implementing control are, in fact, nonviolent members of the ethnic group in question. Strong moderate forces can be interlocutors to the community in general and an alternative for political action that does not involve violence. If moderates side with the government, they offer superb intelligence on radical activities. India and Spain provide examples where governments have worked with moderates against radicals in their own group.[35]

In essence, governments must break the link between mainstream groups and those that would use violence. Political movements are often fronts for terrorist groups or work with them side by side. They provide social services, run businesses, and offer a legitimate face for fundraising and political activities. Moreover, they offer a means of recruiting new members. If regimes can infiltrate, or better yet cooperate with, mainstream groups, they are often able to gain information on radical activities and turn potential militants away from violence.[36]

Control's effectiveness is, in many cases, comparable to conducting a successful counterinsurgency. In addition to breaking up organization and cutting groups off from outside sources of support, governments must try to win over the broader ethnic group and the population in general. Inducements in the form of political rights, economic aid, symbolic benefits, and so on can create goodwill for the government, making it far easier to gather information on potentially violent individuals and groups.[37]

Good intelligence is essential when implementing control. If the government uses force against otherwise passive individuals, it risks turning them into rebels. The military government in Israel also encouraged positive leaders while ruthlessly suppressing those considering the use of violence, in part by gathering extensive intelligence on the Israeli Arab community. The Ba'ath, on the other hand, used violence indiscriminately, thus encouraging passive individuals to rise up. Security measures should be applied consistently and, when possible, with restraint, in order to prevent a backlash that will cause governments to lose the support of the broader, currently apolitical population.[38]

The role of the state also shapes control's effectiveness. As noted above, control is easier if the security forces are drawn from all of a country's communities. The more the state is an agent of change or ethnic hegemony, the more control is required to keep the peace—and the more it will be resented. In Israel, the state was the agent of the dominant Jewish community and was resented as a result. Iraq's experience is the most telling: the state was both an agent of assimilation and controlled by one communal group. The failure of the Ba'ath to keep the peace suggests the limits of control under such trying conditions.

Regimes more respectful of civil liberties will find control measures harder to implement. Democracies around the world wrestle with the question of how much surveillance is acceptable. Even countries in which respect for civil liberties is entrenched, like the United States, allow the investigation of groups that might be using or preparing to use violence.[39] Yet, as Abram Shulsky notes, this creates a catch-22 regarding democratic restrictions and surveillance: "one cannot know about the support group's additional activities because one may not look, and one may not look as long as one does not know."[40]

Israel avoided this problem for much of its history because of the different majority attitudes regarding civil rights for Arabs and for Jews. In the immediate aftermath of the 1948 war, Jews agreed that the Arab population was suspect and required considerable police and security oversight. Over time, as Israeli Jewish attitudes shifted and as legal and political protection for Israeli Arabs grew, the use of control measures against Israeli Arabs became far more difficult.

Final Words

Various types of control are effective in different circumstances, and understanding control's variants improves our ability to determine the cases in which certain types of control will work and encourage a more intelligent use of control measures in general. In some societies, where groups are more bellicose, higher levels of control will be necessary. Thus, some selective control measures, while morally repugnant, can preserve peace. In many societies, however, these measures would be understood for what they commonly are: means of preserving a leader's or group's exclusive power, not of fostering peace.

This chapter discussed the utility and efficacy of control, not the morality of it. It is important to recognize, however, that control can demand a heavy price in terms of human rights.. Arabs in Israel are in effect second-class citizens, despite recent advances in their condition. Kurds everywhere, and other minorities in Muslim countries, are treated far worse, all in the name of social stability. Indeed, preserving ethnic and tribal peace is often used as a justification for ensuring one group's exclusive control over political power. Even when control does not involve discrimination, it often includes infringement of basic political rights such as free speech and free expression. Thus, control policies should be recognized for what they are—tools of last resort, to be used only when kinder and gentler means fail.

Unfortunately, in the aftermath of ethnic conflict, more benign methods of ethnic conciliation do not work. As discussed in other chapters, when the security dilemma is active, measures to resolve conflict, such as elections, devolving power, and creating a new national identity, fail. Fear and hatred often overcome shared bonds among neighbors. In such circumstances, control policies, however unpleasant, are necessary. When societies are deeply divided, groups are organized and able to use violence, and the memory of conflict burns fiercely, it is often impossible to maintain social peace with low levels of control. The deleterious human rights impact of control policies can be offset, or at least softened, when control is combined with more benign measures to keep the peace. Over time, as the wounds of conflict heal, the level of control can be lessened. Until then, a large degree of control may be necessary to keep the peace.

4 Co-optation

An alternative to controlling and repressing ethnic groups is to co-opt them: winning their cooperation through carrots rather than sticks. Using a range of inducements, the leaders of ethnic groups can become proponents of peace rather than instigators of unrest. Co-optation's primary weakness is that its impact is limited. Because it can do little to solve the root causes of violence, co-optation most often reduces the scope of violence rather than stops it altogether. Nevertheless, successful co-optation can mean the difference between an organized, widespread campaign of violence and popular disgruntlement that does not lead to bloodshed or is never mobilized in the first place. Co-optation can also bolster other strategies, increasing their overall effectiveness.

Co-optation involves buying off elites to gain their support. If governments can offer group leaders wealth, status, or power over their communities, they can better ensure loyalty to the central government. When co-optation is successful, grievances such as security, status, or hegemonic concerns may be widespread, but the group cannot mobilize effectively because its leaders are co-opted.

Co-optation takes advantage of elite influence to prevent ethnic violence. In most societies, particularly those with wide disparities of wealth and power, a small segment of the population is disproportionately influential in politics. The views of these elites are crucial to political stability. Organized opposition and violence are almost impossible without effective leadership. If governments can win these elites to their side and prevent them from encouraging conflict, fighting may be mitigated despite widespread hostility on the part of the population at large.

This chapter begins by noting the possible benefits of co-optation, paying special attention to how it might offset several of the causes of conflict discussed in Chapter 2. It then draws on the experiences of Morocco, Syria, and Bahrain to illustrate the relative advantages and disadvantages of co-optation. The chapter concludes by arguing that co-optation is an effective but limited strategy for keeping the peace.

The Promise of Co-optation

Co-optation defuses the destabilizing potential of elites—both entrenched and emerging—by transforming them from potential firebrands into defenders of the status quo. As discussed in Chapter 2, elites often play on ethnic group fears and aspirations, mobilizing their communities to increase their own power. If governments can satisfy elites, whether through bribes, access to power, recognition of their status in society, or other means, these individuals and their supporters will have an increased interest in supporting the government and are less likely to rail against each other—if the government so instructs them. After leaders are co-opted by the central government, their jobs and status often change dramatically. They shift from being independent spokesmen to docile functionaries who depend on the government for their position and fortune. In this way, the leader becomes a force that promotes regime goals rather than the ambitions of the ethnic group. Co-optation, however, differs from true power-sharing. Co-opted leaders do not have a genuine voice in the political process, and as a result their communities benefit far less.

Co-optation also bolsters moderates over radicals. By providing them with more resources and access to government, co-opted elites gain greater influence in their communities, thus magnifying their individual importance while moderating their group's politics. The playing field becomes tilted in favor of co-opted elites. Even though radicals may initially enjoy more support in the community, their inability to deliver the goods will weaken their position over time.

Although co-optation works directly with a group's elites to satisfy their concerns, it also can placate those not co-opted by increasing the group's overall status. One of the measures of a group's place in society is its representation in leadership positions. Although co-opted elites often have little actual influence in decision-making, their very presence in government and society indicates at least some degree of respect for the group at large. The ethnic populace at large may derive reflected glory from those in elite positions. By gaining economic or status positions, a group has less concern about losing ground to a competing minority group. In short, co-optation helps mitigate fears of majority rule: that a government of the majority will only support the majority.

Co-optation in the Middle East

Co-optation is a commonly used tactic for keeping social peace in the Middle East. Area regimes are adept at identifying and bribing potential opponents to reduce their inclination to support political opposition of any stripe, including ethnically based opposition. Critics are given jobs, government contracts, or other rewards in exchange for their support. Sometimes the rewards are more subtle, such as access to preferred housing, better health care, or other benefits. In any event, the tangible result is that bitter regime critics often become active government supporters, and many potentially bellicose leaders use their influence to foster social peace.[1]

Co-optation is effective in the Middle East because elites are particularly important to the region. In part this is due to the authoritarian (both modern and traditional) nature of most Middle Eastern political systems, which restricts participation in decision-making to a chosen few. Another reason for the importance of elites is the high level of stratification of Middle Eastern societies. The middle class is weak in much of the Middle East, and there is little social mobility. This social stratification has encouraged the development of a patronage system focused on landlords, government officials, or key business leaders. Limits on modern educational opportunities have allowed those with the wealth or influence to gain access to modern education to preserve their positions by securing prestigious and influential spots in the civil service and government.

Middle Eastern elites consist of business, military, bureaucratic, intellectual, tribal, religious, and political leaders. In short, they are individuals who command disproportionate power due to their ability to convince, buy, or otherwise force others to do their bidding. Military elites have been particularly important in much of the Middle East. Israel, Tunisia, Egypt, Jordan, Algeria, Libya, Yemen, Syria, Iraq, and Iran have all at times had military figures among their prominent leaders. In many traditional monarchies, the ruling family itself has taken on military leadership roles, in part to forestall coup attempts. In recent years, religious figures have become more important.

The violence and instability that has characterized Middle Eastern politics has reinforced the importance of communal groups in elite politics. Parties, unions, and other formal associations have not proven effective in protecting members from death, imprisonment, or exile during regime changes. Thus, leaders often turn to tribes, ethnic groups, and religious sects for organizational support.[2]

Morocco, Bahrain, and Syria illustrate different aspects of co-optation. In Morocco, co-optation played a major role in keeping the peace between Arabs and Berbers, exploiting the traditional nature of politics there. In Bahrain, co-optation's impact was more limited and more ambiguous, but it still helped to limit communal unrest. Co-optation failed to keep the peace in Syria, but even there it limited the scope and scale of the violence.

Co-optation in Morocco

At the beginning of the twentieth century, the Berbers' relationship with their Arab neighbors and the Arab central government of Morocco was at best uneasy. Most Berbers continually resisted domination by the Arab central government, and even the sultans who were able to subdue them did not succeed in keeping them under control for long. Many Berbers scorned the settled Arabs and were despised in turn. At the same time, tribal war within Berber society was endemic. From this inauspicious beginning, however, relations between Berbers and Arabs in Morocco—and among Morocco's major tribal groups—became a success story of ethnic relations.

Much of this success is a direct result of the policies pursued by the French colonial government and—in a different form and by different leaders—by the monarchy that succeeded it. Although the specific positions, honors, and rewards bestowed by the French colonial government, which governed Morocco from 1912 to 1956, and the post-independence monarchy differed considerably, they both relied heavily on co-optation to win the goodwill of potentially belligerent elites and to demonstrate their commitment to important ethnic groups and tribes. These governments did not rely exclusively on co-optation—both also used considerable control among other methods—but co-optation did play an important role in keeping the peace.[3]

Morocco before the French

The Berbers are the indigenous inhabitants of Morocco and today are the country's largest minority, comprising roughly 40 percent of the total population of 20 million. Historically, Berbers were seldom politically unified. The community was organized entirely on a tribal basis, which was structured in a manner that discouraged overall unity. For example, one collection of brothers and cousins might unite to fight against more distantly related cousins over grazing rights or access to water. These foes, however, would unite to fight against a rival clan that posed a threat to the individuals of the area, and clans, in turn, would unite to fight a rival tribe or outside threat. When the threat was removed, however, fighting among small units of distant relatives would recur.

Arab society in Morocco was a blend of tribal and urban cultures. Arabs came to Morocco as Islam began to spread in the seventh and eighth centuries. Some Arab areas were organized along tribal lines and shared a warrior ethos, a segmentary lineage structure, and heterodox religious practices with their Berber neighbors. Arabs, unlike the Berbers, were urban as well as tribal. Arabs dominated settled areas, towns, and especially the royal court.

Before the French completed pacifying Morocco in 1933, most Berber areas in the country were in a state of dissidence, constantly resisting central government encroachment.[4] Intertribal fighting was even more common than fighting against the government. Berber society approached a Hobbesian state of chaos. For example, in the Rif Berber region in western Morocco, conflict was so rampant that Rifians customarily declared peace rather than war. House-to-house fighting was common, and each family dwelling usually contained a pillbox to defend against one's neighbors. Indeed, conflict in general was an important part of tribal culture. Warfare was an important social ritual, and prowess at arms a supreme source of social recognition. As Al-Hajj Muhammad notes in Henry Munson Jr.'s oral history of a Moroccan family, tribes from different Berber tribal regions lived a life of violence:

> This [the mid-nineteenth century] was a time of violence in the hills of the Jbala [a Berber tribal region of Morocco stretching from the River Sebou

> up to the Mediterranean]. Muslim killed Muslim for the slightest reason: a cow, a goat, a piece of land or a woman. . . . If we did this today, there would be no Muslims left in Morocco. In those days, the *qayyids* [local leaders] did not care if the Jbala killed each other so long as they paid their taxes. Two men would argue as the *fqih* would wake the village by the call to the dawn prayer. And by the sunset prayer, all the men in the village would be shooting at each other. But the Jbala never killed the way the Rifis [a neighboring Berber tribal region] used to kill. The Rifi would kill his own brother over an onion.[5]

The central government never established control over many Berber areas before colonization. Berber areas, being poor, often were not worth the expense of a punitive military expedition to punish nonpayment of taxes, and the fierce resistance put up by local tribes further discouraged the government.[6]

The years leading up to the French protectorate were particularly violent. As the French and other colonial powers increased their meddling in Morocco—the French seizure of the Touat oasis in north-central Sahara was the first loss of Moroccan territory to any Christian power in recent years—the prestige of the sultan and court diminished. Efforts by Sultan Abd el-Aziz (1894–1908) to work with the West to reform Morocco further increased domestic discontent. Each concession Morocco made to European powers, whether in the form of territory, trading rights, or simply symbolic obedience, decreased the respect tribal groups felt for the sultan. Such proof of the state's weakness increased tribal unrest because tribes then took matters into their own hands in order to defend themselves and expel the invaders from Muslim lands.

The long period of French colonial rule, which lasted from 1912 to 1956, changed communal relations forever, laying the groundwork for what has proven to be an enduring ethnic and tribal peace.[7] During the French protectorate era, violent conflict within, between, and by ethnic groups diminished in Morocco.[8] As they pacified Morocco, the French also coopted traditional elites. Marshall Louis-Herbert Gonzalve Lyautey, who led the French government, exploited rather than feared local leaders, using them as intermediaries between the French protectorate and local society. Lyautey believed that such indirect rule was both more effective and less costly than direct French oversight. In a letter to his sister, he wrote that he intended to use traditional systems and rules to ensure French control: "In all human society there is a ruling class . . . Enlist this ruling class in our service."[9] Upon victory, the French worked with traditional leaders and did not change customs, demanding only submission to the sultan's court, which they dominated.

To this end, the French engaged in an extensive campaign of co-optation, providing local leaders with a range of inducements to cooperate with colonial authorities. In the south, Lyautey ruled through the *grands caids*—the local Berber leaders such as Haida ou Mouis, Madani and Thami el-Glaoui, Abdesselem M'Toungui, and El Hadj Taieb Ben Mohamed el-Goundafi. Under Lyautey, *Service des Affaires Indigenes* (SAI) officials, the French officials assigned with administering the protectorate, allowed local tribal leaders tremendous latitude. The French created municipal commissions to run urban areas, which drew their membership from leading merchant and landowning families and oversaw areas ranging from public works to health. Lyautey and his successors often recruited tribal leaders as local leaders after they surrendered. For example, the tribal leader Assu u-Ba Slam was made a local leader despite the fact that he led the local opposition to the French pacification campaign. In the city, the government used local elites to rule. To further minimize resentment, Lyautey gave local leaders all due ceremony when meeting with them, and they also received symbolic honors, such as membership in the legion of honor.[10]

Despite the array of benefits showered on leaders, co-optation did not open up decision-making to the Arab and Berber masses, and even many elites had only token influence. The colonial administration undermined the traditional basis of authority. Previously, leaders in Berber and tribal society rose and fell based on their charisma, prowess in war, and ability to dispense patronage. Suddenly, leadership depended on maintaining good ties to the French colonial government. Local influence over their leaders, and thus over society at large, decreased as a result. Elites also suffered a decrease in their true level of power. Local administration of much of Morocco was nominal at most. In the cities, Moroccans gradually disappeared from many municipal councils. Local pashas presided over other councils, but French members of the council and the French city manager made the important decisions.

Even when they did have influence, co-opted officials often proved to be incompetent administrators. Many traditional leaders expected bribes or other favors in exchange for performing their duties. Moreover, although many Moroccans proved eager collaborators, few had the ability, education, or inclination to become administrators in the French manner. Many traditional leaders proved to be particularly poor administrators, unaccustomed to working with modern bureaucracies. Thus, the French increasingly relied on their own officials in the field to make important decisions, further diminishing local authority. The problem of administration was exacerbated by the dilemma inherent in colonialism: to be effective, local figures had to have popular support, which often was undermined by open collaboration with the French. Loyalty and respect in the community did not always go hand in hand.

In 1956, Morocco gained its independence from France, bringing to the fore the question of who would rule. Two forces dominated the struggle: the Istiqlal Party, composed of nationalists who wanted a figurehead king, and the monarchy of Mohammad V. Although the Istiqlal carried out much of the struggle against the French in alliance with Sultan Mohammed V, it was his refusal to submit to French authority that sparked a popular revolt. The Istiqlal appeared to have the upper hand until the late 1950s. However, in large part due to its failure to win the allegiance of Morocco's Berber population—a failure manifested by ethnic violence—the Istiqlal lost its bid for control over the state.

The Istiqlal rejected co-optation as a policy. The Istiqlal's vision of Morocco became entwined with Arab nationalism, and Istiqlal leaders saw the only good Berbers as the ones who had renounced their Berber identity. Mehdi ben Barka, an Istiqlal leader, typified this sentiment when he argued that a Berber was a man who had never been to school. The Istiqlal, in its preparation for assuming power, began to supplant rival leaders who did not share its vision of Morocco. The Istiqlal filled all the local leadership posts with French-speaking Istiqlal supporters, almost all of whom were Arab and urban.[11] In effect, the Istiqlal's policy was the opposite of co-optation. It tried to use leadership positions to cement its power base, working with allies and excluding potential foes.

The Istiqlal policies caused several Berber tribes to rise against the new Arab-dominated central government. Berbers in the Tafilalt revolted in 1956–57, those in the Rif in 1958–59, and those in the Central Atlas in 1960. These revolts were not similar to past resistance to the central government. The rebels supported the authority of the sultan, who was considered a symbol for Berbers as well as Arabs, and rejected the policies of the Istiqlal. A Berber slogan of the time reflected this sentiment: "We did not achieve independence in order to lose freedom" (to the Istiqlal). Traditional leaders, most of whom the French had previously co-opted, led the revolts. They rightly saw the Istiqlal's rise as a threat to their status positions and to their communities' ways of life. The tribesmen shared their leaders' perception. The relationship between the revolts and ethnic policies can best be understood by looking at the conditions for their abatement. Peace resumed when Sultan Mohammad V, whose position was strengthened by the Istiqlal's failure to win the support of Berber and tribal areas, worked with local Berber leaders and did not try to change Berber culture.[12]

As he consolidated power, King Mohammed V ended the Istiqlal's assimilationist campaign and renewed the co-optation of Berber leaders. In his first government, two out of four members of the Throne Council (an advisory body similar to a president's cabinet) were Berbers. In addition, the monarchy tacitly supported the Popular Movement, a Berber-based political party that claimed to represent Berber interests, giving Berbers a sense of inclusion. The government also gave the lands of the French *colons* to local Popular Movement officials, thus increasing their loyalty and the movement's overall clout. This support bolstered the loyalty of potential political and ethnic opponents of the monarchy, but it also decreased their autonomy and made them dependent on the throne for their continued political influence.

Berber groups responded well to these efforts. In general, tribal areas became staunch supporters of the monarchy. After the 1958–59 revolt, the once bellicose Aith Waryaghar Berber tribe abstained from politics almost completely, having the lowest voting rate in the country.[13] Interestingly, this abstention occurs almost immediately after the tribe had risen against the Istiqlal policies. The issues that led them to revolt had been satisfied, leaving them content with the regime.

Hassan II continued his father's policies upon his ascension in 1961. Like his father, he tried to prevent the formation of independent political organizations in Morocco while strengthening the power of co-opted elites. Through control policies, the monarchy arrested activists, censored newspapers, and otherwise used force to hinder autonomous organization. At the same time, the monarchy used its patronage to create cultural and political organizations that ostensibly represented the interests of various Moroccan groups but in reality served the central government. The king even created several opposition parties to represent various factions and interests in Morocco. All these organizations, however, depended on the goodwill (and often the subventions) of the monarchy for their survival.

This policy of preventing political organization involved quashing any independent association or form of civil society, making it wholly subservient to the monarchy. When independent leaders arose, they were given a simple choice: join the government publicly or be removed from the public sphere. This policy extended from labor leaders to soccer players; after rising to a certain level they were asked to use their popularity to back the monarchy. Efforts to develop an infrastructure on a local level, such as building a bridge or paving roads, also were actively discouraged by the government. The endemic corruption of Morocco—bribes were often necessary to obtain licenses or permits, for example—also inhibited the formation of autonomous organizations.[14]

For both the era of French rule and the modern monarchy, co-optation played an important role in keeping the peace. Co-optation satisfied tribal leaders in particular, transforming them into regime supporters. Communal groups in general also derived reflected glory from their co-opted leaders. During the monarchy, co-optation prevented independent organization, undercutting the ability of elites and would-be challengers to mobilize ethnic chauvinism. Resources and positions received from the government bolstered moderates, increasing their influence. The power of co-optation is suggested by the violence that occurred when the Istiqlal briefly halted it. When the Istiqlal threatened leaders' positions, their followers rose in revolt. When the monarchy restored their leaders into the country's elite, they accepted this inclusion as just.

Co-optation in Syria under the Ba'ath

The Ba'ath government of Hafez al-Asad, which formally took power in Syria in 1970, also used co-optation to maintain itself in power and to prevent communal violence.[15] Unlike in Morocco, co-optation met with mixed success. Asad's regime was led and dominated by 'Alawis (a sect of Islam that has in essence formed a communal identity); much of the opposition consisted of radicals from the Sunni Muslim community, the majority group of Syria, which dominated the country for most of its history and resented 'Alawi preeminence. Asad's regime failed to prevent communal violence from erupting in the 1970s and the 1980s, but co-optation did lessen its scope and helped keep the regime in power.

Co-optation was not the only, or even the primary, tool that the Ba'ath used to keep the peace. To preserve power, the Ba'ath regime employed considerable repression. Regime opponents were routinely arrested, tortured, and killed. No independent media were allowed to either witness or report upon political activity, which was in general banned. The regime kept a particularly close eye on ethnic and sectarian groups, acting quickly to prevent any effective organization. The regime also prohibited any independent political organization and brutalized Syria's once-vibrant civil society. To break the power of the Sunni establishment, the Ba'ath sought control over professional and religious associations. The regime banned independent organizations and supplanted them with loyal institutions led by regime supporters.

Asad also tried to use the Ba'ath Party to dominate society, increasing the influence of co-optation. Party leaders selected election candidates to ensure central control. The party formed separate wings to mobilize peasants, women, and youth. The regime set up parallel institutions to replace and dominate social ones. Although local councils existed to set local priorities, Damascus had the last say on projects and budgets. A parallel party structure also laid down broad lines of policy. Although the regime allowed non-Ba'ath political parties, they were united in the National Progressive Front with the Ba'ath and were not allowed to recruit followers in the army or in the university.[16]

Asad used co-optation in a manner similar to how Israel employed divide-and-rule. Asad co-opted leaders of other minority communities, forming a de facto alliance with Christians, Druze, and other groups against the Sunni Arab community. Based on their percentage of the population, there were three times as many Druze and five times as many Isma'ilis (another schismatic sect of Islam) in leading Ba'ath organizations as one would expect. Such disproportionate representation reflects Asad's attempts to satisfy these minority communities and make them loyal to his regime, as opposed to the Sunni Arab community. Asad also tried to provide token Sunni representation. However, the inner core, particularly in security areas, was held by 'Alawis.

Asad also co-opted potential opponents even as he clamped down on any political activity. The government's growing wealth and control over the economy allowed it to co-opt many opponents among the Sunni merchant community. For example, those who joined the official Syndicate of Artisans could buy inputs from state agencies, participate in the social security fund, and obtain export licenses—healthy incentives for any business. In order to gain the goodwill of the business elite, Asad worked with Syrian capitalists, moderating the revolutionary Ba'ath agenda in many ways.

Government efforts led to increasing ties between the 'Alawis and the Sunni business elite. As access to the state became the key to new wealth, Sunni merchants sought to establish connections with 'Alawi government and military figures. Political and military elites used power to enrich themselves and became embourgeoised, while the merchant elite used wealth to buy political influence. Over time, a military-mercantile complex of officers and merchants developed.[17]

Despite this domination of the economy and its extensive control efforts, the Ba'ath regime provoked anger among the Sunni Muslim majority. The 'Alawi-dominated Ba'ath government proved a double challenge to religious Sunnis. The secular Ba'ath ideology angered many religious Sunnis, and domination by the heretical 'Alawis further horrified them. Sunni critics stressed supposed pagan elements in 'Alawi beliefs and accused them of ignoring, or even worsening, the plight of Muslims in Lebanon and Palestine. What offended most Sunni Arabs, however, was their domination by former inferiors. After the Ba'ath took power, economic and political power shifted from Sunni urban elites to 'Alawis from the region of Latakia. This domination angered Sunni elites and decreased the status of this once-hegemonic community.

Widespread violence began in 1978 and lasted through 1982. For the regime, the worst single incident occurred on June 16, 1978, when Sunni militants killed thirty-two cadets and wounded fifty-four at an Aleppo military school. The vast majority of cadets were 'Alawis. Asad initially responded to the violence by making conciliatory gestures to the opposition, such as replacing several regime officials, including the prime minister, and promising greater respect for the rule of law. The opposition, however, continued the violence, and many Sunni merchants declared a general strike. To quell this dissent, Asad sent in the army. The army killed hundreds and imprisoned many more, leading Sunni militants to respond with a campaign of terror against regime members. Approximately three hundred regime members died in the early 1970s.

Asad responded brutally to this campaign. From 1980 to 1983, perhaps thousands of political prisoners died in regime jails. Rape and torture were common tools to terrorize opponents, and the regime destroyed mosques and broke up Islamic associations. After an assassination attempt on Asad, the president's brother led his unit into a prison in Palmyra and gunned down at least 550 Islamic militants held there. The final showdown occurred in February 1982, in the city of Hama, a traditional Islamic stronghold. To demonstrate its ruthlessness, the regime leveled much of the city, killing perhaps 25,000 inhabitants.

Although co-optation (and control) clearly failed to keep the peace, it did reduce the scope of anti-regime violence. Minorities in general were at most lukewarm supporters of the Islamist insurgents and generally worked with the Ba'ath over its rivals. The Damascus bourgeoisie and bazaar did not join the rebellion, in part because of their economic ties to and dependence on the regime even though Sunni merchants in general supported Islamists. Similarly, Sunnis incorporated into state institutions did not join the rebellion in large numbers. The regime may not have survived had other minorities, the Damascus Sunni community, or Sunnis incorporated into the regime joined the Islamist violence. Their loyalty, bought by regime favors as well as enforced by regime surveillance, enabled the 'Alawis to stay in power. Needless to say, co-optation failed to convince all or even most Sunni Arabs that the Ba'ath were their allies. The continued violence suggests limits to the power of co-optation even as the passivity of many Sunni elites suggests co-optation's power.

Co-optation in Bahrain

The ruling family of Bahrain, the Al Khalifa, has long used co-optation to retain the loyalty of Sunni and Shi'a leaders and, by extension, has won the support (or at least the acquiescence) of the broader communities.[18] As with Syria and Morocco, co-optation was not the only strategy used to keep the peace. The Bahraini government used its security forces and tried to divide potential foes.[19] Co-optation, however, played a crucial role in helping the Al Khalifa, a Sunni Muslim family, rule over a 70 percent Shi'a population, maintain itself in power, and limit social violence. The Al Khalifa's success is particularly impressive, because the country faced economic difficulties and regular meddling by Iran on behalf of the Shi'a.

Since the early 1980s, Bahrain has suffered limited unrest and violence. The Shi'a resented the Al Khalifa, which excluded the Shi'a from power, and sought more status and influence for their community. The Shi'a also suffered economically: unemployment was over 30 percent among the Shi'a, and the Shi'a community in general was poorer than its Sunni neighbors. In addition to indigenous sources of unrest, Iran promoted

Shi'a radicalism. In 1981, Iran sponsored an attempted coup by the Islamic Front for the Liberation of Bahrain, and Iranian support for anti-government radical Shi'a groups continued throughout the 1980s. The Shi'a occasionally rioted to protest their condition, and anti-government sentiment was widespread. Islamist radicals often gained support because traditional leaders were seen as pawns of the regime.

Tension remained high in the 1990s. In 1994, roughly three hundred Sunni and Shi'a elites signed a petition to the amir calling for greater political freedom and for the return of the National Assembly. A second petition these elites circulated gathered over twenty thousand signatures. The government rejected the demands and arrested several organizers, leading to riots by young Shi'a. At the same time, Iran tried to create and organize a Bahraini Hezbollah organization, which would share Iran's Islamist beliefs. Hezbollah then spread anti-regime and pro-Iran propaganda and tried to train a local leadership cadre, but this group was not linked to any of the violence.[20]

Co-optation prevented this widespread discontent from becoming a broader communal conflict. Co-optation shored up the Al Khalifa's power base. Although many Sunnis saw the Al Khalifa as corrupt and unrepresentative, they remained loyal because the regime favored them with high-status positions and with the distribution of government monies. Perhaps more important for preventing communal violence, co-optation was used to win the support of Shi'a elites. Important Shi'a families received government contracts and patronage and other favors. To gain the support of Shi'a elites during the recent crisis, the Al Khalifa expanded the appointed advisory council in 1996, giving it a Shi'a majority for the first time. These measures convinced many wealthy Shi'a to work with the government against poorer radicals. As a result, violence fell because it was often disorganized and leaderless.

Co-optation was particularly effective in Bahrain because the regime dominated the economy. Oil is the primary form of wealth in the country and the region. Most of this wealth was channeled through the central government, which decided how to spend the money and who would receive the contracts. The majority of the citizenry worked either directly or indirectly for the government.[21] As a result, those who opposed the regime had few resources at their disposal.

Co-optation also was effective in Bahrain because the government supplanted civil society. The government security services interfered with political organization and tightly controlled meetings of all organizations. As in Morocco and Syria, the Bahraini government also tried to prevent autonomous organization, whether religious or secular, by sponsoring similar institutions that rely on the state for funding.

Advantages and Disadvantages

Co-optation generally fosters ethnic peace, but in areas where tensions run high, it can only solve part of the overall problem.

In all three cases assessed above, co-optation played a significant role in preventing or reducing violence. Co-opted elites were far more inclined to cooperate with the government, even to the point of working against the wishes of their broader communities. As a result, radicals agitating for violence found it difficult to have their message heard and even harder to organize effectively. Although less important in keeping the peace, some communities also saw the presence of elites in senior positions as proof of their community's overall status in society and government.

In every instance examined in this book, co-opted elites cooperated with the government rather than working toward violence. Co-opted tribal and communal leaders under the French colonial government in Morocco often worked against the nationalists, later supporting the monarchy rather than stir up unrest. In Bahrain and Syria, co-opted leaders

TABLE 3. **Observed Impact of Co-optation**

Effects of Co-optation	*Morocco under the French and the Monarchy*	*Syria under the Ba'ath*	*Bahrain*
Decrease elite grievances	x	x	x
Elites more pro-government	x	x	x
Moderate leaders' strength increased	x	x	x
Satisfy population with symbols of status	x		
Hinder overall organization	x	x	x

regularly worked with the government against militants in their own communities.

Co-optation strengthened moderate elites over radicals. Elites willing to work peacefully within the system gained more resources and a louder voice in government. This gave them an advantage over rivals, particularly in societies whose access to the government is necessary for economic success. In Morocco, for example, co-opted elites could offer permits and patronage to those who accepted their leadership. Radical rivals were left without similar resources. The government's ability to co-opt increases relative to its domination of society and the economy. In Bahrain, where economic activity was almost completely dependent on government largesse, the government could co-opt with relative ease.

Co-optation also decreased the status concerns of communal groups by providing them with visible representation. In colonial Morocco, the large numbers of Berber and tribal leaders in high-status positions reflected their communities' general inclusion in society. Many Berbers in Morocco did not feel discriminated against because they were aware that several Berbers in their community had attained prominent positions in government and commerce. In Syria, traditional elites co-opted by the government, particularly minority leaders, became staunch pillars of the colonial regime and often worked against Sunni radicals. Needless to say, co-optation does not entirely remove status concerns from a community's agenda, particularly if those co-opted are not respected in the community. Over time, many Bahraini Shi'a came to view their co-opted political leaders with contempt, a view that limited the status the community as a whole could then derive from the co-optation arrangement. As a result, unrest continued even though the Shi'a have few leaders.

Despite these benefits, co-optation is far from a perfect strategy for maintaining peace. Most obviously, it does not stop many forms of violence. Although co-opted elites will usually work for peace, leaders and would-be leaders who are not co-opted often turn to violence. Thus, Sunni religious leaders, especially those who were not co-opted but were accustomed to considerable status and influence, proved to be bitter enemies of the 'Alawi regime in Syria. Co-optation also does not completely stop violence when grievances are high. Despite successfully co-opting Sunni and Shi'a elites, the ruling Al Khalifa family endures widespread unrest from the Shi'a community, which resents its lack of status.

Co-optation also inspires resentment if elites lose their positions. Sunni

Arabs, who dominated Syria until the 1960s, not surprisingly became the chief foes of the Ba'ath order that excluded them. Similarly, when the Istiqlal removed Berbers from co-opted positions, they led the revolts against their continued rule.

Syria's experience shows both the strengths and limits of co-optation. On the one hand, co-optation failed to prevent a bloody civil war between the 'Alawi government and Syria's Islamic movement. On the other hand, co-optation weakened the Sunni Muslim cause, hindering its ability to organize and attract followers from among co-opted Sunni groups and non-Sunni minorities. This experience suggests that co-optation works, but that alone it is often insufficient.

Gauging how much to co-opt is often difficult. Governments using this strategy face a dilemma: to be respected and effective over time, co-opted elites must have some degree of independence. Co-opted Sunni Arabs in Syria, for example, had little respect among Islamists, as they were (rightly) seen as pawns of the Ba'ath regime. Elites are more likely to retain respect among members of their communities when they have some autonomy. This independence, however, can be used to counter the government's strategy of preventing effective ethnic organization.

Co-optation in general is less effective when a community has independent institutions on which to draw. Contrasting Syria in the early days of the Ba'ath rule with Syria today is instructive. During the mid-1970s, disaffected Sunnis could use mosques, professional associations, and other forms of civil society to organize politically. After violence became widespread, however, the Ba'ath shattered these independent institutions. Civil society was no longer autonomous and served to increase regime control over political activity. Bahrain and Morocco, in contrast, subverted civil society, replacing autonomous institutions with state-dominated ones.

Widespread poverty or state-dependent wealth also makes co-optation easier. Poorer individuals have more to lose from even token resistance to the government's wishes, particularly in a centralized state. Sunni Arab merchants in Syria and Bahraini elites relied on the government for their well-being, which increased the government's leverage over them. In Morocco, wealthier individuals also were often hesitant to offend the government because their economic well-being depended on government support. Structuring an economy centered around the state, however, can lead to economic stagnation and can interfere with development goals.

Co-optation often reduces administrative efficiency, creating further resentment. The French faced a constant struggle between the demands of administrating and placating local traditional leaders. French colonial officials regularly ignored the greed and corruption of loyal tribal leaders. Even if not corrupt, many loyal leaders were illiterate or incapable of mastering even basic administrative techniques. This lack of efficiency can have political consequences as well as hindering economic development and effective governance. Emerging elites, many of whom are well-educated or have other plausible claims to high-status positions, often resent a system in which birth or loyalty to a particular regime counts more than merit. Under the French colonial government, for example, many newly educated Arab leaders simply sought a place in the system commensurate with their new skills. When the colonial regime relied on traditional leaders instead, they became opposed to its continuation and led the anti-colonial movement.

Co-opted leaders also can be fickle. Many potential elites are eager to gain the plums of patronage that come with co-optation, yet they bear no loyalty to the regime. For this reason they cannot be wholly trusted, remaining candidates for plotting coups and unrest. In essence, governments are demanding loyalty on the basis of self-interest. If the government's ability to provide benefits decreases, or if opposition groups can threaten punishments for those who cooperate with a regime, co-optation is less likely to succeed. Although this book did not examine the British Mandate period in Palestine, the experience there suggests the dangers of relying on co-opted leaders. During the 1920s and 1930s, the British cultivated both Arab and Jewish leaders, seeking to co-opt them to preserve communal peace. Both communities, however, placed tremendous pressures on their leaders. Many co-opted leaders tried to prevent violence, but as tensions rose, they either became politically irrelevant or embraced more radical views to satisfy their constituents, thus limiting the benefits of the co-optation strategy.

At times, government resources are not sufficiently abundant to win the loyalty of potential elites. There are only so many senior military, civil service, or commercial positions available for any society, and by giving even a portion of these coveted positions to individuals from a certain group or class, the regime may alienate the group's traditional rivals or other aspirants for the same positions. This shortage of resources has been particularly acute in recent years, primarily because increases in education have expanded the number of potential elites throughout the Middle East. Moreover, a rise in the standard of living in many countries has led to an expectation of prosperity and status, making the price of buying off potential elites much higher than before.

Ideology and conflicting self-interest have also limited the effectiveness of co-optation. Many individuals are considered unworthy of cooperation with the regime due to their dissenting ethnic background or radical political ideas. The Istiqlal, for example, who were prejudiced against the culture and values of Berbers, refused to accept Berbers into the ranks of the nation's leaders. Similarly, as discussed in Chapter 3, the Iraqi Ba'ath made no effort to co-opt the Kurds, preferring instead to work only with loyal Arab nationalists.

The organization of the ethnic group greatly affects co-optation. Segmented ethnic groups have proved easier to co-opt than ones with a strong national identity. The French colonial government used existing clan divisions to co-opt rival clan leaders and to weaken the ability of the community as a whole to unite. As a national identity that transcended the clans developed, co-optation proved harder to enact. As the number of potential leaders increased and clan identities decreased, identifying the right group to co-opt became more difficult.

Despite these limitations, it is important to remember that co-optation has few disadvantages relative to its rewards. Unlike control, it simply fails rather than backfires. But this general endorsement of co-optation should be tempered with the recognition that its impact is often limited and may decrease over time. Moreover, co-optation is only a partial solution to the problem of communal violence. It decreases elite incentives to mobilize their populations, but it does less to solve more fundamental problems of security or hegemony or to satisfy elites who are not co-opted. Thus, governments trying to heal the wounds of a communal conflict should certainly not hesitate to employ co-optation, but they must recognize that by itself it is not sufficient to keep the peace.

5 Manipulating Ethnic Identities

The collapse of the Soviet and Yugoslav empires is the most horrific recent reminder of the bloodshed and turmoil that can occur when national identities fail to coalesce.[1] As soon as the central government's hold on power slipped, these empires collapsed into bloody war. Despairing after these failures, some scholars have concluded that building an indivisible nation is impossible after communal conflict.[2] Yet ethnic identity is not written in stone. In the worst of times, identities are thrust upon a people; in the best of times, different peoples can unite under the banner of a common identity. A glance through the history books reveals that many once-strong and warlike peoples such as the Etruscans and the Parthians were conquered by, and later subsumed under, the identities of their formal rivals. Similarly, in Western democracies today, once hostile groups live in peace side by side, if not always hand in hand, under a common flag. Britain is home to the descendants of Picts, Angles, Scots, Saxons, Welsh, Normans, and other groups that once warred bitterly but now share a common national identity. If the establishment of new identities can be successfully encouraged in countries that have suffered ethnic war, the destructive history of ethnic conflict may not be condemned to repeat itself.

Although the creation of new identities is common throughout history, scholars often neglect it as a solution for ethnic conflict. Most scholars of ethnic conflict see identity manipulation as a cause of conflict. Belligerent elites, seeking to consolidate or gain power, create or exploit chauvinistic ethnic identities and, in so doing, sow the seeds of conflict. Identity manipulation, however, is a two-edged sword. Just as elites can make a hostile ethnic identity more salient, so too can they depoliticize an identity or create a new, more peaceful one that leads hostile groups to unite.

This neglect is particularly surprising given the long historical record of identity manipulation. Many political leaders have engaged in "nation-building" in an attempt to join formerly disparate and rival peoples into one nation.[3] Such efforts often involve a combination of legal changes that contrive to blur or obliterate ethnic status through regulations forbidding certain types of dress, schooling in a common language with a common curriculum, and the promulgation of national symbols (a flag, anthem, national heroes) that unify residents. To encourage individuals to abandon their original identity, these measures are often coupled with incentives that offer the hope of a better future: better educational or career opportunities, for example. The goal of these policies is to create a population that perceives its mutual identity as a common bond of nationality. Ideally, under these circumstances, traditional rivalries melt away, cease to be politically salient, or, at the very least, do not assume a violent form. These strategies focus on the malleable elements of ethnic identity. Attempts to change ethnic identities do not simply affect the rules by which individuals and groups search for status, security, and resources; rather, they try to change the actual identity and preferences of the players themselves.[4]

Against this hope of a peaceful shared identity is the dark reality of nations forged out of mutually hostile ethnic groups. Soviet man was fashioned out of the bones of millions of dead minorities, but he proved a brittle creature nonetheless. Bangladesh, Turkey, and Indonesia offer other modern examples of attempts at imposing a new identity on traditional peoples—attempts that led to bloodshed, not commonality. As Chaim Kaufmann argues, "[i]n ethnic wars both hypernationalist mobilization rhetoric and real atrocities harden ethnic identities to the point that cross-ethnic political appeals are unlikely to be made and even less likely to be heard."[5]

Manipulating an individual's identity, or offering multiple identities that reduce the salience of ethnicity, becomes more difficult because of this hardening process. For example, a politician might appeal to a U.S. voter as an American, a Minnesotan, an African-American, a Christian, a senior citizen, a social security recipient, or another potential identity. The same voter can respond to all these calls. Individuals have a repertoire of possible identities, drawing on the most useful or meaningful depending on the circumstances (social security recipients share a common interest in higher premiums regardless of race or region while many Minnesotans would support a tax break on snow shovels regardless of their age or religion). When an individual is part of a group that has suffered from mass violence, however, that identity becomes powerful and far more salient than competing ones. Jews, Kurds, Armenians, and other groups that have suffered violence because of their communal identity will not easily put that identity aside. As a result, it is far easier to appeal to this hardened identity and more difficult to play up rival affiliations that might otherwise split a communal group.

The above overview suggests that identity manipulation strategies may contain the potential for disaster, but they also offer great promise. Governments that use these strategies need to understand the intricacies of identity manipulation. How might new identities ameliorate ethnic conflict? What forms of identity manipulation are common? To what degree have these been successful? Under what conditions is identity change easier? What role do outside powers play? These are the questions this chapter answers.

This chapter presents two different strategies that governments have used to manipulate ethnic identities and foster ethnic peace: the destruction approach, used for over fifty years by the Pahlavi regimes in Iran to shatter the identity of the Bakhtiyari people, and the "inclusion" model used by the Moroccan monarchy to join Arabs and Berbers since the time of independence in 1956. These examples illustrate various factors that shape or limit successful identity change. To illustrate the potential for disaster, this chapter presents the case of the Iraqi Arabs and Iraqi Kurds under the Ba'ath regime.[6]

These Middle Eastern cases demonstrate that government manipulation of identities can indeed contribute to ethnic peace. Identity manipulation strategies can work in at least four ways. First, they offer individuals the promise of successful assimilation: individuals of an ethnic group gain a greater chance of acquiring social and economic status by assimilating than they would if they retained their current identity. Second, they reduce the ability of ethnic groups to organize, as many of their members feel more in common with former enemies and identify less with their original people after changing their identity. Third, identity change strategies can decrease mutual security fears: the reduced organizational ability of groups whose members defect and assimilation make ethnic mobilization harder while the gradual change in identity creates new perceptions of brotherhood that replace more hostile images. Fourth, assimilationist policies can placate hegemonic groups, satisfying them that their way of life is indeed preeminent.

These potential benefits must be weighed against the certainty of several costs. Even when identity change is successfully implemented, it is often incomplete and generates tremendous resentment. The promulgation of new identities threatens to disempower traditional elites, who often are more willing to lead revolts than to give up power. Moreover, identity manipulation attempts often harden communal identities that had not yet jelled, thus creating a greater potential for division. To overcome these problems in the short term, identity change attempts require large amounts of coercion and co-optation to succeed. Elites must be bullied and bribed into cooperating with the government. Furthermore, these policies often only work under rare conditions. Identities are easier to manipulate when past levels of intercommunal violence were low; when the groups in question share a high culture; and when other social groups accept the newcomers as relative equals. Moreover, outside powers can also strengthen ethnic particularism, leading individuals to see themselves as members of an ethnic group first, and citizens of a state last.

This chapter has five remaining parts. The first part relates the debate about whether identities can or cannot change. The second section explores why identity manipulation might in theory lead to a decline in ethnic violence. The third examines instances of identity manipulation in Iran, Morocco, and Iraq, noting the degree of success and failure and the problems encountered. The fourth section reviews the arguments made previously as to how identity manipulation can lead to lasting peace by weighing the evidence from these three Middle East cases. It also notes the important role of outside powers in determining whether identity manipulation succeeds or fails. This is followed by an attempt in the final section to derive "lessons learned" from the Middle East experiences about the conditions under which manipulating identities is easier and more difficult.

Can Identities Change?

The extent to which communal identities can be changed is a subject of considerable debate. The primordialist approach asserts that ethnic groups derive their cohesion from some inherent biological, cultural, or racial traits. Ethnic groups are islands unto themselves. Birth defines membership, and socialization confirms it. The regulating principles that define distinctions between groups may vary, but what is crucial is that they determine both the boundaries and the meaning of tribal membership in such a way that the "in-group" and the "out-group" can always be clearly demarcated. If change occurs, it does so at a glacial pace, making identity manipulation worthless as a practical policy.[7]

The modernization school argues that identities can be created and manipulated, but that they become more cohesive over time and are difficult to erase. Drawing largely on the Western nation-building experience, this school observes how identities are created, often from remarkably little material, into a powerful emotional and political force.[8] Literacy, and the written national history that comes with it, take what was a loose identity and make it more solid.

The perennialist school would, in essence, agree with the modernization school, but its focus is on why identities, once made, are so stable.[9] Thus, governments and other powers can foster new identities, but will find it difficult to manipulate them once they take hold. A variant of the perennialist school has recently been developed in the work of Chaim Kaufmann, who argues that massive violence tends to harden identity. As a conflict becomes more intense, group perceptions of their enemies become more bitter while chauvinists often rise to the fore among all parties. Such hardened identities are far more difficult for governments to manipulate, particularly with regard to former enemies.[10]

Hegemonist scholars would argue that government officials can manipulate ethnic identities.[11] Under certain conditions, the state may create ethnicity as a vehicle of political mobilization or simply to preserve what appears to be certain ethnically structured patterns of exploitation. The state may embark on such efforts in order to assert its own autonomy or with an eye toward bolstering its prospects for survival. Such manipulation is common in colonial cases. Colonial powers often provide incentives that in turn strengthen particular identities to the exclusion of others.

The hegemonist view of identity, drawing on a more general "constructivist" school of analysis, sees identity as highly flexible.[12] As Jack Snyder notes, answers to questions about which group people will join, their sense of obligations, and their sense of threat "hinge in part on facts, but in the social realm, facts almost never speak for themselves. Facts require interpretation and the application of moral judgments."[13] By defining an identity in a certain way, states try to create an understanding of the obligations, interests, and preferences of their citizens. Elites in particular construct identities. Their goal, in so doing, is to bolster their own political and social supremacy.[14]

The strategic manipulation school makes a related argument, contending that individuals choose their identities in part on the basis of rational self-interest.[15] Individuals have multiple heritages and identities, and they call upon the most salient (and the most useful) one as the conditions warrant.[16] When individuals can gain by being an ethnic group, they will organize as such: but so too will they organize as a "class," as a "nation," or as other identity categories as appropriate. Ethnic identity, in this approach, is a commodity that individuals and leaders use to organize in the struggle for resources, status, and power. In its essence, the strategic manipulation school is a complementary reverse of the hegemonist approach: where hegemonists focus on the incentive structure presented by the state, strategic manipulators focus on how individuals react to, and alter, this structure.

The Western historical record strongly favors the view that identities can change. In 1648, when the Peace of Westphalia inaugurated the era of the nation-state, many states that exist today were collections of dialect groups that had little in common with their neighbors. For example, France had to transform a region of French, Celtic, German, Flemish, Basque, Spanish, and Italian speakers—to say nothing of dialects—into the ethnically homogeneous France of today.[17] When Italy was unified in 1870, only a small portion of the population spoke standard Italian; as Massimo d'Azeglio famously observed: "We have made Italy, now we must make Italians."[18] Although pessimists can note that Scots, Basques, and other peoples proudly proclaim their distinctiveness, in general the levels of violence in these countries are extremely low, and popular sentiment does not favor secession.

Nation-building attempts have been especially common in the Third World during the decolonization period, but their success is much less clear. States existed after colonial governments relinquished power, but the peoples living in them did not always consider themselves to be one nation. D'Azeglio's observation about Italy and Italians could be made for much of the Third World after decolonization, or even today. Most governments in the Middle East and Africa struggled to create a loyalty to the nation-state that transcended loyalty to one's tribe, ethnic group, or religious sect. These attempts have often failed. Again and again, African, Asian, and Middle Eastern states have faced tribal and communal conflicts.

Of course, saying that identities can change should not suggest that this process is easy. Although individuals carry within them multiple sources of identity, typically they do not shed these lightly. In addition, acceptance of a new identity often requires the willing cooperation of the state and other group members. If others will not accept assimilation or other forms of identity change, then the web of reinforcing expectations (the heart of the constructivist argument on how identity is formed) becomes torn. Indeed, when the state or other group members rebuff an identity change attempt, it often stokes the fires of status conflicts, leading to increased ethnic tension.

Kaufmann's caution about how ethnic violence can limit identity change also has strong support from recent history. Violence in Yugoslavia, Rwanda, and Iraq has hardened the identities of these countries' communal groups. Similarly, Jews, Armenians, and other peoples who are victims of great crimes are understandably reluctant to forget the suffering that resulted from their ethnic distinctiveness. As one Rwandan who survived the genocide noted, "People come to Rwanda and talk of reconciliation. It's offensive. Imagine talking to Jews of reconciliation in 1946. Maybe in a long time."[19]

In summary, the historical record suggests that identity change is a common process, but the deliberate manipulation of such identities has proven difficult in the Third World and after cases of massive violence. Thus, rather than ask whether identities can change after communal violence (for obviously they can), it is more useful to determine when change can occur and what conditions make it easier or harder.

The Promise of Identity Change

To improve our understanding of whether and how identity manipulation could work to keep communal conflict from recurring, it is necessary to lay out the mechanisms of this process. In theory, identity change policies could work in four ways: reassuring individuals about their security, helping individuals achieve higher status goals, interfering with violent communal organization, and placating hegemonic groups.

Identity change policies can reduce fear. As noted in Chapter 2, a common reason that ethnic conflict breaks out is that a security dilemma can develop between suspicious ethnic groups. If assimilation succeeds, however, the mutual fear necessary for the security dilemma to hold is absent. The Bretons in France today, for example, appear to be almost extinct as a corporate group even though in the past century the possibility of Breton secession was a constant fear in Paris.[20] The concept of organizing as Bretons is increasingly far-fetched because so many Bretons see themselves as Frenchmen.

Identity change policies can bypass group status concerns by appealing directly to the individuals who compose the group. Ethnic conflict often occurs because groups seek a greater degree of recognition for their cultures.[21] Assimilation policies, however, can give individuals an incentive to subordinate, abandon, or change their communal identity in favor of another. When successful, assimilation allows group members to achieve their social status goals as individuals by letting them partake in a greater share of resources, education, and leading social and political positions. Assimilating individuals are ones who recognize that their best hope for advancement lies with changing their political identity (to join the dominant side) rather than with fighting a rival. The group, however, will not have its status claims recognized as a group per se. Again, the French example is instructive. Many of France's distinct regional groups came to accept a French identity and the French language because that acceptance offered them prospects for social and economic advancement.[22]

Identity change, when successfully implemented, can interfere with attempts at ethnic organization, thus making mobilization for conflict far more difficult. As a distinct national myth is adopted, a new language is spoken, or a distinct religion is practiced, rallying along traditional lines becomes more difficult. Maintaining the image of a rival group as an enemy is more difficult if one is slowly adopting the customs, language, and indeed the name of that rival group. Those assimilating become less hostile to this ethnic group, and even those not assimilating might be more sympathetic toward their formal rivals as their ethnic brethren slowly join their ranks. When groups cannot organize effectively, they cannot use violence successfully. Thus, the effect of identity manipulation can be similar to control even though the cause is quite different.

Finally, identity manipulation can placate hegemonic groups. Hegemonic groups often use violence to force other groups to accept their dominant position and to conform to their ways. If the state seeks to defend and even to extend the hegemonic group's identity, then the group itself is more likely to be satisfied. In Turkey under Mustafa Kemal (Ataturk), the state promulgated and enforced a Turkish identity on the country's minorities. Although Kurds and Turks of Greek extraction suffered mightily, the regime's enthusiasm for assimilation satisfied Turkish chauvinists.

Cases of Identity Change

To illustrate whether identity manipulation can be used to keep the peace, this chapter reviews attempts by the governments of Iran, Morocco, and Iraq to change the identities of communal groups in their countries. These cases were chosen for four reasons: the prevalence of conflict, the length of time involved, the variation in government policy, and the difference in outcomes. Each of the countries in question suffered communal violence in the past. As a result, all can inform our general question of how to resolve ethnic conflict. Each country also involves many years of identity change policies; thus, we can determine how policies worked in the long term. However, each case is different with regard to the type of identity sought and the level of success achieved. The variance in these cases illustrates a range of identity manipulation strategies and conditions under which different strategies are more likely to work.[23]

The Destruction Model: The Bakhtiyaris in Iran[24]

Persian history and culture are immediately identified with Iran even though the country barely has a Persian majority.[25] This identification is not surprising: for most of the twentieth century, Iran's Pahlavi rulers tried to impose a Persian culture and identity on Iran's ethnic mosaic. Under Reza Shah Pahlavi and his son Mohammed Shah, the Iranian government emphasized Persian culture and attempted to rally Iran's disparate tribal and ethnic groups under the Persian banner.[26]

The Bakhtiyari people of Iran, once important political actors in the early years of the twentieth century, have almost disappeared as an independent political entity. The Iranian government's assimilation policies changed many Bakhtiyaris into Persians. Successful identity change, however, took generations to complete and required various Iranian governments to destroy Bakhtiyari institutions, repress Bakhtiyari cultural expression, and impose the dominant Persian culture on them through a high level of repression. The Bakhtiyari experience suggests that identity change policies can succeed in fostering lasting peace if the government is willing to shatter the culture in question. The Bakhtiyari case may seem obscure, but this is precisely the point: it is obscure today because of the Persian government's successful destruction of this distinct identity over the course of the twentieth century. Just as once-vibrant Western communities such as the Picts and Lombards are no longer active political entities, so too are the Bakhtiyaris becoming a shadow of their former selves.

The Bakhtiyaris are a traditional people whose homeland is the central and southern Zagros mountains of Iran. As of 1986—the last year that reliable data is available—they consisted of 34,333 households or roughly 200,000 people.[27] Like Iran's dominant Persian community, the Bakhtiyaris are Shi'a Muslims of the Twelver sect. The Bakhtiyari language is an offshoot of Persian. The Bakhtiyaris are a nomadic people organized along tribal lines.

Until Reza Shah took power in the early 1920s, fighting within the Bakhtiyari community and between the Bakhtiyaris and other ethnic groups was rampant. The Bakhtiyaris continually feuded with neighboring Persian, Qashqai, Lur, and Arab tribes over revenues and land. The few historic records that mention the Bakhtiyaris do so in the context of conflict: the need to punish them for nonpayment of taxes, their quarrels with other groups over territory, and their general resistance to the wishes of the central government.

When Reza Shah came to power, the Bakhtiyaris were near the peak of their historic strength vis-à-vis the central government. In 1894, they had stabilized the rotation of power within the tribal confederation, thus reducing internal conflict. William Knox D'Arcy's 1908 discovery of oil near Bakhtiyari lands and the building of a major road through their territory further bolstered the Bakhtiyaris vis-à-vis the central government. The Bakhtiyaris "guarded" the concession and road for the British in exchange for payoffs.[28] Before Reza Shah took power, Bakhtiyari khans governed seven major cities, including Kerman, Isfahan, Yazd, and Kashan. One khan had been prime minister, another a minister of war.

Using the new powers of the centralized state, Reza Shah Pahlavi crushed the Bakhtiyaris. Newfound oil revenue enabled Reza Shah to build a strong army and a bureaucracy that far exceeded the Qajar state's powers. His policy was one of forced assimilation, using the repressive powers of the state to coerce the Bakhtiyaris into a new identity. Reza

Shah was not magnanimous in victory after defeating the Bakhtiyaris. He disarmed the tribes, forcibly settled many of them, and removed their leaders. Tribal rebellions were put down with extreme brutality, creating deep resentment among the tribal peoples. He also changed the social structure by redividing pastoral lands and separating Bakhtiyari areas administratively.

Under the Pahlavi regime, the Iranian government promoted urban, Persian culture at the point of a bayonet. To remake society along his new national lines and assimilate the Bakhtiyaris into the national identity, Reza Shah attacked local shrines, enforced military conscription, replaced tribal rulers with local administrators, reorganized the tax system, disarmed many tribes, and imprisoned local khans. He also prevented migrations, thus converting tribesmen into agriculturists, and forced a change in native dress. At times Reza Shah even deported entire tribes. Under Reza Shah the government was not an impartial arbiter among social groups; rather it favored one particular group: the Persian majority.

Reza Shah tried to create a new Persian identity that reflected both his admiration for the West and for Persian chauvinism. He used fines and the threat of unemployment to force women to unveil. Using fascist Germany as a model, he set up the Society of Public Guidance to instill a national consciousness through the use of journals, textbooks, papers, and radio. In the same vein, he played up Persian culture, renaming the country "Iran" to emphasize its Aryan heritage, and commemorated Persian poets and monarchs. He directed architects to use a Persian style for buildings, changed Arabic names of cities to Persian ones, and used a Zoroastrian rather than an Islamic calendar, because the Zoroastrian religion was native to Iran.

Reza Shah not only used force to compel the Bakhtiyaris to become Persians. He also worked with local leaders who cooperated with the regime, and he regularly co-opted elites with money and privileges. Local leaders often served as government administrators. Reza Shah abolished the titles, but protected the privileges, of the local aristocracy who did not directly oppose him. Unlike his predecessors, Reza Shah sought not only social peace but also to forge a strong nation united under a Persian identity. As the British military attache in Iran at the time reported: "[Reza Shah's policy] . . . is a complete break with the traditional policy of the past, and is to establish complete political and military control over all parts of Persia and to effect the disarmament of the entire civil population. The tribal system of the country forms the greatest obstacle to the fulfillment of this policy."[29]

Modernizing reforms complemented and reinforced this promotion of a strong national identity. In 1926, Reza Shah introduced land titles, thus strengthening the power of local tribal leaders. These titles, however, came at a price: leaders now were tied to the land and to the state. Although their power increased among their fellow tribesmen, it weakened compared with the central government. Key social changes under Reza Shah, such as the development of infrastructure, also facilitated Persian hegemony. Reza Shah developed the infrastructure in remote areas, but he did so selectively, to further central government power at the expense of outlying regions. Infrastructure development served to refocus trade on the Persian center and helped Reza Shah send troops throughout Iran. Reza Shah also used education as a means of assimilation. For him, education was a means to integrate citizens into society, making them loyal citizens devoted to their shah and state. Persian identity was transmitted through education: textbooks were standard throughout Iran, and a special emphasis was put on knowledge of Persian. Reza Shah also tried to increase literacy in Persian.[30]

Mohammed Shah, Reza Shah's son who took power after World War II, also vigorously repressed dissent, but he increased the use of sinecures as well. Bolstered by oil revenues, the new shah bought off dissent by employing huge numbers of Iranians in the state. Of an estimated middle class of 630,000 in 1970, roughly half were civil servants and another 200,000 were teachers or school administrators. Mohammed Shah continued his father's vigorous education policy. The number of students at elementary schools increased from 286,598 at the beginning of his reign to roughly 5,200,000 when he left power.[31] Mohammed Shah also employed Bakhtiyaris in leading positions and integrated them into the symbolic life of the state. His second wife, Soraya, was the daughter of a Bakhtiyari chieftain. General Teymour Bakhtiar served as the military governor of Tehran during much of the 1950s and later headed SAVAK, the shah's secret police.

The Persian people did not resist the incorporation of Bakhtiyaris into their identity. A similar language, common ties of Shi'a Islam, and historic interaction between elites of the two communities made it easier for the Persians to accept the Bakhtiyaris as equals. Persians and Bakhtiyaris shared a pride in Iran's past, a common artistic aesthetic, similar values concerning ontological questions, and other features that made their common incorporation into one people possible. This acceptance stands in contrast to the Persian disdain for Iran's Kurdish community, which many Persians considered culturally backward.

The Bakhtiyaris looked for more autonomy in 1979 when the shah was overthrown and the Khomeini-led clerical regime took control, but they did not take up arms to do so. Central government authority effectively collapsed in many parts of Iran during the revolution. During this time, both the Bakhtiyaris and the neighboring Qashqai tribes pushed for more autonomy; the Qashqai lost a few members in clashes with regime forces. The Bakhtiyaris, however, stockpiled weapons but never used them.[32] Both groups' relative passivity stands in sharp contrast to the Iranian Kurds, whose uprising against the government took four years to subdue and cost thousands of lives.[33]

The Bakhtiyari tribal structure remains intact today, but is no longer a source for independent political action. Over a hundred thousand Bakhtiyaris regularly make the biannual migration,[34] and tribal groups still align themselves along the two major moieties, the Ilkhani or the Hajji Ilkhani. Nevertheless, the Bakhtiyari role in Iran today is conspicuous by its silence. Sixty years of repression and assimilation have limited the Bakhtiyaris' ability and desire to act as a corporate group.

The Bakhtiyaris could not resist assimilation because they were not able to organize. Pahlavi co-optation drove a wedge between Bakhtiyaris. By the 1960s, most Bakhtiyaris claimed their khans were now "city people" who no longer shared tribal identity or represented tribal interests. Subsequent land reform measures under the shah tied the tribesmen-turned-peasants' fortunes to that of the state rather than to those of tribal leaders. Education also increased the Bakhtiyaris' perception of having a shared history with their Persian neighbors as well as increasing their knowledge of the Persian language. As a result, corporate identity among the Bakhtiyaris fell, while a common identity between Bakhtiyaris and other Iranians grew.

The biggest indicator of assimilation, however, was a silent one: an identity change shrouded in demographic redefinition. As the overall population of Iran grew rapidly, that of the Bakhtiyaris remained steady. The numbers of Bakhtiyaris have remained roughly the same over the past hundred years even though the population of Iran skyrocketed during the same time. This silent measure suggests that many Bakhtiyaris are redefining themselves as Persian, whether voluntarily or through intermarriage.

The case of Iran's Bakhtiyari population illustrates the tremendous potential of identity change policies: they can and do at times work to foster ethnic peace. This peace, however, as seen in the case presented here, was a brutal one even though the Pahlavis had many advantages in their campaign to transform Bakhtiyaris into Persians. Thus, although Iran's experience with the Bakhtiyaris demonstrates the possibilities of using identity change to foster ethnic peace, it also suggests the difficulties and limits to such a policy.

The Inclusion Model: A Growing National Identity in Morocco, 1956–1999

The Moroccan monarchy has tried to slowly bolster a Moroccan identity as part of its effort to manage ethnic relations between the country's Arabs and Berbers and among the country's once-fractious tribal groups.[35] Rather than impose this identity on recalcitrant peoples as did Reza Shah, King Hassan II, and to a lesser degree his predecessor Mohammad V, tried to encourage a Moroccan identity indirectly by playing up sources of national unity and by minimizing organized expressions of Berber identity—a policy that has helped keep the peace but has met with mixed success in its broader nation-building ambitions. The monarchy combined three elements in its ethnic relations strategy. First, it co-opted Arab and Berber leaders and made symbolic gestures to both communities. Second, it repressed almost all expressions of independent political activity and civil society in order to ensure its control over political dialogue. Third, it promoted a Moroccan identity through language and education. The result was a decline in autonomous tribal and linguistic organization and an increase in Moroccan identity.

Morocco, like Iran, suffered from considerable violence in the early twentieth century. As described in Chapter 4, it was not until 1933 that the French effectively pacified Morocco. Until this time, conflict was a vital part of tribal culture. Warfare was an important social ritual, and prowess at arms a supreme source of social recognition.[36]

King Mohammad V, upon taking power from the French in 1956, used a mix of coercion and co-optation to maintain social peace. As noted in Chapter 4, the monarchy co-opted many Berber and tribal elites by providing them with high-status positions in government and in society. The king's bribes and token representation efforts helped mitigate the concerns that had led Berbers to revolt against Arab domination in the past. Reinforcing this policy of inclusion was the threat of punishment for those active in politics. The king arrested, jailed, and harassed political opponents on a regular basis. As a result, most Moroccans of all ethnic groups came to consider politics a dangerous, unrewarding business.

Under Hassan II, Mohammed V's son and Morocco's ruler since 1961, repressive policies always operated in the background to discourage political agitation. In the 1960s and 1970s, state control was particularly harsh. In the 1960s, there were hundreds of forced disappearances of potential and actual government opponents.[37] In 1973, the king did not hesitate to crush a Berber tribal revolt near Gwilmima in the Atlas Mountains before it assumed major proportions. Censorship was widespread. In 1978, for example, one activist was arrested for publishing an article on Berber history—an action that served to remind various cultural associations that their continued activity depended on the goodwill of the government.

The Moroccan government used several overlapping police and security organizations to maintain public order—a policy that succeeded in diminishing political activism. Reports of torture and police brutality regularly persist, although the scale has been reduced in recent years.[38] The government also suppressed even peaceful gatherings. According to an activist, the former Minister of Interior Driss al-Basri once bragged, "If there is a mouth open, I will shut it. If there is a hand out, I will cut it off."[39]

These control mechanisms severely inhibited ethnic organization, allowing the monarchy to attempt nation-building regardless of the will of community leaders. Interviews indicate that many Berber leaders feared arrest, particularly if they strongly protested government policies, and that they believed that the fear of punishment prevented many people from joining their cause. As one activist lamented to me: "You can say all you want about how people love the King or the Muslim tradition of accepting authority. Yet in reality it all boils down to fear. I'm afraid to directly protest against the government even though I oppose it. My people in the countryside are afraid to even join my organization though many say they support it."[40] Hassan II also tried to prevent the formation of independent political organizations in Morocco. In part he did so by arresting activists, censoring newspapers, and otherwise using force to prevent organization.

This blend of repression and absorption proved especially effective with regard to Arab nationalist parties. Although the Arab nationalist Istiqlal Party and its successors tried to maintain a pretense of independence, several Moroccan experts interviewed dismissed these parties as little more than token groups. These same experts believe that Arab nationalism has very real support in Morocco—what they dismissed was the idea that the parties effectively channel or represent this sentiment. Arab nationalists thus proved unable to force the government to promote an Arab nationalist identity to the exclusion of all others.

To complement the suppression of political action and the co-optation of Berber and Arab elites, the monarchy promoted a national identity with itself as the center. Hassan II, like his father, claimed the mantle of Berber culture as well as an Arab heritage. The king's wife was a Berber, and he regularly noted the Berber heritage of Morocco in his speeches. The king also tried to stress issues that unite Moroccans regardless of language or tribe: the 1975 Green March, where thousands of Moroccans mobilized behind the king's call to claim the Western Sahara after the Spanish withdrew, was one example in which the king succeeded in uniting Moroccans. These efforts created some loyalty to the regime. Even Berbers of former areas of dissidence such as the Rif proved loyal to the Moroccan state and have supported Moroccan foreign policy on national issues such as the dispute with Algeria.

Among Berbers, the government also sought to foster a Moroccan identity, in part by minimizing exposure to Berber culture and cultural activism. Arabic remains Morocco's official language of government and schooling, and the government tried to prevent the official use of Berber. In February 1996, for example, the government banned performances by an independent Berber cultural organization—the fourth time the Interior Ministry had banned a public activity by this group.[41] No academic resources were provided for the study of Berber languages or culture even though classes ranging from French to Hebrew could be found.

As in Iran, religion acted as a source of unity. Berbers and Arabs recognized their joint Islamic heritage as a bond that unites them. As one interlocutor noted, "Sure we have our differences, but we do not forget that we are all Muslims."[42] Furthermore, as the language of Islam, Berbers respected Arabic as a language of learning. Indeed, the teachings of ancient Berber political leaders have only survived in Arabic.

Education was another force for national unity in Morocco. During the 1970s and early 1980s, the number of primary school students grew at an average annual rate of 6 percent and secondary school students by 10 percent. University enrollment more than tripled. Education produced subtle identity changes. It fostered a common language, a common history, and shared political values. Arabic today is taught at school, and most Berbers speak it daily.

As a result of these forces, traditional identities diminished and at least some sense of a Moroccan identity developed. Several of those I interviewed noted that many Moroccans, particularly those educated in the past thirty years, derive their identity in part from the state as well as from their region and family. As one Arab official noted: "The process is difficult, but we have made great progress. Today, many of the children of both Arabs and Berbers see themselves as Moroccans."[43] Several Berbers in government echoed this sentiment and noted that their social and professional advancement came about in part by embracing a Moroccan rather than a Berber identity.

Many Moroccans today see ethnic disputes as an irrelevant subject in Morocco, in part because of the national identity that the king has slowly constructed. Several Moroccans interviewed noted that Islam or national identity brought Arabs and Berbers together, thus reducing the chances of any conflict. Interviews suggested that those who claim "we're all Moroccans" were less likely to see ethnicity as even a potential source of conflict. These individuals do not perceive a strong security or status threat from other communal groups.

Yet social barriers between Arabs and Berbers remain strong. Many urban Arabs held Berbers in contempt or fear, primarily due to rural-urban differences. The Berbers, for their part, saw themselves as part of the Islamic world and downplayed their ties to the Arabs around them. Although urbanization of Berbers may have the potential to change social ties, it has not yet done so. Most city folks retain ties to tribal homelands. So far, these differences have not become political. Moroccan elites still debate the question of the Berber role in Moroccan identity. No political party has yet formulated a coherent approach to the issue.

In short, the Moroccan experiment with building an identity was far less complete than the Iranian experience with the Bakhtiyaris, but it also required far fewer resources and has engendered less resentment. On a basic level, the Moroccan experience was a success, since the monarchy was able to maintain social peace. Like the Pahlavis, Morocco's monarchs destroyed the ability of ethnic groups to organize independently through a combination of co-optation and coercion. In addition, like Iran, a common culture helped smooth the path toward a common identity: the shared high culture of Islam made both Arabs and Berbers more willing to accept each other as equals. Promoting a national identity decreased communal fears and hostility while increasing individual identification with non-ethnic institutions.

Morocco's experience, however, also suggests that nation-building is an imperfect process. Even though Berber identity never jelled into a strong, cohesive identity that excludes other political identities, it has not disappeared either. Despite years of government attempts to foster a common national consciousness, the Berbers remain a large and often distinct part of Morocco's population. Other nations seeking to use a common identity to transcend ethnic differences are likely to confront similar problems.

Identity Hardening in Iraq, 1968–1991

Arab-Kurdish relations in modern Iraq are a sad chronicle of battles and bloodshed.[44] The Ba'ath regime in Iraq used a combination of brutal force and harsh assimilation policies to compel Iraqi Kurds to accept an Arab identity. (The Ba'ath's brutality is also discussed in Chapter 3.) This attempt backfired, leading to repeated Kurdish uprisings and hardening the particularistic Kurdish identity. The cease-fire attained when the Ba'ath took power in 1968 quickly collapsed, leading to fighting that did not end until 1975. Revolts recurred with greater intensity whenever the central government was weakened. During the Iran-Iraq war, and following Iraq's defeat by the U.S.-led coalition in 1991, the Kurdish region erupted into rebellion, seeking to escape the Ba'ath's clutches. If anything, Kurdish identity in Iraq is stronger today than at any time in its history. The Iraqi case illustrates the danger of identity manipulation when the government bungles its implementation and when conditions are not propitious.

The Ba'ath used massive force to shatter Kurdish organization and institutions. Entire villages were devastated, with surviving villagers being deported to Arab-populated parts of Iraq. To destroy Kurdish identity, the regime provided financial awards to Arabs who took Kurdish wives, changed Kurdish place names to Arabic ones, and Arabized the faculty and curriculum of Kurdish schools. The regime transferred Kurdish civil servants and police out of Kurdistan. Torture, mass arrests, and executions ensured that everyone obeyed these brutal orders. Any Kurd trying to return home after being deported was summarily executed.

The regime did not assure Kurds of their role in Iraq. The government did not allow Kurdish as a language of instruction nor did it give Kurdish representatives even token input into decision-making. The only development spending that occurred in the region was for roads to facilitate military movements. Arab Sunnis dominated the Ba'ath government. No Kurd joined the Revolutionary Command Council until 1982, and that Kurd—Taha Muhyi al-Din Ma'ruf—had little personal or political weight.

The high level of discrimination further impeded attempts to transform Kurds into Iraqis. The regime made so few efforts to incorporate Kurds into the government or into Iraqi society that the benefits of changing one's identity were almost nonexistent. Kurdish elites had no incentives to cooperate, because they were frozen out of political power. The high level of discrimination strengthened communal differences.

Foreign intervention also hindered Ba'ath identity change policies. Assimilating Kurds into an Arab-dominated "Iraqi" identity proved difficult, since the Kurds had brethren across Iraq's borders with whom they were in regular contact. Cultural materials, ranging from books and poems to political tracts, traveled across borders. Iranian military and political support also made secessionist violence a more plausible alternative.

Brute force and rampant discrimination hardened Kurdish identity. The widespread rebellion in Iraqi Kurdistan in 1991 included members of almost every tribe and region, including those that in the past had worked with the central government. Moreover, the violence associated Iraq and Arab identities with the horrors of Ba'ath repression, further increasing the appeal of Kurdish identity. As a result, the Kurds became even less likely than before to remain at peace with their Arab neighbors. Being Kurdish, a concept that only a few Kurdish intellectuals embraced earlier in the twentieth century, now resonates deeply in the hearts of most Iraqis who speak Kurdish.[45]

Identity Change Mechanisms and Ethnic Relations

The cases above suggest that identity manipulation can lead to ethnic peace by interfering with communal organization, improving the status of individuals, reducing group security fears, and placating hegemonic groups.

As Table 4 indicates, identity manipulation can have a potent effect on ethnic relations, particularly in the long term. As noted in Chapter 2, or-

TABLE 4. **Observed Impact of Manipulating Ethnic Identities**

Effects of Identity Manipulation	*Bakhtiyaris in Iran*	*Morocco under the Monarchy*	*Iraq under the Ba'ath*
Interfere with violent communal organization through assimiliation	x	x	
Help individuals achieve higher status goals	x	x	
Reassuring individuals about their security	x	x	
Placate hegemonic groups	x		x

ganization is essential for sustained ethnic violence. In Iran, however, the Bakhtiyaris gradually lost the ability to act as a corporate group. Even when central government power collapsed, as it did during the 1979 Islamic revolution, the Bakhtiyaris could not organize themselves to take up arms. Many Bakhtiyaris had assimilated, and group cohesion had fallen. Similarly, Berbers in Morocco were less able to organize as a communal group due to the regime's manipulation of identity. Although the government's maintenance of a high level of coercion contributed to this reluctance to organize, my interviews suggest that Berbers also saw themselves as Moroccans as well as members of narrower communal groups.

Security fears can also fall if governments successfully manipulate identity. Because it is harder for groups to organize in general, their rivals have less to fear. This can cause a spiral of peace: perceptions of weakness lead to a relaxation in self-defense preparations, which in turn creates a greater perception of weakness. Furthermore, in Morocco and Iran, the growth of stronger national identities created confusion over the identity of former enemies. If Bakhtiyaris rose up today, many of the Persians they would be fighting would be former Bakhtiyaris. Interviews in Morocco indicate that many Moroccans see members of other tribes and ethnic groups as part of the same people and thus have questioned the possibility of whether communal conflict could recur. In their eyes, the potential parties to a conflict had changed. The fierce tribes of nineteenth-century Morocco have gentled, and their members live side by side in peace.

Identity manipulation also contributed to the end of conflict by increasing the material and social status of individuals. Berbers in Morocco and Bakhtiyaris in Iran sought out the better jobs and leadership positions that came with a knowledge of the dominant language and acceptance of the identity favored by the state. Because both the government and other social groups accepted this assimilation, an individual's status could be improved simply by changing one's cultural identity.

Finally, identity changes at times can satisfy the ambitions of hegemonic groups. Persians in Iran, long a hegemonic group, felt no need to use violence to assert their hegemony, since the state was already enforcing hegemonic policies. The Iraqi case, however, demonstrates that attempts at identity manipulation can often inflame security and status fears, antagonize communal elites, increase a group's ability to organize, and actually strengthen ethnic identity. Because the Ba'ath tried to brutally extinguish Kurdish culture without providing any benefits to leaders or followers to assimilate, Kurds in general had little incentive to change their identity. Kurdish tribal leaders and newly educated intellectuals in particular had little reason to subsume their identity, because they would lose power and status if they did so. Moreover, the Ba'ath regime created a security dilemma between it and the Kurds; after years of slaughter, Kurds came to fear the Arab-nationalist dominated state as a threat to their security. Finally, the regime's combination of discrimination and brutality made it easier for the Kurds to organize. That strategy strengthened communal identity and gave individuals a material incentive to join resistance groups that promised an end to discrimination. Not surprisingly, Kurdish identity today is stronger than in the past.

Outside powers can play a key role in preventing an identity change. Iranian support to Iraqi Kurds increased their hope of resisting assimilation through military rebellion. Intervention, however, crosses a cultural dimension as well as a military one. In Iraq, outside powers and diaspora communities offered the country's Kurds a distinct literature, history, and language—assistance that helped keep Kurdish identity alive in the face of government efforts to extinguish it. In addition to strengthening particularistic identities, outside support also deepened the divide between Arabs and Kurds, respectively, since it led many among the dominant Arab community to see minorities as a potential fifth column.

Outside powers can act as the guardian of a minority or non-dominant group's identity. Outside powers (or diasporas) abroad can help preserve an identity deliberately, by fostering a group's traditional culture and way of life. Preservation can also happen by accident, however, whenever an outside power allows the traditional language and culture to flourish. Comparing the fate of the Iranian Kurds and the Bakhtiyaris is instructive here. The Kurds, in contrast to the Bakhtiyaris, had many brethren across Iran's borders in Iraq and Turkey. From these countries, Kurdish literature and Kurdish nationalist ideas flowed even though the governments of these countries guarded against Kurdish particularism. On the other hand, the Bakhtiyaris had no kinsmen across the border who were outside the reach of the Iranian central government. Thus, no element of the Bakhtiyari people could escape the central government's control over education and society. This condition helped facilitate the assimilation of the Bakhtiyaris.

Conditions under Which Identity Change Is More Likely to Succeed

The most important factor determining the success or failure of government attempts to change identity is the strength of the government relative to that of the groups in question. When the central government is strong enough to compel individuals, over time identity change policies begin to take effect. The Iranian regime's use of force shattered the Bakhtiyaris' ability to fight other groups or to resist the central government. Thus, incentives for individual Bakhtiyaris to become Persians had time to work. Similarly, in Morocco, communal groups also realized that resistance would fail, leaving them with little choice but to cooperate with the government. When groups are divided internally by clan or region, the government's influence becomes even stronger. Coercion in the short term made successful identity manipulation possible over time.

Coercion alone is not the sole cause of ethnic peace in the cases examined: by any standard the Ba'ath used considerable coercion to force an Arab identity on the Kurds, but this effort backfired. To win the support of leaders, some co-optation is necessary. In Morocco, the government proved adept at winning over community leaders with subventions and positions of responsibility. Even the rather brutal Pahlavi government was willing to work with Bakhtiyaris (who would become their puppets) and to co-opt vast segments of the population with government-funded jobs. This co-optation reduced elite and popular incentives to take up arms against a regime. However, in Iraq, Kurdish leaders lost the high-status positions they had attained in their community while they received nothing in return. Not surprisingly, Kurds were bitter toward their Arab neighbors and were in a near-constant state of rebellion.

Dominant group attitudes (and those of their leaders) are also vital to the success of identity manipulation. The Iraqi Kurds also rejected an Arab nationalist identity because it did not bring sufficient status with it. Because the regime's cronies controlled political and economic power, the Kurds gained little for becoming Arab in Iraq. In contrast, the Bakhtiyaris in Iran who assimilated rightfully believed they would gain sufficient status in society. The Persian majority was not hostile to their incorporation into society, making the change in identity advantageous for individuals. Thus, for individual Bakhtiyaris, their status was more assured by assimilating into the dominant community than by remaining second-class citizens.[46]

The Moroccan and Iranian cases suggest that the presence or absence of a large intelligentsia with a well-developed written history and culture has a strong effect on attempts to change cultural identity. Moroccan schools emphasized the common heritage of both Arabs and Berbers. Furthermore, the high culture of Berbers is written in Arabic, and Arabic is accepted by Berbers as the chief language in Morocco—a choice reinforced by government policies. The Bakhtiyaris in Iran also share a high culture with their Persian neighbors and lack an independent intelligentsia of their own. These commonalities help smooth the path for a new identity. Elites can keep their position, as the new identity does not automatically bring with it a new social pecking order. In general, the disruption identity manipulation does to a society and its symbols is reduced when the cultures involved are similar.

A long-term view is necessary when assessing assimilationist policies. Identity change policies require generations to take effect. Learning a new language and accepting the symbols and history of a new culture can take years or generations to incorporate. The demographic redefinition of Bakhtiyaris into Persians was only noticeable by comparing total Bakhtiyari numbers today to what these numbers would be if the Bakhtiyaris remained unassimilated. Indeed, initially the resentment created by attempts to change daily rhythms probably strengthened Bakhtiyari identity, as suggested by the repeated Bakhtiyari clashes with Reza Shah in the early twentieth century. Over time, however, the continued futility of clinging to a lifestyle that brought little economic reward or social status and continued political repression became apparent. Morocco suggests a similar pattern; new identities took decades to develop, and even after all that time their solidity is unclear.

As Kaufmann's work argues, identity change policies are particularly difficult to carry out if a group has suffered a massive tragedy, usually characterized by great bloodshed and widespread emigration. One such tragedy, of course, is the memory of an extremely violent ethnic conflict. Iraqi Kurds today confront decades of massive killings that have hardened Kurdish identity. The violence touched all Kurds. Moroccan Arabs and Berbers, in contrast, did not face a legacy of overwhelming bloodshed, with one group as victim and the other as perpetrator. The Bakhtiyaris did suffer great violence, but total deaths fell well short of the Kurdish experience. Again, the intelligentsia plays an important role, since it can preserve memories of conflict and use them as tools for mobilization, making it harder to reconstruct cultural and social histories in ways that emphasize the specific identity that the government wants to foster.

The importance of the intelligentsia and of outside powers suggests that identity manipulation will become harder in the future. As literacy spreads, so too will recordings of conflict and strife endure. Similarly, the presence of diasporas abroad—and their growing ability to communicate with people in their home country—will help keep cultural identities alive in spite of government efforts.[47]

Disadvantages to Identity Manipulation

Identity manipulation policies suffer from several serious disadvantages, reducing their attractiveness to policymakers and to those interested in human rights. As the Iraqi case so sadly illustrates, nation-building often inflames the status and security fears of other groups. Few groups willingly accept assimilation into another culture; the very process implies a renunciation of their own culture. The heavy hand of the state that is required to enforce an identity change often leads to a fierce security dilemma. After trying to Arabize the Kurds, the Iraqi government came to be seen as the enemy. Any hope of an impartial government vanished, making it almost impossible to end the security dilemma. The deaths of hundreds of thousands of Kurds testify to the dangers inherent in identity manipulation.

Identity change policies almost invariably enrage community elites, leading to an increased threat of unrest from these groups. As the Ba'ath discovered to its dismay, tribal elders, newly educated intellectuals, and other leaders have a tremendous interest in the survival of the traditional order. Their status, power, and wealth often depend on the survival of a distinct culture, which they of course will lead. If they can, they will resist attempts to usurp their favored positions. When these elites are strong and can punish those who change identity, then state efforts are more likely to fail. If elites are weak, however, or if the state can more effectively coerce or bribe individuals to change, then identity manipulation becomes easier.[48]

Identity manipulation also is costly in terms of cultural diversity. As the distinct cultures and identities of Bakhtiyaris and other tribal groups slowly fade, their unique way of life ends. Although this book focuses on lives lost rather than cultural survival as its measure for the successful resolution of ethnic conflict, it is important to note that even successful nation-building has many drawbacks. Destroying distinct identities may lead individuals to identify with one another, but it also comes at the price of humanity's cultural richness.

6 Participatory Systems

Ethnic groups with a voice in government are often able to resolve their differences peacefully through the political system rather than resort to war. Many Quebecois, Catalans, and Scots seek their own state, a greater share of government resources, more autonomy, and assurances that their distinct cultures will flourish. In many ways their ambitions mirror those of Kurds, Palestinian Arabs, and other minorities in the Middle East, Africa, and other parts of the developing world. Yet in general, violence by ethnic groups in Western democracies is extremely rare despite the often-contentious nature of political debates in these countries. As a result, many scholars are optimistic about democracy's potential for keeping the peace among different ethnic groups. Sammy Smooha and Theodor Hanf typify this sentiment when they argue that "Liberal democracy fosters civility, a common domain of values, institutions, and identity, at the expense of communalism. It equates nationalism with citizenship and the state with civil society. All citizens, irrespective of their national or ethnic origin, are considered equal nationals."[1] Scholars are not alone in their enthusiasm. Promoting democracy is the knee-jerk answer that policymakers and international organizations and humanitarians in general proffer when asked how to resolve communal tensions.

Democracy, however, is more troubled in deeply divided societies, particularly when security fears are prevalent (the rule, not the exception, after an ethnic conflict has occurred). Attempts to build participatory systems have foundered on a lack of trust among communities, a tendency of ethnic groups to adopt maximal positions vis-à-vis one another, and weak political institutions.. Free elections lead to tyrannies of the majority or to other undemocratic results, and communal leaders often exploit democratic freedoms to trumpet messages of hatred and intolerance. Furthermore, the presence of many minorities with different ways of life and fundamental beliefs can lead participatory systems to dissolve into a civil war or to foster an authoritarian regime. Not surprisingly, despite the apparent promise of participatory systems in maintaining ethnic peace, democracy is rare in divided societies.[2]

This chapter has four parts. The first part notes the potential benefits of power-sharing systems, explaining how, in theory, they can alleviate many of the causes of ethnic conflict described in Chapter 2. The second part notes why the transition to democracy is difficult and argues that it often exacerbates, rather than mitigates, various causes of conflict. The third part explores two variants of power-sharing: the consociational democracy of Lebanon and the hegemonic democracy of Israel. The fourth and final part assesses the relative advantages and disadvantages of each system, as suggested by the two cases.

The Potential of Power-sharing

Democratic systems, when successfully institutionalized, give ethnic group members the opportunity to select the political elite, attain economic success, or capture status positions without limitations, stemming from their ethnic background. Political participation thus defuses ethnic violence driven by a hope for status. Individuals and groups can use the electoral system to gain official support and respect for their communal institutions, such as language and holidays, by voting for sympathetic candidates and withholding support from chauvinists.

Democracy can be particularly effective at satisfying the desires of aspiring elites. When people use the ballot box rather than the gun to gain power, would-be leaders are better off seeking power through peaceful mobilization than through war. Moreover, participatory systems create jobs and status positions for local elites.

If the electoral system is properly designed, it can also foster ethnic moderation, leaving firebrands isolated and out of power.[3] Working with elected officials from rival communities can help a group maintain an electoral coalition, pass contentious legislation, or protect group prerogatives. Successful cooperation in turn aids future relations, demonstrating that groups can work together and that they share common interests.

Participation, under rarer circumstances, can also satisfy the ambitions of hegemonic groups. When one group controls the state—or can easily control the state if its privileged position is threatened—a chief hegemonic ambition is secured. Thus, when a democratic system ensures one group control over decision-making, it can reduce conflict stemming from hegemonic concerns. In these circumstances, less democracy can prove more effective in keeping the peace than a fairer system, which would allow any group to have unimpeded access to political power.

Certain forms of democracy are more likely to result in true power-sharing in highly divided societies. Liberal democracy relies on an ever-changing majority to avoid a tyranny of the majority. Different coalitions of individuals, unified temporarily on the basis of economic interest, region, social interests, and other factors, unite and divide, ensuring that all voices are eventually heard. Majority rule works when the majority changes from election to election, as it does in the United States and other Western democracies. In divided societies, however, voting blocs are more rigid, and majorities are less likely to change. The largest ethnic group may never lose power, since ethnic group members vote as a bloc. Liberal democracy, in such circumstances, produces aliberal results.

Thus, measures to offset majority power are needed. Proportional representation systems and ones with a high degree of federalism provide local ethnic groups with more influence than does a "winner take all" system, where a majority group can dominate the entire government. In theory, these mechanisms to offset majority control reduce incentives for conflict by giving minority groups and their leaders more power with respect to fundamental concerns such as education, taxation, and law and order. Ensuring minority representation in the legislature helps balance majority power, as does a "grand coalition"—the sharing of executive power among ethnic groups—and a minority veto over sensitive issues.[4]

Efforts to offset majority rule, however, often go against the desires of hegemonic groups, thus preventing it from being implemented effectively. The same blandishments used to reassure minorities—setting aside certain positions, recognizing their distinct culture, or allowing them a veto over decision-making—are often the very grievances cited by the hegemonic group. In theory, it is possible for a hegemonic group to monopolize most but not all of society's resources and for other groups to accept this. However, this balance is uneasy. Rival demagogues often seize on any special privileges—real or perceived—to attack the political status quo. Thus, in a highly divided society, any system is likely to be attacked by at least one group as unfair.

Getting There: The Difficult Transition to Democracy

Although democratization can foster social peace, it is a Janus-faced phenomenon: unrest, strife, and even outright war often occur during attempted transitions to democracy.[5] Democratic institutions are often poor vehicles for organizing the equal division of power and privilege among hostile ethnic groups. Hence, loser groups are often even more dissatisfied under democracy than they were under the previous authoritarian regime. Democratic freedoms (of speech, press, assembly, and so on) also provide political space to determined chauvinists, giving them more room to organize for war. Democratization thus unleashes communal conflicts that had lain dormant under previous authoritarian regimes. Not surprisingly, social scientists have found a strong correlation between the transition to democracy and instability.[6] Several recent conflicts and outbreaks of violence, including those in Azerbaijan-Armenia, Chechnya, Georgia, India (Kashmir), Pakistan, South Africa, and Tajikistan stemmed in part from attempts at democratization in ethnically divided societies.

Minorities often fight democratization because they fear that majority rule would install in power a permanent elected majority that allows the minority no voice in decision-making. In Georgia, democratization produced war by causing minority fears of majority tyranny. The minority Abkhaz feared that their distinct cultures would be overrun by a power-monopolizing Georgian majority. Hence, they opted for violent resistance when Georgian nationalists appeared poised to win elections. The experiences of Sri Lanka and Northern Ireland teach the same lesson. In Sri Lanka, the majority Sinhalese long monopolized power at the expense of the minority Tamils, provoking a bloody rebellion. In Northern Ireland, the Protestant majority monopolized power at the expense of the Catholic minority from 1969 to 1992, fostering violent Catholic nationalism.[7] All are "democratic" in that elections were held, but aliberal in that certain groups were effectively shut out of power.

The promise of pluralism can also threaten the position of hegemonic groups. In Rwanda, France and other outside powers pushed for greater pluralism, posing a threat to chauvinistic Hutu elites who dominated the country. Rather than accept a more open system, these elites raised the specter of a Tutsi threat, creating the conditions for the subsequent genocide.[8] When the hegemonic individuals within a group dominate, they are likely to resist opening up decision-making.

Elites also can easily manipulate democratic freedoms, particularly when democratic institutions are weak. Chauvinists in almost every country, if freed from authoritarian constraints, exploit the media and the right to assemble freely, using these opportunities to mobilize their followers. The Chechen experience illustrates the risk that radicalized groups will take to exploit democratic freedoms to promote separatism. After suffering repeated cruelties by Russian rulers, many Chechens wanted no part of the Russian state, regardless of its government type or its respect for minority rights. When given the right to assemble and speak freely, Chechen leaders rejected any ties to Moscow—a position that triggered a brutal Russian crackdown in which tens of thousands of Chechens and Russians died. Indeed, necessary conditions for elite competition (as discussed in Chapter 2)—the political space to express views and mobilize followers—is created by democratization.

Communal leaders also often oppose the institutionalization of a democratic system. Because the very act of participation can imply accepting the system's legitimacy, radicals within the group often oppose the idea of elections and cooperation with other groups. In Northern Ireland, Spain, Ethiopia, and elsewhere, ethnic radicals often opposed attempts to hold elections, arguing that participation was tantamount to submission. When radicals boycotted elections, those who participated risked being labeled traitors.

Groups are particularly fearful of their security during democratic transitions—something that democracy itself does little to affect. Building institutions depends on creating mutual expectations of cooperation and non-aggression,[9] but these expectations require time, and peace, to take root. Moreover, regardless of the stakes involved or the desire of the parties for peace, successfully implementing a peace settlement involving democracy is difficult to carry out because combatants fear for their own security.[10] The freedoms inherent in true democracy—such as the right to assemble and to speak freely—facilitate ethnic mobilization and raise security fears. Thus, even when democratic institutions are established to keep the peace, often they are not sustained because of security fears. In Angola, for example, the National Union for the Total Independence of Angola (UNITA) refused to lay down its arms, in part because it feared revenge by the Popular Movement for the Liberation of Angola (MPLA). Similarly, despite the existence of a democratic compromise to end Lebanon's civil war, peace did not return to this country until 1990, when Syria moved in to ensure order (and secure its own control). Before then, even a small armed community could, and did, spoil any cease-fire. Not surprisingly, democratization is often more successfully institutionalized by outsiders who can ensure security: colonial powers, or interested neighboring states.

Because of these problems, democratization often founders during the transition. Minority mistrust, dominant group resentment, and the elite exploitation of freedoms all contribute to ethnic tension and, frequently, to ethnic conflict. Conflict is particularly likely when a government is weak—a common problem during any political transition—and cannot deter conflict or suppress radicals. Thus, when tension is high, democratization is often impractical because it cannot be implemented.

Two Variants of Participation

Every democratic system varies in its particulars. In the Middle East, only two countries, Israel and Lebanon, qualify as having (or having had) participatory systems, and the systems in both of these countries differ considerably from each other and from the models familiar to most Westerners. In Israel, Arab citizens living within Israel's pre-1967 borders can vote and elect members to the Israeli parliament, but until recently they could not realistically aspire to even approach the summit of political power because no major Israeli political party would form a governing coalition with Arab elected officials. Although Israeli Arabs have influence, Israeli Jews dominate the country: an arrangement I label *hegemonic democracy.*[11] In Lebanon, from 1943 to 1975, a form of communal power-sharing—so-called *consociational democracy*—helped once-warring communal groups live together in peace but collapsed under the weight of region-wide information. This system was revived, with important variations, after 1989 and has helped maintain an uneasy peace in Lebanon. These experiences provide valuable lessons when seeking how democratic systems can, and cannot, be used to keep the peace.

Hegemonic Democracy in Israel, 1967–1995

As discussed in Chapter 3, democracy in any true meaning of the term was lacking for Israel's Arab community during the era of the military government, which stretched from 1948 to 1966. The late 1960s, however, marked a turning point for the Israeli Arab community. Israeli Arabs gradually increased their participation in Israeli society and politics. Although Israeli Arab activism at first took the form of supporting parties that rejected Zionism—a sign that democratic freedoms bred the potential for radicalism—Israeli Arabs became increasingly pragmatic in their voting choices as the potential for true political influence increased. By the late 1980s, the Israeli Arab community had become a stronger, more self-confident minority that used the democratic process to press for more rights and privileges. During this time, Israeli Jews increasingly recognized that Israeli Arabs were loyal citizens who did not support violence. The result shows the potential advantages of an imperfect democracy. Israel's democratic system ensured the power of Israel's Jewish community but, in the process, it improved the condition of the country's Arab population and decreased the likelihood of violence by both communities.[12]

The transformation of the Israeli Arabs from a powerless community to a self-confident one took decades. The military government that oversaw the Israeli Arabs until 1966 had left the Israeli Arab population weak and disorganized. Within the Arab community, Christians, Muslims, Druze, and other subgroups were divided not only from each other but also internally. No independent political institutions existed, and political elites remained co-opted. Economically, Israeli Arabs were concentrated in lower-paying jobs such as construction and farming and held few administrative or professional positions.

Even after the end of military government, Israeli Arabs mostly voted for the Labor Party and its allies because they could deliver government patronage. Labor and its electoral allies controlled the Ministries of Education, Agriculture, Religious Affairs, and Interior as well as the Arab Department of the Histadrut. Therefore, these bodies controlled much of the funding and many of the jobs that went to the Israeli Arab community. Not surprisingly, the Labor Party won 53 percent of the Israeli Arab vote from 1949 to 1973.[13]

During this time, Israeli Arabs had little say in decision-making. In 1971, almost 30 percent of Arab villages had no local councils, compared with 1 percent of Jewish villages.[14] In 1976, of the 1,860 officials in Israeli government and non-government major institutions, only 26 were Arabs, and almost half of these were employed in religious courts. Clans dominated Israeli Arab politics, and the major parties had almost no Arabs on their guiding committees.

This lack of influence made Israeli Arabs highly cynical about politics, and they began voting for pariah parties in protest. Because the ending of military government did not correspond with material improvements or status positions—and Labor's hold on power seemed secure—Israeli Arabs increasingly rejected mainstream parties, using their votes to protest their condition and exclusion from power.[15] From 1965 to 1977, Israeli Arabs increasingly voted for Rakah, a pro-Arab Communist party, in order to express their discontent with discrimination. Rakah gained popularity because it was non-Zionist; this non-Zionism, however, made it an outcast with the mainstream Israeli parties, which would not ally with it in the Israeli parliament. Rakah gained only 10 percent of the Israeli Arab vote in 1959, but in 1977 it received over 50 percent.[16] Furthermore, in the early 1970s, more radical Israeli Arabs formed Abna' al-Balad (Sons of the Village), which grew out of the Al Ard movement. Abna' al-Balad rejected Zionism more openly than Rakah and had an aggressive Arab nationalist agenda. It also rejected electoral participation and tried to discourage Israeli Arabs from voting.

New Israeli Arab elites also began to emerge. Increasingly, Israeli Arab communities rejected traditional leaders, many of whom were (rightly) perceived as co-opted by the government. New leaders, many of whom were educated by the Jewish state and influenced by Israel's vibrant political debate, began to gain influence in their communities.

Communal violence also reared its head in 1976. On March 30, 1976, a strike led by the National Committee for the Defense of Arab Lands, a Rakah front, turned violent. Police killed six Arabs and arrested and injured hundreds of others.[17] To this day, many Israeli Arabs commemorate the day as the holiday known as Land Day. What is notable to an outsider, however, is not the scope of the violence in 1976, but rather how limited it was. Given the past violence of the Arab revolt, and the future violence of the *intifada,* the Land Day violence of 1976 pales by comparison. Nevertheless, it was clear that Israeli Arabs' inferior status (and perhaps agitation from abroad) was leading to increased violence.

The Land Day protest, however, roughly coincided with the end of Labor's electoral dominance, when the more conservative Likud Party won the 1977 elections. Israeli Arabs were at a crossroads. On the one hand, they could continue down the path of outsider politics, supporting Rakah and carrying out violent protests such as the Land Day demonstration. On the other hand, Labor's defeat enabled them to use the democratic system to improve their position.

As a result of Likud's victory, the Labor Party became more responsive to Israeli Arabs, and smaller parties stepped up their competition for the Israeli Arab vote. The narrowness of Likud's victory led all parties to compete more heavily for Arab votes. Labor soon had to meet the needs of its Israeli Arab constituents or risk losing more Israeli Arabs to protest votes. More dovish Jewish parties were even willing to ally with Arabs, and voting for them promised results for Israeli Arabs. Thus, electoral necessity changed the attitudes of the dominant Jewish parties.

After this breakthrough, Israeli Arabs increasingly chose to work with the system, not against it. From the end of the 1970s, Israeli Arabs used their votes to gain political influence rather than to protest Zionism. Rakah did worse in the 1980s than in the 1970s as rival Arab parties emerged and as the rewards of voting for sympathetic Zionist parties increased. In 1981, Israeli Arabs increased their votes for Labor because the Likud government favored harsher policies against Arabs in general—the first increase in Labor's percentage of the Israeli Arab vote in decades. In 1984, the Progressive List for Peace (PLP), which had an agenda similar to Rakah but deemphasized communism, became a major rival to Rakah. The PLP's success can also be seen as an indication of the growing tolerance among Israeli officials: one of the party's founders was also a founder of the previously banned Al Ard movement.[18] Over time, however, Israeli Arabs increasingly voted for small, dovish parties that were clearly committed to Arab interests but were also able to ally with Zionist parties. Support for traditional Zionist parties fell in 1984.[19] Voting for parties allying with liberal and dovish Israeli parties also represented a shift from seeking patronage to looking for a chance to gain a voice on national matters.

Gradually, the Israeli Arabs came into their own politically. By 1984, the Israeli Zionist parties' gentlemen's agreement not to ally with Israeli Arab parties began breaking down. In 1984, Labor did not put a separate Arab list out but gave Arab politicians a realistic place on the overall ticket. Labor also supported government participation by Arab-dominated groups such as the PLP. Other parties focused on the support of components of the overall Israeli Arab vote—some put a Druze high on their list, others a bedouin leader. In 1988, the first strictly Arab party came into existence when an Arab Knesset Member of the Labor Party, Abdul Wahab Darawshe, broke off from the Labor Party in protest and formed the Democratic Arab Party. Islamic parties have also developed within Israel.

The success of Israeli Arabs in joining Israel's political life on an independent basis can be illustrated by comparing their failed effort in 1980 to form a country-wide Arab political party and Darawshe's 1988 success in doing so. In 1980, Prime Minister Begin crushed efforts by the mayors of the largest Arab towns and villages to form a political party, the Congress of the Arab Masses, to work for Israeli Arab rights. This suppression occurred without resistance from other parties, primarily because the Labor Party feared being labeled "Arab lovers" by the Israeli Jewish population more than they feared losing Arab political support. In 1988, Darawshe formed his own political party, which had an almost identical political platform to that of the Congress of Arab Masses, with little opposition. Similarly, Israeli Arabs have established a wide range of community-based organizations that promote human rights, education, culture, and other issues. Some institutions now exist to defend the rights of Israeli Arabs whose villages were destroyed—organizations that would have been unthinkable during the years of the military government.

The realism of Israeli Arab political parties is honed by the constant knowledge that greater repression awaits those who are intransigent. After several Israeli Arab students endorsed the Palestine Liberation Organization's (PLO) use of violence in the early 1970s, Israeli officials, including then Foreign Minister Dayan, made threats reminding Israeli Arabs of the fate of the Palestinians in 1948.[20] As one Israeli Arab politician noted: "We are under no illusions as to our position in Israel as a whole. If violence happened, the Jewish parties would band together against us. The rights we have worked for decades to achieve could vanish instantly."[21] Even religious militants learned this lesson. After years of being harassed by the secret police, fundamentalist Israeli Arab leaders shifted from clandestine political activity to calls for increased attention to routine patronage and greater rights. Religious militants even called for "two states"—a policy that would have been heresy for their brethren in the West Bank and Gaza who support only the return of Israel to Muslim rule. Since entering the political arena, Islamic parties in Israel have stayed completely within the law, making painstaking efforts to do so, even while they expand contacts with Islamic militants elsewhere. As Sheikh Abdallah Darwish, a leader of the Islamic movement among Israeli Arabs, noted with regard to Islamic movements in the Occupied Territories, "Identification—yes; violence—no."[22]

In addition to participating in elections, Israeli Arabs also began to form their own political institutions independent of Israeli authorities. In 1971, Arab students founded the National Union of Arab University Graduates, and in 1975, an Israel-wide organization for Arab university students was founded. In subsequent years, Israeli Arabs formed dozens of voluntary associations in areas such as education, youth, and health.[23] New organizations such as the Committee for the Defense of Arab Lands and the Committee of the Heads of Arab Local Councils, both of which were founded with the backing of Israeli Arab intellectuals, were considered by a majority of Israeli Arabs to be representative, unlike the old party lists under the military government.[24]

Despite this surge in Israeli Arab influence, Israeli democracy remained unequal for Arabs and Jews. Institutional protections of minority rights are weak, particularly when security concerns can be invoked to justify human rights violations;[25] nor do most Israeli Jews favor an equal society. According to polls taken in the late 1980s, over two-thirds of Israeli Jews believe that the State of Israel should prefer Jews to Arabs in general; 72.3 percent of Jews reject equal admission to universities; 74.2 percent reject equal admission to public workplaces; and 85.9 percent reject Arab inclusion in senior government posts.[26] Furthermore, although Israeli Arabs can participate in politics as individuals, they are shut out from much of the symbolic life of the state. Israel's national symbols and history are at best ambivalent symbols for Israeli Arabs.

THE LIMITED BENEFITS OF HEGEMONIC DEMOCRACY. Israeli Arabs are better off today than they were in the past: their status in society has grown, they enjoy more political freedom, and they suffer less harassment than twenty-five years ago. In addition, both Arabs and Jews have more positive attitudes toward each other and increasingly reject violence.

Starting in the 1980s, the government began making progress on Israeli Arab issues as a result of their growing influence in government. Over the years, Israeli Arabs have increasingly joined the labor market on equal terms as well as such important institutions as the Histadrut and Jewish political parties. Furthermore, they increasingly use the same beaches, cinemas, parks, and other public facilities as Israeli Jews. The average ratio of Jewish locality budgets to Arab locality budgets was 13 to 1 in the 1970s, but this shrank to 2.5 to 1 in the 1980s.[27] Israeli Arab villages no longer had structures demolished without villagers first having their say, and even a bit of land expropriated from Arab villages in Galilee was returned. In 1985, the Israeli Knesset enacted a law to exclude parties that seek to negate Israel's democratic character and incite racism—a law used to prevent the participation of the anti-Arab religious party Kach. As never before, Israel's Arabs are becoming masters of their own fate. In 1988, over 75 percent of Israeli Arabs surveyed thought the political struggle of Israeli Arabs was proceeding well.[28]

If anything, the early 1990s showed even more dramatic improvements in the status of Israeli Arabs. In 1992, the Israeli government depended on Israeli Arab Knesset members to survive; as a result, the Labor Party signed a Memorandum of Understanding with several Arab parties, committing itself to work for greater Arab-Jew equality, to close municipal budget gaps, to eliminate education and housing disparities, and to improve religious endowment property. The government also almost tripled development spending on Israeli Arabs, committed itself to absorbing Israeli Arab graduates into the civil service, provided child assistance that previously had been reserved for families who served in the army, appointed several Israeli Arabs as government officials, and admitted publicly that past policies toward Israeli Arabs were mistaken. Israeli Jewish politicians began courting Israeli Arabs in person.[29]

Israeli Arabs' status in absolute terms improved dramatically, particularly for Israeli Arab elites. Most of these elites live in private, high-standard houses, have the full range of modern municipal services, and are well educated. Moreover, they increasingly enjoy a free press, the right to run for office, and freedom of movement and association. In 1995, Ali Abeed Yihyia was named the first Israeli-Arab ambassador.

Opinion surveys suggested that few Israeli Arabs saw violence as productive, and most supported the moderation of their political leaders. Over 55 percent of Israeli Arabs believed that elections and other democratic means were improving their situation. Since the 1970s, there was a steady decline in support for unlicensed demonstrations.[30] Over 70 percent of Israeli Arabs were against the use of force as part of political action, and a majority opposed unlicensed demonstrations. Interviews of Israeli Arab political elites, including leaders of former pariah parties such as Rakah, suggested that they see their role as influencing Israeli Jewish public opinion and, when trying to help Palestinians in the West Bank and Gaza, they do so within the system of Israeli politics.[31] Thus, over time the Israeli Arab community has become less radical.

Communal tension remained high but did not result in widespread violence. Roughly two-thirds of Israeli Arabs felt they suffered frequent discrimination.[32] Anti-Arab legislation was routinely proposed, although rarely passed, in the Knesset. After terrorist attacks, Arabs were beaten on the streets. Personal humiliations of Israeli Arabs were common—Israeli Arabs, for example, were often forced to pay in cash while Jews can write checks.[33] Israeli Arabs, however, do not appear to fear massive communal violence, although they regularly complained of sporadic hostility and attacks.

Even after decades of peace at home, Israeli Jews still mistrusted Israeli Arabs. Survey data suggested that Israeli Jews attributed far more extreme attitudes to Israeli Arabs than actually existed. Most Israeli Jews believed that every Arab hates Jews, and the vast majority believed that Arabs in Israel cannot be trusted. Furthermore, over 80 percent of Israeli Jews believed Israeli Arabs threaten national security to some degree.[34] As one expert noted, "[T]here is a common belief that Arabs in Israel are only loyal to the state because we are strong and the PLO and its allies are weak. Many Israelis feared that should Israel be threatened, the Israeli Arabs would defect."[35] Jews saw Israeli Arab support for a Palestinian state in the West Bank and Gaza as proof that Israeli Arabs cannot be trusted; Israeli Arab leaders' attempts to gain PLO blessings for their electoral campaigns have only reinforced this fear. Ironically, the *intifada* heightened Jewish suspicions of Israeli Arabs even though Israeli Arabs did not take an active part in it.[36]

Despite this high level of mistrust, Israeli Jews, like Israeli Arabs, were also moving away from extreme attitudes. In March 1978, Jewish students at Haifa University prevented Israeli Arab students from holding a conference on the situation of Israeli Arabs on the grounds that "this is an Israeli university and not a *Fath* [the leading PLO grouping] training camp."[37] By the 1990s, however, such conferences were commonplace. Support for Israeli Arabs living in Israel either as a national minority or as a minority with full civil rights increased, while support for extreme views such as expulsion fell. In the 1980s, opposition against the use of general strikes by Arabs dropped and support for an increase in surveillance of Israeli Arabs also fell. Increasingly, Israeli Jews were willing to accept an Arab superior in the workplace, have an Arab friend, or endorse the idea that Arabs can be equal citizens in Israel. In general, Israeli Arabs were far more in favor of mixed neighborhoods and schools than Israeli Jews, but both groups were moving in this direction.[38] One important factor behind Israeli Jews' more charitable attitudes toward Israeli Arabs stems from the Jews' control of the police and the military. As one Israeli expert noted, "Jews in general know that the police are their police. Should violence break out between Arabs and Jews, they know the police will side with them."[39] Israel's progress from almost constant communal fighting during the period of the British Mandate to peaceful, if tense, communal relations today demonstrates the strong impact that government policies can have on ethnic relations. This peace is particularly remarkable given the threat felt by the Jewish population from neighboring Arab states and from Palestinians in the West Bank and Gaza strip. The Israeli democracy is highly imperfect, yet it has managed to keep the peace for decades now.

Israel's democracy is remarkable not just because it has led Israeli Arabs to choose peaceful means to express their grievances, but also because it has mollified Israel's Jewish population and withstood the pressures of outside powers. Political necessity led Jews to violate the unspoken prohibition against Arab-Jewish electoral cooperation and, over time, decreased Jewish suspicions of their Arab neighbors. Even more impressively, this cooperation has continued even as Israel fought several wars with its Arab neighbors and was engaged in a long-standing campaign against Palestinian terrorism and violence. Thus, hegemonic democracy, despite its imperfections, still provides a valuable example of how democratic systems can bring a measure of peace to deeply divided societies.

Israel's success in satisfying aspiring elites through greater participation may be in jeopardy in the future. Regular concessions to the Israeli Arab community have helped satisfy Israeli Arab leaders even though they constantly complain about their second-class status. Israel, however, may be nearing the end of compromises it can make that would not anger Jews who seek to preserve Jews' dominant position in Israel. Treating Israeli Arabs as full partners, necessary if elites in the future are to be satisfied, would anger those who see the state's existence as ensuring a Jewish identity and political presence. Tension and violence between Israeli Jews and Palestinians in the West Bank and Gaza raises further problems. Israeli Arabs are inevitably caught in the middle, branded by Jews as dangerous turncoats if they openly sympathize with Palestinians while lambasted by Palestinians as traitors if they do not actively back their cause.

Consociational Democracy in Lebanon

Consociational democracy—a form of democracy that emphasizes communal consensus and autonomy over majority rule—is a much-touted form of power-sharing for highly divided societies. Consociational democracies combine electoral participation with a high level of local control, dispersing the points of political power and helping each group obtain a share in the system. Arend Lijphart has identified four characteristics of consociational democracy: a grand coalition of the political leadership of all significant segments of society; a mutual veto that requires agreement among leaders; proportional representation of major groups in decision-making bodies and the civil service; and a high degree of subcultural autonomy.[40] Austria, Belgium, the Netherlands, South Africa, and Switzerland all are examples of consociational successes. Failures of consociationalism include Cyprus (from 1960 to 1963, ending in civil war) and Nigeria (which ended in military rule).

In the Middle East, only Lebanon has attempted a consociational democracy.[41] Although this attempt clearly failed, with Lebanon suffering a brutal civil war from 1975 to 1990, consociational democracy did help keep the peace for decades before 1975. Moreover, many of the reasons for the collapse of Lebanon in 1975 had little if anything to do with the political system there. Thus, although Lebanon's experience points to several obvious shortcomings of the consociational model, it also highlights many of its advantages.

For over three decades, the consociational system of Lebanon helped to keep the peace. Indeed, before its collapse into anarchy in 1975, Lebanon seemed to offer a model demonstrating how different ethnic groups could live together in harmony. Its admirers often touted it as "The Switzerland of the Middle East." Many of the conditions scholars have identified as conducive to consociational success were present in Lebanon: the country was small, making decision-making easy; a tradition of accommodation and compromise was in place; and a rough balance of power was present among major social groups.[42] Embodied in Lebanon's unwritten 1943 National Pact between Christians and Muslims was a political system that balanced power-sharing with stability.

This accomplishment is impressive, especially because Lebanon's political history has been an attempt to cope with the fears and aspirations of the country's religious and ethnic groups. Lebanon is home to many religious and ethnic communities: Armenian Catholics, Assyrian and Chaldean Catholics, Greek Catholics, Maronite Catholics, Roman Catholics, Syrian Catholics, Armenian Orthodox, Greek Orthodox, Syrian Orthodox, Protestants, Bahais, Jews, 'Alawis, Druzes, Shi'a, and Sunnis all can be found in Lebanon. In the mid-nineteenth century, Lebanon's Druze and Maronite Christian populations engaged in a sustained war, in which thousands died.[43] Moreover, the Lebanese state was wholly artificial, carved out of Syria by the French colonial power to ensure the position of favored minorities, particularly Maronite Christians. Finally, waves of Arab nationalism, and the subsequent onset of the Arab-Israeli conflict, placed Lebanon in a dangerous neighborhood. In particular, Lebanon's Christians feared living as unequal citizens under the protection of Islam. Thus, on the surface, Lebanon would seem a candidate for war since its creation.

To mollify Lebanese fears—and to ensure Christian control—in 1943 Lebanese elites brokered the so-called National Pact, which divided power among Lebanon's major communities. The agreement ensured that the republic's president would be a Maronite Christian, its prime minister a Sunni Muslim, its speaker of parliament a Shi'a Muslim, and his deputy a Greek Orthodox Christian. Of the 77 parliamentary seats, 42 were to be allocated to Christians. Thus, the Christians, particularly the Maronites, were assured a dominant role. Of the 35 Muslim seats, Sunnis received 16; Shi'a 14; and the Druze 5. The initial allocation was based on a 1932 census that indicated a Christian majority in the population as a whole; within the Muslim population, Sunnis supposedly outnumbered Shi'a. Yet in subsequent years, emigration and different birth rates led to a Muslim majority and a Shi'a plurality.[44]

Consociationalism, however, helped keep the peace during this turbulent period. Voters voted with few impediments, communities organized, political expression was relatively free, and other essentials of a democratic life were present. Most important, consociationalism ensured the status of major Lebanese groups. Indeed, the National Pact was designed to do just that: it explicitly provided a recipe for balancing Lebanon's many communities. Although Christians, and Maronite Christians in particular, retained a favored position, other communities had a say in national decision-making as well as a high degree of local autonomy. Perhaps most important, political rewards were given according to a confessional formula, giving each community a slice of the pie.

Consociationalism also ensured the status of traditional elites, actually helping them bolster their power. The system allowed elites to control their communities rather than the other way around. Several families led Lebanon's communities for generations. Electoral restrictions gave traditional leaders advantages over their newer rivals.[45] The government co-opted leading families, giving them honorary administrative positions, access to government largess, and big salaries. In exchange, these leaders controlled dissent in their villages and clans. Moreover, elites of different communities often worked with one another to preserve the existing order. Those who did not accept the traditional leadership found themselves cut off from state resources.

EXPLAINING LEBANON'S COLLAPSE. Despite the carefully constructed political system, a brutal civil war plagued Lebanon from 1975 to 1990. Roughly 170,000 Lebanese died in the war, 300,000 were wounded, and perhaps 800,000 displaced. Lebanon collapsed into 15 years of civil war for a variety of reasons, only some of which can be placed at the doorstep of its political system.

As critics of consociationalism rightly note, Lebanon's system proved unable to encompass new demographic and political realities. The system froze politics at a time when the country needed to forge a new grand compromise and when the various groups needed to change their own leadership. Increasingly powerful communal groups lacked status that reflected their demographic strength. New elites in particular felt the pinch and resorted to outbidding to gain power. Critics of consociationalism, however, ignore that many of the factors that led to civil war would have strained even the most flexible and stable of systems. By the time Lebanon collapsed in 1975, it was host to thousands of armed Palestinian guerrillas who were in a constant struggle with Israel within Lebanese territory. The presence of the Palestinians exacerbated divisions within Lebanon, fostering an intense security dilemma that the weak consociational government proved powerless to stop from spiraling out of control.

Part of the Lebanese fiasco is explained by the inflexible nature of the political system. According to Arend Lijphart, consociational democracy's main weakness in Lebanon was

> the inflexible institutionalization of consociational principles. The segmental allocation of the highest offices and the "preset" electoral proportionality, both of which favored the Christian sects that constituted a majority in the 1932 census, were incapable of allowing a smooth adjustment to the gradual loss of minority status by the Christians to the Muslims.[46]

When the system was created, the Maronites theoretically were the most populous group in Lebanon. As time went on, however, emigration and lower birth rates pushed the Maronites down to third place demographically, while the Shi'a became the largest minority and Sunnis the second largest.[47] The system was not open to change, therefore institutional failure was inevitable. Muslims began demanding that the system reflect their greater numbers, but Christian groups resisted, fearing that this would weaken their status in Lebanon. The consociational system proved unable to accommodate aggrieved groups: it preserved certain rights, but it would not bend to provide new ones. The system that had worked after 1943 failed by 1975.

The emergence of new elites also heightened conflict. Modernization, education, urbanization, and other sources of politicization produced a crop of new leaders who had gained little from the National Pact. Particularly among the previously passive Shi'a, new leaders began to emerge. Although many traditional Shi'a elites supported the system that reinforced their power, the spread of politicization gradually weakened their power and hold over their communities. New leaders demanded more influence for their communities, demands that discredited traditional elites and that polarized the country. The spread of violence (discussed later in the chapter) also led to the emergence of new elites wedded to conflict. Power began to flow from the barrel of the gun.

Security concerns also played a major, if not leading, role in causing the Lebanese conflict. The presence of Palestinians mobilized and alarmed all parties, creating a new security threat that made compromise difficult and, as time went on, polarized Lebanese politics. Before 1967, the Palestinian presence in Lebanon numbered around 180,000. By 1969, it had risen to 235,000; by 1982, the number leaped to 375,000. Initially, refugees were mainly workers, fishermen, and peasants. However, they were also Arabs and Sunni Muslims and, in time, they arrived heavily armed. The Palestinians also championed a Sunni Arab brand of Arab nationalism that found only limited sympathy among the Shi'a and none among the

Christians. The Maronites in particular saw the Palestinians as intruders and foreigners; they were concerned that the armed Palestinians would support the Lebanese Muslims and strip the Christians of their power. The Lebanese government was aware of the problem. As then President Fu'ad Shihab's 1960 report stated, "In other words, the Palestinian problem is bigger than Lebanon. For Lebanon will either repress the Palestinians or be repressed by them—no third solution exists."[48] The Palestinian problem worsened after "Black September" in 1970, when the PLO shifted its base from Jordan to Lebanon.

The heavy hand of the Palestinians in the parts of Lebanon they controlled quickly alienated many Lebanese. As Druze leader Kamal Jumblatt noted:

> From time to time, Lebanese citizens and foreigners were arrested and imprisoned, on the true or false pretext of having posed a threat to the Palestinian revolution. Such actions were, at first, forgiven, but became increasingly difficult to tolerate . . . it all mounted up and began to alienate public opinion, especially conservative opinion, which was particularly concerned about security.[49]

PLO groups sought to preserve their freedom of action and their ill-gotten gains and resisted efforts by the Palestinian leadership to prevent crime and extortion.

Because the Lebanese government was unable to provide adequate security, the security dilemma for all communities proceeded to grow. Political leaders of all communities had opposed a strong state, fearing that it would interfere with communal autonomy and with their own political position and might even be used by their rivals to dominate the country. After the 1967 war, the debility of the Lebanese government became apparent to all concerned. The Palestinians began launching attacks on Israel out of Lebanon, roughly half of which involved cross-border attacks by rockets or mortars rather than infiltration. Maronite officers led the army into clashes with Palestinian commandos but, by 1969, the army was forced to retreat and give the PLO de facto military autonomy in the so-called Cairo Agreement. At the same time, a change of government among the Maronite factions in 1970 resulted in purges of the army and intelligence services, thereby reducing the information available on Palestinian commandos.

Increasing attacks on Israel by the Palestinians led to harsh Israeli responses, which further highlighted the Lebanese government's weakness and raised the threat felt by groups in Lebanon. In 1968, Israeli forces raided the Beirut airport and killed several Palestinian leaders. After the murder of Israeli athletes in the Olympic games in Munich in 1972, Moshe Dayan announced that Israel would not simply retaliate but would preempt Palestinian military action, striking Lebanon at will. Between 1968 and 1974, Israeli violations of Lebanese territory averaged 1.4 incidents a day. By 1974, Israel was regularly patrolling Lebanon and bombing PLO camps, with the government of Lebanon powerless to stop it.[50]

As the army's inability to shield Lebanon from Palestinians and Israelis became apparent, the major ethnic groups began to enlarge their party militias. The better-organized and more fearful Christians were the first to develop militias in response to Palestinian activity. Both the Phalange and Chamoun's National Liberal Party began building large militias in the late 1960s. In 1969, Tony Franjieh formed a third Maronite militia, the Giants Brigade. By 1973, these militias were attacking Palestinians on their own.[51] Once the civil war erupted, several other small Maronite groups sprang up, such as the Guardians of the Cedars and The Organization. As the violence mounted, the overall sizes of the militias also increased. By the late 1970s, the Maronite militias were larger than the Lebanese army. The Palestinians had upset the internal Lebanese balance of power. In order to increase their control and influence in Lebanon, the Palestinians began to train radical Lebanese militias, extending the cover of the de facto autonomy granted by the Cairo Agreement to these allies. In 1973, leftist and Nasserite Lebanese militias fought alongside the Palestinians against the Lebanese army, leading all Lebanese groups to prepare for a clash, gather arms, and seek foreign allies for funding and supplies. By 1974, even the formerly quiescent Shi'a set up training camps in the Beqaa as the fighting spread, complaining that the army was not protecting southern Shi'a from Israeli attacks.[52]

The timing of Shi'a mobilization and arming strongly suggests that the civil war and Palestinian-Israeli conflict played a key role in mobilizing the Shi'a far more than concerns about the justice of Lebanon's political system. The year when the Shi'a militia Amal was formed—1974—coincides with high levels of Palestinian and Israeli violence and follows the formation of militias by other groups in Lebanon. Palestinian attacks on Israel in particular had angered the Shi'a population, which bore the brunt of Israeli retaliation. Amal grew tremendously as villagers joined the movement seeking protection against the Palestinians, whose presence would bring Israeli wrath. Shi'a attitudes toward the Israeli invasion of 1982 illustrates what motivated the Shi'a. Many Shi'a initially welcomed the Israeli invasion since it drove out foreign forces, leading people to think that their personal security would be enhanced. For a time, the Israeli Defense Forces and Amal even cooperated together against the Palestinians in the south. However, as it became clear that Israel itself would not simply remove the Palestinians and leave, tension mounted and the Shi'a mobilized in huge numbers.

The conflict within Lebanon died down dramatically after the Syrians asserted their power in 1990. On May 22, 1991, the Treaty of Brotherhood, Co-operation, and Co-ordination was signed between Lebanon and Syria. This treaty accepted the Pax Syriana in Lebanon. Once the Syrians established order and security—at the point of a gun and at the price of Lebanon becoming a Syrian satrap—groups were not compelled to arm to protect themselves. Indeed, arming could endanger a group's security, for it brought Damascus's wrath.

Superior force, not institutional merit, created peace. The final power-sharing arrangement rewarded Sunni Muslims over other groups, even though the Shi'a now are Lebanon's most populous community. The October 22, 1989, Ta'if Agreement, which became the basis of the Syrian-dominated peace, allowed the Christians to keep the presidency, but with significantly reduced powers. A Sunni Muslim remained prime minister, and the Christians and Muslims had parity in the legislature. Previous power-sharing arrangements proposed in the 1980s were roughly as just as the final settlement, but they did not lead to peace until Syria laid down the law.

Lebanon after Ta'if: A Return of Democracy, 1991–2000?

In October 1989, many Lebanese communal leaders signed the Ta'if Accord, which revamped Lebanon's political system. The Ta'if Accord formed the basis for revising Lebanon's National Pact–based government. The new structure followed the old in many ways, although power was significantly redistributed among Lebanon's communities. The 128-seat parliament is divided equally between Christians and Muslims. Shi'a Muslims have twenty-seven seats of the Muslim total of sixty-four. The prime minister and the cabinet both are stronger, while the presidency, still held by a Maronite Christian, is weaker.

The negotiations at Ta'if, however, did not end the civil war. The violence ended in 1991, not 1989 when Ta'if was concluded, because only then did Syria crush resistance in Lebanon and consolidate its position there. Syria imposed order on Lebanon. It disarmed Lebanon's militias, allowing only Hezbollah to retain its paramilitary structure in south Lebanon. To keep all groups weak and subservient, Damascus has encouraged subcommunal divisions, trying to create rivals to potentially strong organizations like Hezbollah.[53] To prevent unrest and ensure its control, Damascus displayed thirty thousand or more troops in Lebanon, along with many intelligence operatives.[54]

THE BENEFITS OF THE TA'IF SYSTEM. The Ta'if system, like the National Pact before it, was a form of consociational power-sharing. As discussed below, it was at best an imperfect form of consociationalism given the Syrian role. Nevertheless, the Ta'if Accord ensured that all major communities had a voice in the system and that no community could dominate the others. As a result, it ensured all communities a certain level of status in society. Groups received official recognition, with certain rights and privileges respected. Leaders, particularly ones approved by Syria, also received government respect and support.

Over time, elections began to play a part in power-sharing. After the initial Syrian consolidation of power, communities initially saw elections as little more than window dressing for Damascus's control. Some communities also feared that electoral participation would legitimate the Ta'if division of power, which they felt shortchanged them. The leading Shi'a Muslim group Hezbollah, for example, initially viewed elections with suspicion and participated only as an expedient. Over time, however, it sought to use electoral participation to gain a role in government and to join the Lebanese establishment.[55] As Laura Zittrain Eisenberg argues, "In parliament, Hezbollah representatives have demonstrated a readiness to 'check their ideology at the door,' eschewing the classic fundamentalist stances of inflexibility and a refusal to compromise."[56] Similarly, even conservative Christians who rejected the legitimacy of Ta'if increased their participation over time.[57]

Ta'if also encouraged groups to cooperate with each other in parliament. In order to pass legislation, collect their share of the spoils, and otherwise conduct politics, groups participated in politics and at times formed electoral alliances. However, this cooperation is often forced. Syria often imposes deals on groups to ensure that its will is carried out. Damascus, for example, imposed an electoral arrangement on Hezbollah and Amal in the 2000 parliamentary elections, a deal that diminished Hezbollah's electoral clout.[58] Without Syria's heavy hand, it is not clear if cooperation would continue.

A FAÇADE OF PEACE? The Ta'if system is an imperfect creation, and it faces an array of challenges. The biggest question is whether Lebanon's peace is a creature of Syrian occupation or has the strength to stand on its own. Neither Lebanon's government as a whole nor individual politicians dare to act independently of Syria.[59] Indeed, it is questionable whether the Ta'if system could have been created, or could endure, without Damascus's heavy hand. In essence, Syria has acted as a brutal Leviathan, using its troops and intelligence service to enforce order and prevent any unrest. As long as Syria's military presence is so visible, and its willingness to use it so apparent if unrest resumes, groups need not fear other groups. Similarly, although elite militancy along ethnic lines has been stifled, this is in large part due to the surety of punishment rather than any increase of goodwill on the part of leaders.

Several of Lebanon's communities are dissatisfied with the Ta'if division of power. Maronites still resent their loss of dominance in Lebanon, while the Shi'a have even greater cause for complaint. Although they represent at least 40 percent of Lebanon's total population (and may even be a majority), they have only 27 seats in the 128-seat parliament. The speaker of parliament is a Shi'a, and although this position is stronger than it was before Ta'if, the speaker remains less powerful than the Sunni prime minister.[60]

In general, the electoral system has not brought Lebanese together. Politicians represent their sect and community, not the nation. Most officials are largely in power because of support from within their own sect: they do not rely on outsiders to get elected, reducing their incentives to court and know other communities.[61]

If anything, communal identity is more important than ever in Lebanon. As Augustus Richard Norton notes, in Lebanon "One's life chances are shaped by the accident of being born a Sunni Muslim, Greek Orthodox, Maronite Christian, Shi'a Muslim or belonging to one of the 15 recognized confessions that comprise Lebanese society."[62] Being Lebanese means little. War hardened Lebanese identities, and returning to even the uneasy harmony of the past is difficult. As one Lebanese wrote, "the country became more and more religiously segregated . . . I have felt repeatedly that religion has worked rather like the stamp with which cattle are branded . . . And so are we all, like it or not, branded with the hot iron of our religious ancestry."[63]

CONCLUSIONS. The return of consociationalism under Ta'if is a shaky success story. Ta'if has helped stop the killing and restore a workable government to Lebanon. Given the violence and devastation of the civil war, it was perhaps the best of many bad alternatives for restoring a government to Lebanon.

Yet it has not brought Lebanese together under a new identity or entrenched norms of power-sharing. Most worrisome, it depends heavily on Syria's iron hand to keep the peace. Should Syria remove its troops and otherwise diminish its influence, a return to war is a distinct possibility. Aggressive elites would draw on the legacy of conflict to whip up communal resentment. The imperfections of the power-sharing arrangement would give them fertile soil in which to sow words of hatred.

IMPLICATIONS FOR CONSOCIATIONAL DEMOCRACY. Consociational democracy's greatest strength is that it drastically reduces group concerns about their status and satisfies traditional elites. Under the National Pact, high levels of autonomy left groups accepting of, if not necessarily happy with, their status for many years. Similarly, elites—at least traditional ones—were satisfied with their positions in their communities and saw the system's preservation as in their best interests. The Ta'if Accord also satisfied elites and communities in general as to their status, at least to the point that they did not take up arms.

Consociationalism, however, is difficult to square when a group's ambitions for status or hegemony grow or are threatened. In Lebanon before the 1975 civil war, Maronites saw any change in the system as a threat to their dominance; Sunnis and Shi'a considered change necessary to reflect their proper status in Lebanon. Similarly, Shi'a are dissatisfied with Ta'if because it does not reflect their community's demographic dominance. Once a grand compromise is reached, engaging in negotiations again is difficult if not impossible.

A consociational state, by itself, cannot end the ethnic security dilemma by force or crack down on elites because the government is too weak. Under the National Pact, the Lebanese army would not and could not control the country because Christian leaders kept it weak, fearing that a strong army could be used by Muslims to dominate the country. When the Palestinians first came to Lebanon in force, Lebanese leaders could not agree to commit the army in the south for fear of polarization.[64] Similarly, the high level of autonomy prevented the government from stopping communal leaders from organizing or spreading their messages. Indeed, if anything, consociational democracy can also increase the ability of a group to organize and to use violence, since the high level of local autonomy granted for more mundane issues enabled communities to organize more easily in times of crisis. This weakness is not limited to Lebanon but rather extends to consociational democracy in general: by keeping government weak, and communities strong, the government's ability to control unrest is limited. The security dilemma ended during the Ta'if government only because Syria used its muscle to back up the weak Lebanese state.

Consociational democracy is especially fragile when outside powers join the fray. Arguably, the growing power of the PLO and the fear that this caused among the Maronites made civil war inevitable. Because the state offered no hope, the Maronites took actions into their own hands. Similarly, the constant Israeli attacks undermined the central government, reducing its credibility in the eyes of Lebanon's communities.

Advantages and Disadvantages of Ethnic Democracy

The experiences of Israel and Lebanon suggest a range of lessons for the use of democracy in fostering ethnic peace. In many ways, the Israeli and Lebanese systems were polar extremes. The Lebanese system was the ultimate in power-sharing and consensus-building. The Israeli system, on the other hand, was completely exclusive until 1966, and even today remains dominated by the Jewish community. Between them, however, they offer insights into the advantages and limits of democratic systems in keeping the peace.

For power-sharing systems to be introduced in the first place, security must be increased. In Lebanon, the National Pact was forged during a time when France was keeping order, thus ensuring security for the communities while cooperation gradually took root. Almost fifty years later, limited power-sharing again occurred after Syria forcibly suppressed any opposition: the parties in question would not agree among themselves before Damascus weighed in. The Israeli experience offers particularly useful lessons, as Israel itself overcame the transition problem. The Israeli democratic experience, unlike that of Lebanon, did not spring up due to outside control. Rather, years of social peace as part of an undemocratic system gradually led to democracy. In Israel, more than twenty years of peace among Israeli Arabs was a necessary condition for the shift toward a more inclusive system—one that could truly be called democratic—in the 1970s.

The security dilemma must be limited for democratization to survive beyond its introduction. Israeli Jews, even though dominant in society, needed to be assured of the loyalty of the Israeli Arab population and that, should this loyalty vanish, the Israeli security forces could easily prevent unrest from becoming widespread. Not surprisingly, both Israeli Arabs and Jews were aware that any violent organization would lead to a quick crackdown. The constant atmosphere of suspicion made it clear to Israeli Arabs that political participation would be tolerated if, and only if, their loyalty to a Jewish state was assured.

A tense outside security environment can disrupt consociational democracy, but hegemonic democracy is a tougher beast. Outside intervention can easily disrupt social peace in a consociational democracy, which by definition has a weak government. The hegemonic democracy of Israel, in contrast, has weathered cross-border raids, terrorism, and war with neighbors who proclaim themselves kin to, and defenders of, Arabs in general and Palestinians in particular. Over time, however, Israeli Jews became less suspicious of their Arab neighbors, though tension at times increased when Israel faced violence from neighboring Arab states or Palestinians in the West Bank and Gaza. This change in attitude suggests an obvious implication for other states: when a state's security is imperiled, the hegemonic model, although perhaps inferior in terms of equity, is more likely to survive than consociational democracy.

As Table 5 indicates, power-sharing offers a variety of advantages. If security concerns can be overcome, successful participation increases a group's sense of having a stake in the political system, thereby reducing concerns about its status. Opinion polls of Israeli Arabs over the years show a direct correlation between whether Israeli Arabs believe that the system can improve their position in Israel with both decreased support for the use of violence and greater acceptance of Israel's existence. Lebanon's system was predicated on ensuring a basic level of status for all the major communal groups in the country. Even though the system was inflexible, for decades the major social groups tried to work with, rather than against, the political system. Peace may even have lasted if Lebanon was not in such a violent neighborhood. Although the degree of support for the political system in Lebanon under the Ta'if arrangement remains an open question, even violent radical groups like Hezbollah are playing a constructive role.

In addition to reducing status concerns, even restricted participation in decision-making helped limit the dangers of elite politics. For many years in Lebanon, input into decision-making provided the country's existing elites with a stake in preserving the political system although its static nature alienated emerging elites. New elites emerged, decreasing (but not eliminating) the impact of the co-optation of existing elites. Participation, while at times restricted for Israeli Arabs, nevertheless induced Israeli Arabs to use the Israeli political system, not to reject it, in their struggle for rights. Polls and interviews conducted in the 1980s and 1990s indicated that Israeli Arabs believe that they can use the political system to improve their condition. As this belief grew, support for violence fell.

Success builds on itself. True input into decision-making strengthened moderates over radicals, proving that peaceful participation in the system can deliver the goods. Rejectionist Christians and Hezbollah in Lebanon both increased their participation in elections over time, recognizing the many rewards of playing the game. As the benefits of participation grew, Israeli Arab attitudes become more favorable toward the Israeli political system. As time went on, Israeli Arabs increasingly voted for mainstream rather than rejectionist parties such as Rakah. Similarly, the continuation

TABLE 5. **Observed Impact of Participatory Systems**

Effects of Participatory Systems	*Israel, 1967–1999*	*Lebanon, 1943–1975*	*Lebanon, 1991–1999*
Decrease group status concerns	x	x	x
Satisfy aspiring elites	x		
Satisfy existing elites	x	x	?
Encourage intergroup cooperation	x	x	?
Decline in security fears over time	x		?
Assure hegemonic groups	x		

of domestic peace led Jewish parties to cooperate with Arab parties, something unheard of before the 1980s. By the late 1980s, even the Islamic parties, which initially rejected the very idea of Israel, participated in national elections.

Power-sharing systems, if successfully implemented, decrease group status concerns and increase incentives for groups to cooperate with each other. In Lebanon, communities cooperated for thirty years before the civil war and the decade after it, in large part because the system encouraged groups to work together, or at least to not actively oppose one another. In Israel, Arabs have played a growing role in Israeli society and politics, demonstrating to Jews that the community can be a reasonable partner in state politics.

Lebanon's troubles, however, demonstrate both the dangers of immutable "grand bargains" and how outsiders can disrupt fragile ethnic bargains. Security fears increased in Lebanon as outside powers meddled and as Lebanon became a war zone for the Israeli-Palestinian conflict. The frozen national accord also proved insufficient, as modernization and the emergence of new elites led to widespread dissatisfaction over how national resources were distributed among communities and within individual communities over who represented the people.

Power-sharing systems based on ethnicity also magnify the salience of communal identity, making it harder to create cross-cutting ties. As Jack Snyder and Robert Jervis note, power-sharing can reify contending groups, encouraging political mobilization along ethnic lines.[65] In Lebanon, the National Pact and Ta'if Accord suffered from this weakness, discouraging any sentiment of being "Lebanese" and elevating the salience of ethnic identity.

Democracy may be the best solution to the problem of ethnic tension, but it is also the most difficult to implement and sustain. Nevertheless, because democracy has proven successful in keeping the peace—and has a host of other benefits, ranging from human rights superiority to personal satisfaction to reduced government corruption, it must be considered first as a solution. But this preference should not blind us to democracy's fragility. At the very least, ethnic democracy requires peace at home. Moreover, we must remember that when no colonial or outside power will guarantee a transition, an electoral system and other democratic institutions may take decades to truly serve democratic purposes.

Given its problems, democracy must be implemented along with other solutions discussed in this book. As noted in other chapters, control and co-optation helped Israel build the trust necessary to give Israeli Arabs a true voice in decision-making. Manipulating identities also can make it easier for former enemies to participate peacefully. When combined with these other tools, democratic systems can help keep the peace in perpetuity.

7 The Promise and Perils of Partition

Should the United States and the world community always try to preserve nation-states torn by violence, or should they sometimes support the partition of these states?[1] Afghanistan, Angola, Bosnia, Burma, Burundi, Iraq, Liberia, Rwanda, Sudan, and Congo are only a few of the prominent examples of countries that face (or have faced) bitter communal violence that could easily erupt again or continue indefinitely. Does there come a time when these states should be declared failures and new states with better borders be put in their place? Critics of partition argue that such so-called solutions are at best temporary and at worst might set off an explosion of violence and strife in multiethnic states throughout the world.

The options of partition or preservation are present every time the United States and the world community decide between propping up weak governments in countries with a history of civil strife or working toward the peaceful dissolution of a state. This dilemma arises again and again. Yesterday, Iraqi Kurds struggled for independence only to meet with brutal repression; today, Muslims, Croats, and Serbs in Bosnia contest territory while the United States and the international community struggle to preserve a much-diminished state; tomorrow, perhaps Burundi will join the list of nations that the world must decide whether, by action or inaction, to support or let collapse.

The arguments for and against partition are both powerful.[2] Partition's proponents contend that the memory of conflict leaves communal groups highly sensitive to their security, making them likely to take up arms again.[3] Furthermore, regimes often mistreat losers in communal conflicts. This mistreatment, combined with the memory of violence, keeps communal groups mistrustful of one another and reduces communal cooperation. Democracy, and even basic political functions of a government, are difficult if not impossible. Thus, both repressive government and continued violence are common when the winners and losers of communal conflicts remain together in one state.

Yet partition is hardly an ideal answer. Successor states are almost never perfectly homogeneous. They, too, will face the problems of communal mistrust and a lack of cooperation: only the names of the oppressor and the oppressed will change. The international community should not necessarily reward groups that use violence. Recognizing a new state in one region might prompt other, currently peaceful peoples to take up arms and demand their own states. Finally, partition may only result in the transformation of a conflict from a civil war to an international one.[4]

The historical record on partition is mixed.[5] Norway, Singapore, and Slovakia all obtained their independence without violence, and parts of the Austro-Hungarian and Ottoman empires were partitioned after World War I with relatively little bloodshed. Azerbaijan, Ethiopia, Georgia, Korea, Poland, Ireland, India, Moldova, Palestine, and Cyprus, in contrast, all suffered tremendous violence when, or after, the partition was enacted.

The mixed historic record suggests that neither partition nor preservation is a panacea for communal conflict. Moreover, judging partition by this record is difficult. The true question is not whether partition prevented all bloodshed, but whether it reduced bloodshed compared with other feasible alternatives. Even countries that suffered from violence during partition might have suffered far more had the partition not occurred at all.[6] Partition, however, is not on today's international agenda. When policymakers consider whether or not to intervene, the question is always whether to prop up a government, not whether to partition the state. Partition, however, is often the best of several bad options. The United States and the international community should support partition if a civil war cannot be resolved, or if it can be resolved only through unending brutal repression.

This chapter weighs the general question of when partition is a better choice than preservation by exploring the 1948 attempt to partition Palestine into two states, one Jewish and one Arab. It also assesses the de facto partition of northern Iraq since the end of the 1991 Gulf War. From the Israeli and Iraqi experiences, it notes the relative advantages and disadvantages of partition and suggests ways to implement it more effectively.

The Israeli Experience

On the surface, the Israeli experience serves as a bitter indictment of partition.[7] Both directly and indirectly, partition led to considerable violence. There have been five Palestinian Arab-Israeli Jewish conflicts. The first two—the Arab revolt of 1936–39 and the 1947 civil war—occurred before partition was established but were spurred by the possibility of partition. The third, the Israeli invasion of Lebanon, involved Palestinians living outside Israel and many of whom ended up in Lebanon and degenerated into a long guerrilla war between Israel and the Lebanese Hezbollah. The fourth and fifth conflicts are the two *intifadas*. The first began in December 1987, and the second, the so-called "Al Aqsa" *intifada,* began in September 2000. The two *intifadas* were far more limited conflict in terms of lives but provoked major divisions in Israeli society.[8] To this day, terrorism and violence plague Israel and the Palestinian-inhabited territories. In addition to these direct conflicts, partition contributed to wars between Israel and its neighbors in 1948, 1956, 1967, 1973, and 1982. Not surprisingly, the Israeli experience is often cited as proof that partition leads to even greater bloodshed.

Despite this bitter history, it remains difficult to declare the Israeli experience a failure. Although it is impossible to answer with certainty the question of "how would history have changed had there been no partition?" a civil war almost certainly would have occurred in the Palestine Mandate area, leading either to the massacre and expulsion of the Jewish population or to a de facto partition similar to the one that occurred in 1948 (with all the subsequent strife as well). In addition, many of the subsequent Arab-Israeli wars focused not on the particulars of partition but rather on the very existence of Israel itself. Sorting out conflicting claims is difficult, and this chapter makes no pretense of providing ultimate answers. Nevertheless, the Israeli experience suggests that while many of the criticisms of partition are accurate, the alternatives are often few and equally troubled.

Critics of the partition of Palestine ignore the bloody and seemingly unstoppable fighting that preceded it. Violence broke out several times between 1920 and 1935 before it exploded into the Arab revolt of 1936–39. The violence had a simple cause: the presence of two groups with hegemonic ambitions that demanded dominance over their own states. When the British Mandate began after World War I, Arabs comprised 92 percent of the population and owned 98 percent of the land. Jewish immigration and land purchases threatened this dominance. Any British attempts at balance were doomed: Jews protested that any benefits they received were not enough, while Arabs criticized any losses of Arab status. Even the most trivial of issues, such as the language on local stamps, led to violent disagreements. For Arabs, the idea of partition meant abandoning their goal of hegemony over Palestine, which they felt was their right given their greater numbers and historical presence. For Jews, partition was a first step toward building the homeland they sought—a homeland that had no room for Arabs.

Violence began almost immediately after the creation of the Mandate. In April 1920, an Arab religious procession in Jerusalem turned violent, resulting in the death of 5 Jews and the wounding of 211 more. In putting down the riots, the British killed 4 Arabs and wounded 32 others. In May 1921, a doctrinal quarrel among demonstrating leftist Jewish groups led to wild rumors among the Arabs that Jews were organizing to attack. In response to these fears, Arabs attacked Jews in Jaffa and in various parts of the Ramleh area, killing 47 and wounding 146. Once again, suppression of the riots led to more deaths: this time, 48 Arabs died and 73 were wounded. The level of violence grew once again. In 1929, after a dispute over communal rights at the Western (Wailing) Wall, excited Arab mobs stormed into Hebron and killed over 60 Jews there. Rioting by Arabs elsewhere in the colony killed dozens more. When the British restored peace, over 133 Jews had been killed and 339 wounded; 116 Arabs were killed and 232 wounded.

Not surprisingly, even this limited violence polarized the already divided communities, straining any hope for a peaceful settlement. Both communal groups tried to organize reciprocal boycotts, thus reducing commercial ties. The violence also led individuals to move to more homogeneous areas to protect themselves. Perhaps most important, the violence discredited moderates on all sides. New Arab movements, both Muslim and secular, appeared and began criticizing traditional elites for working with British authorities. Radicals intimidated conciliatory figures and occasionally even murdered them.

The scope and scale of the Arab revolt of 1936–39 went far beyond the sporadic violence of previous years. Between 3,000 to 5,000 Arabs died in the revolt, and up to 15,000 were wounded; hundreds of Jews also died. The revolt also led to tremendous internecine violence among Arabs. At least a quarter of the Arab casualties were inflicted by other Arabs, and many Arabs fled their homes in fear of the violence and radicalism.

The revolt's immediate causes were hardly major provocations: a series of demonstrations and counterdemonstrations over the death of two Jews, who were probably killed by Arab bandits. After Arab merchants declared a general strike, various local groups sprang up and pushed Arab leaders, many of whom opposed a major conflict, to form an executive committee—the Arab Higher Committee—and declare a general revolt. Low-level violence, such as sniping and the derailing of trains, became rampant and trade in the Arab sector came to a halt. In response to the crisis, the British appointed a Royal Commission to investigate solutions to the dispute. Surprisingly, the commission recommended partition—and thus formal recognition of a permanent Jewish home in Palestine. This decision led to immediate violence by outraged Arabs. The British responded by arresting Arab leaders, but this only caused the revolt to spread to the countryside, where it became a mass of separate struggles.

This revolt isolated moderates on all sides and fractured the Arab side. Both communities developed autarchic economies, reducing economic bonds. Arab rebels killed or intimidated landowners who sold land to Jews or officials not considered sufficiently nationalistic. Arab leaders, attempting to motivate religious peasants to join the revolt, began to portray it as a religious dispute as well as a national one. This portrayal, however, alienated many Christian Arabs and led to a decline in Arab unity.

The violence led the Jews to expand their own militias. By 1936, the *Haganah*, the largest paramilitary organization, had ten thousand men with forty thousand more available for rapid mobilization. In 1937, the more extreme Irgun Zvai Leumi was founded in part to engage in a counter-terror campaign against Arabs, British, and leftist Jewish figures. As the Arab revolt spread, the British worked with the *Haganah* to defend Zionist settlements and government installations. The British trained Jews as supplemental police, greatly increasing the number of trained recruits for Zionist militias.

As long as the British remained in Palestine, communal tension could be contained. The British, after all, could enforce order. Even more important, their presence was not anathema to the Arab community, which could endure continued British rule, but not domination by their rivals. When the British decided to withdraw, however, the question of who would rule arose. To this, unfortunately, there was no answer. Both the Arabs and Jews were hegemonic: both sought a state where their institutions, ways of living, and people were dominant. In addition, both communities feared the other and worried about their status in post-colonial Palestine. Firebrands on both sides preached the inevitability of conflict, leading both communities to mobilize for war. In short, all the causes of conflict (see Chapter 2) prevailed, making any peaceful solution difficult if not impossible.

Not surprisingly, the British withdrawal led to immediate conflict. The 1948 War of Independence resulted in roughly six thousand Jewish and ten thousand Arab deaths as well as the displacement of over one million people. The violence spread as the British prepared to depart the country. All sides sought to seize strategic points that Britain abandoned while avoiding a direct conflict with British troops. After the November 1947 announcement of the United Nations partition plan, the mufti of Jerusalem proclaimed a Holy War to drive the Jews out of Palestine. Many Arabs also organized on a local level, working with their clan members and village leaders to fight their Jewish neighbors. This action in turn fostered a brutal war of terrorism and irregular combat, with car bombs and other forms of terror leading to hundreds of deaths. On the Arab side, thousands of poorly armed, untrained peasants fought sporadically, but fiercely, against Jewish settlers and militias.

The Arab side also had organized fighters under arms. Under the leadership of Fawz el-Kaukji, who had led irregular troops during the Arab revolt, neighboring Arab states formed the Arab Army of Liberation (ALA), headquartered in Damascus and composed of both Palestinian Arabs and Arab volunteers from neighboring states. The mufti of Jerusalem also formed the Arab Army of Salvation (AAS), which received relatively little outside support and was a rival of the ALA. At its peak, the ALA had 7,700 men under arms and the AAS had two contingents of less than 1,000 each.[9]

As the UN passed partition resolutions, fighting broke out throughout the area of the British-ruled Mandate. In January 1948, both ALA and AAS forces began mounting larger and more massive operations against Jewish settlements. Irregular local Arab forces also conducted sporadic operations from November 1947 to March 1948. Thousands of Arabs and Jews died in this combination of terrorist attacks and civil war. The situation then shifted to include an outside invasion as well, when Arab armies declared war in May 1948. Egypt, Syria, Jordan, Lebanon, and Iraq all sent troops to fight the Zionists (and to prevent their rivals from gaining the upper hand in the region).

The Zionists emerged victorious from the wars, but their victory was not complete. The restoration of Palestine became a rallying cry in much of the Arab world for decades, creating an atmosphere of hostility that contributed to several subsequent wars. The 1948 war also created a Palestinian diaspora which, although weak militarily and politically, nevertheless remained a constant source of instability in the region.

After the 1949 armistice, cross-border violence continued—much of it between former Arab inhabitants of what was now Israel and the new Israeli state. Roughly half of the Arabs who lived in Palestine had fled during the war, and the vast majority of them settled in neighboring Arab states, particularly Jordan. Most of the Palestinian refugees had little in the way of food, land, or a way of making a living in their new home. As the war died down, some refugees crossed the new border and returned to their old lands out of desperation, while others hoped to reclaim their property after a cease-fire and a settlement. Other refugees returned simply to visit relatives who had remained in Israel. These returnees were not all peaceful. Some stole, vandalized property, or attacked settlers. At times, organized terrorists crossed the borders as well.

Although a small part of the overall number of those crossing the border, these attacks caused tremendous concern in Israel and led to many deaths. Between 1949 and 1956, the infiltrators killed between 200 and 300 Israelis, and dozens of Israeli soldiers died in clashes with Arab soldiers during retaliatory strikes. Infiltrators also destroyed or stole hundreds of thousands of shekels' worth of property. Benny Morris estimates that Israeli security forces—and mines and booby-traps—killed between 2,700 and 5,000 infiltrators, both violent and peaceful, during this period.[10] The new state was forced to spend even more beefing up its army and border forces and otherwise preparing for violence.[11]

Neighboring states, radical religious groups, and organized Palestinian groups in exile often promoted raids to kill settlers and to damage Jewish property. The Muslim Brotherhood, a militant Islamic organization, as well as the former mufti of Jerusalem both sponsored raids into Israel. In the immediate aftermath of the 1948 war, neighboring states opposed these raids, fearing Israeli reprisals. Starting in 1954, however, neighboring states, particularly Egypt, also organized Palestinian infiltrators, primarily for espionage but occasionally for limited sabotage.

Israel relied on third parties, particularly Arab military commanders, to stop the cross-border infiltration. As Moshe Dayan declared:

> We cannot guard every water pipeline from explosion and every tree from uprooting. We cannot prevent every murder of a worker in an orchard or a family in their beds. But it is in our power to set a high price on our blood, a price too high for the Arab community, the Arab army, or the Arab government to think it worth paying. We can see to it that the Arab villages oppose the raiding bands that pass through them, rather than give them assistance. It is in our power to see that Arab military commanders prefer a strict performance of their obligation to police the frontiers rather than suffer defeat in clashes with our units.[12]

Although the Israeli reprisals initially led neighboring Arab states to hinder, or at least not support, cross-border attacks in the years after independence, over time the Israeli raids raised regional tension and eventually contributed to the outbreak of war between Israel and its neighbors in 1956. Repeated Israeli retaliation, which was often quite bloody, against Egypt in response to Palestinian cross-border infiltration led to a spiral of violence. The raids and responses hardened both sides, discrediting moderates and supporters of peace in general. Israeli leaders often felt forced to retaliate to satisfy the Israeli public, which demanded action in response to the killing of Jews. Israeli reprisals, however, discredited neighboring Arab militaries, leading them to seek action against Israel to restore their honor. Starting in 1954, Egypt began to sponsor Palestinian guerrilla attacks on Israel and to use Egyptian military personnel to support this—a dramatic shift from Cairo's previously restrained attitude toward Palestinian infiltrators.

Egypt also worked with Palestinians in Syria and Lebanon to coordinate Palestinian attacks and tried to recruit in Jordan as well. This led to a cycle of raid and response, with both sides building up their militaries and preparing for war. To a lesser extent, a similar cycle strengthened extremists in Syria as well. Most tragically, Jordan, which for many years had tried to control cross-border infiltration, became radicalized by the violence and by 1956 eventually came to actively back Palestinian guerrillas.[13]

The harsh reprisals and active Arab support for cross-border attacks contributed to the 1956 Arab-Israeli war.

The 1956 war, in a sense, put an end to neighboring states' sponsorship of attacks and independent Palestinian operations for many years. After the war, and the consequent rise of Arab nationalism, Palestinian Arabs looked first and foremost to the Arab states to liberate them. This faith in the Arab states, however, ended after the 1967 debacle, when Israel overwhelmingly defeated the armies of neighboring Arab states.

Shortly after the 1967 war, Palestinian cross-border strikes—and anti-Israel terrorism in general—again became a grave problem for Israel. Jordan once more became a key base of Palestinian operations. To stop the attacks, Israel again relied on a combination of direct strikes on Palestinian targets and applying pressure to the Jordanian government. As in the 1950s, this back and forth created the specter of instability in Jordan. If the Palestinians were allowed to expand recruitment in Jordan and defend themselves more vigorously, they might become stronger than the Jordanian government itself.[14] The result was "Black September" (named after the month King Hussein cracked down on radical Palestinian activity in the Kingdom in 1970), leading to the expulsion of the Palestinian movement to Lebanon.[15]

After Black September, the venue for the struggle shifted to Lebanon. As noted in Chapter 6, continued Israeli raids and retaliation contributed to the collapse of the Lebanese state into civil war. Israel repeatedly struck Palestinian targets in Lebanon in the 1960s and 1970s. In Lebanon, Israel followed the path it took in Jordan and elsewhere: make the state responsible for activities carried out in its territory. This policy failed in Lebanon because, in contrast to Jordan, the state was not strong enough to impose its will on the guerrillas. As a result, in 1982 Israel took direct action and invaded Lebanon in an attempt to end Palestinian cross-border attacks once and for all. This invasion greatly reduced Palestinian attacks on Israel, although it unleashed a new menace: Lebanese Shi'a Muslim radicals, who were zealous in their efforts to expel Israel.

The Israel-Palestinian conflict known as the *intifada,* began on December 9, 1987, and ended in 1992. The dispute had myriad causes. Meron Benvenisti notes that the Palestinians' very existence as a community was threatened: the Israeli government had expropriated more than half the land on the West Bank, taken water, settled Jews in traditional Palestinian areas, closed universities, deported leaders, and generally subordinated the economy and culture of the region to the needs of the Jewish state. On a personal level, the Palestinians felt humiliated by their relationship to their Jewish neighbors. The status of both leaders and the community as a whole was gravely threatened.[16] The second, "Al Aqsa" *intifada*, began on September 28, 2000. Again, it had myriad causes that went beyond the immediate trigger for the revolt. The scope and scale of the unrest surprised most observers, particularly as it came on the heels of peace negotiations that appeared close to success. This *intifada* involved the security forces of the nascent Palestinian state as well as large numbers of Palestinian youths. Much of the violence focused on Israeli settlements outside the 1967 boundaries of the state.

Despite the tension and the hatred, both *intifadas* resulted in relatively few deaths. Hundreds died and thousands were wounded in the demonstrations—large numbers, but limited ones compared with Israel's past. Israeli military authorities carefully controlled the use of firepower, a situation far different from the desperate days of the 1948 civil war.[17]

The irony of the two *intifadas*, of course, is that many Palestinians sought the restoration of the original partition. Although in their hearts many demonstrators might have preferred an absolute end to the Jewish state, in their minds they recognized that this was not practical and, in the end, simply sought the restoration of their own state.

Conclusions

The partition of the Palestine Mandate area left a bitter legacy that was in part responsible for several interstate wars and continuing Palestinian-Israeli tension. Balanced against this heavy price, however, are several important observations. Most important, policymakers in 1948 had no realistic alternative to partition. Any other solution that did not involve continued (and costly) British rule was likely to fail. In addition, the partition helped pave the way for a strong and viable democracy in Israel, a development difficult to imagine if the Mandate had tried to keep the land unified. The death tolls from the war, terrorism, and counter-insurgency operations, while high, probably were less than would have occurred if there had been no partition and a village by village civil war had broken out.

Partition enabled Jews to mitigate many potential causes of ethnic conflict. Once Israeli Jews gained control of their own state, their fears about their Arab neighbors (within Israel), their concerns about status, and the desire for hegemony all were satisfied. Jews and Arabs were no longer forced to live side by side, reducing intermingling and eliminating some security concerns. The relatively small number of remaining Arabs, which ranged from 12 to 18 percent of the total population, posed little threat to Jewish control.[18]

In Israel itself partition led to an effective end of civil violence and, eventually, to greater communal power-sharing. Although the Israeli Arabs often bitterly resented Jewish rule, they remained peaceful. After years of peace, the Israeli Arabs began to play a greater role in decision-making in Israel, and in recent years they have exercised considerable influence (see Chapter 6).

Needless to say, the status and hegemonic desires of Palestinian Arabs and their leaders were not satisfied: stateless, they engaged in cross-border attacks, subversion, and terrorism to regain their territory. In addition, much of the community became radicalized, and elites competed with one another to demonstrate their resistance to any compromise with Israel. Thus, while partition satisfied many Jews, it left the overwhelming majority of Palestinian Arabs dissatisfied and strengthened more radical leaders. Many of the Palestinian problems, however, stemmed from their lack of a state, which created grave status problems for the Palestinians as a community and threatened to erase their separate identity.

The De Facto Partition of Northern Iraq, 1991–1999

At the end of the Persian Gulf War in February 1991, northern Iraq, home of most of the country's Kurdish population, exploded into civil war. Kurdish guerrillas and other fighters, joined spontaneously by many Kurdish villagers and tribal members, fought to topple Saddam's regime and establish control over Kurdish-populated regions of Iraq. Beginning on March 4, towns and cities in northern Iraq fell into the hands of Kurdish fighters. The Kurds' success was short-lived. On March 22, the regime began its counter-offensive, and tens of thousands of Kurds, rebels and civilians alike, died. Over one million fled to Iran and Turkey, while thousands more were stranded in the mountains of northern Iraq.[19]

In response to this crisis, the United States and several allies created a safe haven of three provinces in northern Iraq, which contain 13 percent of Iraq's total population. Under UN Security Council Resolution 688, U.S., French, and British forces secured refugee camps and barred Iraqi forces from consolidating their control over parts of the north. By May

1991, many Iraqi Kurds had returned home. To deter Iraq from reconsolidating its control, the United States established a no-fly zone and encouraged Kurdish groups to work together against Baghdad. Washington avoided, however, an explicit commitment to the Kurds' security.

U.S. and international support for the Kurdish enclave effectively partitioned Iraq. The Kurds exercised de facto sovereignty. Although the Kurds possessed neither an internationally recognized state nor government, Baghdad did not control their activities. Partition, however, was far from complete. Turkey, Syria, and Iran opposed anything that might suggest that a recognized Kurdish state was about to emerge.[20] As a result of these fears, as well as their own preference for upholding existing borders, the United States and other major powers did not push to separate the Kurdish north formally from the Iraqi state. Thus, although the Kurdish experience of the 1990s sheds light on the benefits, and costs, of partition in general, its unique status calls for carefully assessing any lessons learned for their broader applicability.

The Kurds' uncertain political status hindered efforts to develop political and economic institutions in the enclave. The UN could not directly assist Kurdish factions who act as the local government in developing the institutions of a state, as this would amount to a recognition of the Kurdish state. Iraq's neighbors in general opposed steps that would create strong and unified Kurdish military forces.[21] Although part of the UN-administered money from Iraqi oil sales went directly to the Kurdish parts of northern Iraq rather than working through Baghdad, in general the area's economy did not develop over the decade. Black market trade with Iraq and oil smuggling provided much of the Kurds' money.

The Benefits of the Safe Haven

Despite the many limits to the safe haven's development as a state, the enclave produced numerous benefits for Iraqi Kurds. Most obviously, ethnic violence, regime repression, and ethnic cleansing have abated. Despite Baghdad's forays into the north, the level of suffering is far less than at any time since the Ba'ath came to power. Kurds for the most part live in peace, and the tribal fighting and power struggles do not approach the scale of killing that existed before the safe haven was created.

Separation has, for now, reduced the security concerns that Kurds perceived toward their Arab neighbors to the south. Although the U.S. protection of the no-fly zone is a dubious guarantee at best, it has deterred

Iraqi forces. As a result, Kurds are far more confident of their individual security than in the past.

The Kurdish areas also enjoy a modicum of democracy, particularly when compared with the rest of Iraq. In May 1992, leaders of eight leading Kurdish political factions and tribal groups competed in elections that, while hardly paragons of democracy, were generally regarded as free and fair.[22] Iraqi Assyrians living in the enclave received five seats in the 105-member parliament.[23] Leaders of Kurdish factions, while not always democratically elected within their subcommunities, generally enjoyed support from their followers. Under U.S. pressure, these leaders have cooperated (if fitfully) with one another. The result is a division of power among these leaders, with a high degree of autonomy enjoyed by various local communities.

Kurdish leaders and the community more broadly enjoyed tremendously enhanced status. Kurds have their own schools, newspapers, television and radio stations, and other forms of cultural expression. Kurdish dress is allowed, and Kurdish culture is flourishing. Iraqi Kurds also have their own currency. As a result, Kurdish identity and culture are far more vibrant than in the past.[24]

Many of the possible drawbacks of partition have not come to pass. Kurds treat minorities in the Kurdish areas such as the Assyrians and the Turcomen far better than did the Ba'ath regime. In general, these communities are secure and enjoy a high degree of autonomy.[25] Nor has a demonstration effect occurred, triggering unrest elsewhere. The Kurdish Workers' Party's struggle against the Turkish government declined at the end of the 1990s, while Iran's Kurds show no signs that they are ready to renew their struggle against the clerical regime.

The Pitfalls of the Safe Haven

Although the safe haven offers many advantages to Iraq's Kurds, it enrages many of Iraq's Sunni Arabs, particularly the hard-line nationalists who support Saddam Hussein. Statements like that of Iraqi minister Abdul Razak Hashemi, who declared that "The north part of Iraq is Iraq and is going to be part of Iraq," typify Iraqi government rhetoric.[26] Ensuring control over territory is a priority for any government, and in Iraq, governments and leaders have risen and fallen in response to past Kurdish crises. Saddam's credibility as a leader is thus in jeopardy as long as the north retains its autonomy.[27]

Baghdad has engaged in occasional military incursions against the enclave, reinforcing the argument that partition contributes to international war. In August and September 1991, Iraq built up troops in the north and made forays against the Kurds that resulted in occasional firefights. Fighting continued throughout the fall, and in winter Baghdad applied economic pressure, denying fuel and food to much of the region.[28] In 1996, Iraqi troops swept into northern Iraq, occupying the Kurdish city of Irbil. Iraqi security forces arrested hundreds of opposition members, and thousands more fled to the United States. In essence, the Kurdish-Arab conflict became internationalized, with conflict occurring over the border of the enclave rather than within the state itself.

The safe haven has required substantial U.S. military support, both to establish and to sustain. The initial U.S.-led effort, Operation Provide Comfort, involved more than twenty thousand U.S. and allied troops. In the following years, the United States and its allies have flown thousands of sorties in support of Operation Northern Watch, the northern no-fly zone, that has come to symbolize the U.S. commitment to the Kurds.[29]

The Kurds also have not come together as a people. The main Kurdish factions are divided from each other by family, region, and ideology, hindering the emergence of a powerful leadership or a strong, unifying identity that embraces more than a rejection of Arab, Persian, or Turkish nationalism.[30] Although the May 1992 elections created a legitimate government, the leaders of the factions did not trust each other and refused to work together to create common "Kurdish" institutions.[31] Despite the imminent and vivid threat from Iraq, Kurdish factions fought regularly with each other from 1993 to 1997. Disputes over land, revenues from smuggling, and personal rivalries led to the deaths of several thousand Kurds and the further division of the region into spheres of influence controlled by the parties and local warlords.[32] Baghdad's 1996 incursion was encouraged by the Kurdish Democratic Party (KDP), which sought to gain an advantage over its rival the Patriotic Union of Kurdistan (PUK). In part due to U.S. mediation, the Kurdish parties have maintained an uneasy truce since late 1997, but a broader political unity remains elusive.[33]

Nor are the boundaries of the de facto state clear. Baghdad, of course, rejects the very existence of the safe haven. The Kurds, for their part, would almost certainly seek to expand the borders of the safe area to include areas where there are large Kurdish populations. Such an expansion would place the Kurds in opposition to almost any conceivable Iraqi government, as several Kurdish-populated areas such as Kirkuk are rich in oil resources.

The Path Not Taken: Kurdish Reintegration into Iraq

Although the Kurdish enclave is hardly a sterling success for partition, any alternatives would probably be far worse for Iraq's Kurds. Had the international community not established a safe haven in 1991, the results would almost certainly have been tragic. If the 1988 and 1989 Operation Anfal operation (where Iraq brutally secured its power over the Kurds after the end of the Iran-Iraq war) is a precedent, tens of thousands of Kurdish fighters, community leaders, and noncombatants might have been killed if the safe haven had not been created. Forced deportations and relocations, and the exemplary punishment of hostile villages and towns, also would have occurred.

The Kurds also would have been under assault economically, politically, and culturally. Iraqi Kurds now enjoy a fair share of Iraq's oil wealth due to UN supervision—a share that was far smaller before the Gulf War.[34] The Arabicization policies of the late 1980s, which tried to destroy the Kurds' distinct language, dress, and sense of identity, would have continued. Similarly, the Kurds would be under the brutal rule of the Ba'ath Party and would have enjoyed no freedoms whatsoever.

The fate of Iraqi Shi'a is instructive. Although the United States and its allies also have a "no-fly zone" in southern Iraq, where many Shi'a live, the Shi'a do not enjoy even a pretense of autonomy from Baghdad. Saddam's regime has brutally put down the Shi'a after their 1991 revolt, arresting and killing Shi'a leaders and having the Shi'a bear the brunt of Iraq's economic woes.[35] The Shi'a have also faced brutal discrimination and the attempted suppression of their distinct identity.

Conclusions

The Kurdish experience in Iraq illustrates several important points about partition. First, it is feasible for outside powers to create, and enforce, the borders of a partitioned state. Although this requires considerable force, partition is an option that can realistically be considered in the aftermath of a brutal ethnic conflict. Second, outside powers have a tremendous impact on the nature of the new state. The Kurdish entity's weak political, military, and economic institutions are due in part to the wishes and pressure of its neighbors. Partitioned peoples with kin across many borders can expect similar pressures. Finally, although partition is hardly an ideal alternative, it is often the best of several bad options. Reincorporating the Kurds into Saddam's Iraq would have been a humanitarian nightmare that would have led to thousands of death and continued oppression.

The Difficult Transition

The Israeli and Kurdish experiences indicate that feasibility is the first question that must be considered when weighing whether to partition a country. Partitions, however, are difficult to enact. Civil violence and the failure of other solutions are often necessary to create the will, both domestically and internationally, to partition a state. Once the decision to divide a state is made, force is often necessary to ensure that those states and local factions that oppose partition or its particular terms do not interfere.

In both Palestine and Iraq, war was part and parcel of the partition. In Palestine, the British and the fledgling UN had a partition plan to implement, but it was the 1948 war that led to the population transfers, more intelligible borders, and other changes that dramatically affected the viability of the new Israeli state. Moreover, the momentum for the new state would never have occurred without the 1936–39 Arab revolt and the post–World War II Israeli attacks on Britain.[36] In Iraq, a military defeat was necessary in order for Baghdad to relinquish its hold, even temporarily, on the north.

One of the most enduring lessons of the Palestine and Iraqi experiences is that if a partition is not managed carefully, it can create tremendous problems. The partition of Palestine proved bloody in part because no power was present to ensure the security of individuals during population transfers.[37] When security forces are available to guard the transfer and succor refugees, much of the humanitarian nightmare can be averted. U.S. and coalition forces helped protect Kurdish refugees after the war, preventing Iraqi government attacks and even simple banditry. Similarly, during the partition in India, the British often had far too few men and frequently sent refugees directly through the combat zone: both those mistakes would have been avoided had the British conducted the transfer properly.[38] (For further discussion on ways for outside powers to better manage a population transfer, see Chapter 8.)

The chance of war between successor states and neighbors in general also makes partition difficult. Borders of the new state are likely to be in dispute. Moreover, whichever group is stronger at the time of the partition has a tremendous incentive to strike and seize what territory it can, to ensure that its rivals do not become more powerful in future years. Neighboring states also may try to increase their influence by grabbing territory or placing their proxies in power. As with population transfers, however, this uncertainty can be reduced (but not eliminated) by effective outside management. If outside powers are willing to guarantee borders or otherwise coerce the successor states into accepting them, interstate conflict need not follow partition.

Arguments for and against Partition

Assuming partition is feasible, should it be done? The rocky experiences of Israel and northern Iraq reveal that although partition is problematic, it still should be considered for intractable conflicts. Clearly, the international decision to partition Israel contributed to civil violence before and during Israel's founding, to cross-border terrorism and reprisals in subsequent years, and to several wars between Israel and its neighbors. In Iraq, the de facto partition has resulted in an uneasy peace, punctuated by occasional incursions.

The violence and misery that came with Palestine's partition and the creation of the enclave in Iraq suggest many cautions for those who seek to use partition as a means of preventing communal conflict from recurring. Perhaps most important, partition sowed the seeds of international war. Because of the problem of Palestinian infiltration—and the broader question about the fate of the Palestinians—Israel regularly engaged in cross-border conflict with its neighbors. This problem of raid and response directly contributed to the 1956 war and to the Israeli invasion of Lebanon in 1982. The Palestinian issue became a *cause celebre* in the Arab world, heightening tension in general. Iraq has made no move to abandon its claims to its northern area, and any formal declaration of statehood would almost certainly be contested, both by words and by force.

In addition to outright war, the boundaries of the new territories were not clear—a problem when all the parties in question both aspired to more than just their partitioned rump state. After the 1948 victory, many Israeli leaders sought to expand the state's territory, for both ideological and strategic reasons.[39] Even today, militant religious Zionists dream of annexing all of historic Judea and Samaria, perceiving this as the true boundary of a Jewish state. Palestinian and other Arab leaders proved even more intransigent. Many Palestinian leaders reject Israel's existence, and even relative moderates seek far more territory for their new state than Israel is willing to provide. Not surprisingly, Israeli settlements outside its 1967 borders are particularly contentious. In Iraq, Kurds may seek to increase the territory beyond the enclave, to include other Kurdish areas, places where populations are more mixed, and oil-rich regions. Iraq's case is particularly instructive as the Kurdish area is relatively homogeneous. Thus, the fact that borders remain in dispute suggests this will be a problem affecting almost all the partitioned state. Uncertainty about borders is likely to provide an unending source of complaints affecting any compromise solution.

The criticism that partition does not eliminate concerns about minority rights but instead simply creates a new minority in the new states whose rights are not respected in turn is borne out by the Israeli and Kurdish experiences—but only in part. Donald Horowitz, for example, has argued that "the only thing secession and partition are unlikely to produce is ethnically homogenous or harmonious states."[40] The new Israeli state followed this pattern, discriminating systematically against its Arab citizens. Although by the standards of other civil wars, the treatment of Israeli Arabs—Arabs who remained in Israel after 1948 and became Israeli citizens—was benign, the Israeli Arabs in effect became second-class citizens. For them, status problems in particular remained intense, leading to lasting hostility. (A more comprehensive description of the Israeli Arabs' treatment after 1948 can be found in Chapters 3 and 6.) In Iraq, the Kurds are far less hostile to minorities than was the Ba'ath government, but this standard is low and Kurdish attitudes might shift if the enclave did not depend on international goodwill for its continued existence. Both Israel and the Kurdish "governments," however, were relatively gentle with the new minorities in their territories.

In general, democracy is at least possible and perhaps even more likely in partitioned areas. Israel's democracy is robust for Jews and still real, if imperfect, for Israeli Arabs today. Kurds in Iraq enjoy more power-sharing and participation than ever before in their history, although democratic institutions are weak. In general, large empirical studies suggest partitioned states appear to fare better regarding democratization after a successful partition.[41]

Another potentially damaging criticism of partition is that it rewards aggression and thus encourages violence by ethnic groups elsewhere.[42] Many pundits opposed partition in the former Yugoslavia, for example, on the grounds that it rewarded Serbs for their killing. Such a criticism is valid but overstated. The demonstration effect of partition is not clear. India, Czechoslovakia, Norway, and Palestine are among the twentieth century's partitions, and these precedents are hardly on the lips of every secessionist demagogue. Iraqi Kurds' relative freedom has not inspired a revolt among Kurds in Iran or Turkey, let alone minorities elsewhere in the world. Moreover, refusing to recognize partition does not necessarily discourage aggressors: the international community began considering partition in Bosnia because the Serbs committed atrocities, not before these crimes occurred. Finally, although partition would indeed reward a minority group using violence, the current bias toward preservation implicitly rewards brutal states that use repression to prevent any unrest. Thus, both alternatives can be criticized for rewarding violence.

The best argument for partition, however, is that it often has no feasible alternative. This is particularly true once the central government can no longer keep order, as happens when a colonial power withdraws or a government collapses for other reasons, and when a range of ethnic conflict causes are present. In such circumstances, many of the options discussed in previous chapters—control, co-optation, and identity manipulation—are not available to governments. Although imposing a democratic government, where communities share power, is a preferred solution, this is often difficult to implement (see Chapter 6).

So too with the war-causing impact of partition. While real, many of the alternatives to partition would have probably led to war as well. A plausible argument can be made that a civil war would have broken out in the Palestine Mandate area in any event, regardless of the partition. War is very common when colonial powers withdraw: regional animosities, long-suppressed, spring up with a vengeance while neighboring states try to fill the power vacuum.[43] The British had spent years trying to work out a compromise solution, suggesting various forms of autonomy and power-sharing. Both sides rejected compromise solutions and sought ultimate control of the state.

A clash with outside powers also was likely. In 1948, the Palestinians were weak and divided among themselves. King Abdullah of Jordan sought to expand his kingdom, and planned to fill the power vacuum left by the British withdrawal. Similarly, neighboring Arab states sought to ensure their own influence—and to limit King Abdullah of Jordan's.[44] With such a scenario, it is highly likely that interstate war of some form would have occurred. Indeed, given the hostility of the neighboring Arab states to the very idea of a Jewish presence in the region, it is hard to blame the many wars in the area on partition alone.[45]

In Iraq, partition was clearly avoidable, but only at the cost of sanctioning murder and human rights violations on a massive scale. The Kurds' past brutalization at the hands of the Ba'ath and the systematic slaughter of many Iraqi Shi'a point to the heavy costs associated with allowing Baghdad to reassert its control over Kurdish areas.

Partition, in addition to being unavoidable at times, offers many potential advantages to those who would foster ethnic peace. Most important, by giving a group a state of its own, partition can eliminate many of the problems that occur when groups must live side by side. Partition can fulfill status aspirations, satisfy hegemonic aspirations, relax security concerns, and provide a venue to power for ambitious elites. Israeli Jews are, for the most part, satisfied with their position and do not agitate for violence. Kurds are far, far better off than they were under Sunni Arab dominance. The problems that partition caused in these countries should not blind us to its benefits.

Given the problems of partition, many critics endorse federalist solutions as an alternative.[46] In theory, federalism offers several of the benefits of partition without many of the problems. Ideally, federalism can satisfy a communal group's aspirations, placate group leaders who seek positions of influence, and create new, cross-cutting cleavages that will foster interethnic cooperation.[47] By granting each group a region of its own, the theory goes, they will have less incentive to organize to use violence.

Federalism, however, can increase a group's capacity, and at times its propensity, for conflict. Federalism backfires when the security dilemma is active, outside powers regularly meddle, and rival nationalisms exist—the very problems that plagued Palestine before independence. All these problems lead ethnic groups to use resources gained from federalism to mobilize their populations for conflict rather than see these resources as a sign of their inclusion. Federalism also makes mobilization easier. By giving groups control over institutions, they also gain control over taxation, administration, and manpower, all of which are essential for mobilizing for conflict. The Lebanese government discovered this to its chagrin (see

Chapter 6), when it found itself unable to impose its will over Lebanon's well-organized, highly autonomous communities.

Conclusion

State borders should not be seen as permanently fixed if their continuation will do nothing but foster more hatred, oppression, and violence. Yet the other extreme, abandoning current borders at the slightest hint of conflict, is just as ill-advised. When weighing the decision of whether to support partition or preservation, policymakers should look at a number of factors. Is there a realistic hope for peace in the country in question? If the government is strong, and if it is able and willing to employ other strategies suggested in this volume, then preservation is probably the best option. However, if the government is too weak to impose its will and the communities are hegemonic, then peace is highly unlikely and partition becomes more sensible. Another important question is whether groups can manage by themselves. If they depend militarily or economically on others, leaving them on their own is a recipe for disaster. Finally, what are the attitudes of a state's neighbors toward communal conflict? If they fear a strong state, then they are likely to support the renewal of fighting. If they are likely to champion one side, then partition may lead to a series of international conflicts.

Although this chapter argues that partition should only be considered in rare circumstances, it remains a plausible option for keeping the peace. However, there remains a tremendous bias for the continuation of current borders even in the face of constant unrest and repeated mass killing. Such a bias ignores the largely arbitrary nature of many of the world's boundaries, forgetting that colonial power politics often mattered more in drawing borders than in settlement patterns. Moreover, this bias often assumes the existence of a national identity that matches that of the state, when in fact such nation-building frequently does not occur. It is time to correct this bias. Even if the world decides not to embrace partition, it must not blindly support preservation regardless of the cost.

If partition is to become a serious policy option, both the United States and the international community must change their doctrine, their response to refugee flows, and their policies toward nascent states. These actions will help transform partition from an idea debated by academics to a viable policy option. As such, they are necessary steps toward helping end bitter communal conflicts and restoring reasonable governments to afflicted regions.

The first step is for policymakers to recognize that partition is, and should be, an option when communal conflicts erupt. Sudan, for example, has scarcely known a year of peace since decolonization. Most of the causes of ethnic conflict identified in Chapter 2 are present. The current international reluctance to consider partition only prolongs the agony of the Sudanese. When governments consider intervention in a communal civil war, they should also weigh whether letting a state collapse is better than propping it up to fight another day.

In cases where partition is desirable, the world community should help carry out any necessary population transfers, provide for border security, and press for guarantees of minority rights. Without population transfers, partition will increase conflict by creating incentives for ethnic cleansing. Historically, population transfers—such as those between Pakistan and India and between Turkey and Greece—have imposed tremendous hardship on the communities involved. Simple humanitarian aid, however, can alleviate many problems ranging from water supplies to temporary housing. International media attention and troops can also help protect minority communities from violence during the transfer. Nor can we blithely assume away the problem of new minorities. A population transfer, while brutal, still may be preferable to the burden of guaranteeing minority rights in a new state. Similarly, by guaranteeing borders outside powers can prevent a land grab by regional states and reduce irredentism among the various rump states.

Creating facts on the ground is an important part of carrying out partition. Recognition of a community as a *de jure* government by itself does little if a beleaguered ethnic group does not have the resources to create a state. Indeed, recognition is counterproductive because it raises the expectations of embattled communal groups while doing nothing to aid their causes. The British Commission that recommended partition in 1937 fueled the Arab revolt but did little to move the partition process forward—the worst of all worlds. Often the most important step in helping a community is military aid: the United States and the international community can arm a weak nascent state while denying arms to its rivals, thus helping to create a military balance. Similarly, a new state will lack political and economic resources ranging from a constitution to financial institutions. Foreign financial aid and technical expertise can help fill this void.

When implementing partition, military factors should often override political concerns. For partition to mitigate the security dilemma, groups must be assured about their security—an assurance that comes when borders can approximate militarily defensible zones. Many of the Israeli-Arab struggles immediately after 1948 resulted from this problem. When historic claims conflict with sensible borders, the latter must take precedence. Only then will groups be confident of their security—a necessary condition for partition to work.

Scholars too can play a role. Partition is an understudied phenomenon, and successful instances of partition are often overlooked. When the idea of partition is raised, conflicts in Israel, Korea, and India are inevitably cited as examples of the cases against it. These bloody partitions are assumed to be failures while scholars ignore the counterfactual question of whether conflict would have occurred even if these states had remained unified. Furthermore, the success of partition in Scandinavia and Czechoslovakia is seldom examined. The Soviet Union, where some republics have left the Union peacefully while others have not, deserves particular attention.

Stability and human rights both are fostered in states where ethnic conflict does not recur and where the state does not preserve itself by repression alone. Many of the civil wars today, however, have the potential to recur endlessly or might only be ended if a brutal government takes power. We should recognize that some civil wars will poison any peace. In such situations, upholding a universal policy of state preservation only enforces what may be an unjust and unstable status quo. Intervention to bolster such failed states is as immoral as it is hopeless. Helping deconstruct these states, on the other hand, may be the most practical and humane solution to recurring civil wars.

8 Military Intervention in Ethnic Conflict

Until this chapter, this book has focused on what governments can do to prevent conflict from recurring in their own countries rather than on what neighboring states, the international community, or other outsiders can do. This emphasis is for a reason: in almost all cases regimes can do far more to affect conflicts in their own lands than can outside powers, no matter how strong or motivated. Chapter 2 related how outside powers could create security fears, inspire belligerent elites, raise status concerns, and otherwise inflame conflict. But this power to incite is not matched by an ability to calm ethnic tension. By themselves, outside powers cannot offer groups in another country social status (or dominance), or give potential elites a leading position in society and politics.[1]

This does not mean outside powers lack any influence. In fact, they have an array of options at their disposal to press or to encourage governments to initiate policies that will improve ethnic relations. For example, outside powers can place economic sanctions on regimes that discriminate against minorities, offer legal assistance in designing constitutions that will promote minority rights, provide training for police and military forces to enable them to control violence without human rights abuses, give grants and loans that enable a government to co-opt potential belligerents, and so on.

Intervention, however, can also be used to solve one of the knottiest problems raised in this book: what to do when governments are part of the problem rather than seeking a solution. If governments seek to initiate or prolong a conflict, then none of the strategies described in Chapters 3–7 will be considered, much less used. In the former Yugoslavia, for example, the Serb-dominated government of Milosevic fostered ethnic hatred in Kosovo rather than working to reduce ethnic tension. In addition, some governments are too weak to use control, manipulate identities, or employ other strategies. In such cases, outside powers can fulfill three roles: they can protect and succor the victims of the oppressive government; they can help alter the balance of power on the ground, enabling a group to defend itself (often as a prelude to or part of a partition plan); or they can help change the government, putting in power a new regime that will be more willing and able to create peace among hostile communal groups.

Outside military intervention can often play a valuable role in solving many of the difficult tasks involved in dealing with a communal civil war. Light ground forces, engineers, military police, medical personnel, transportation experts, signal units, civil affairs specialists, psychological operations units, and water purification specialists are particularly valuable when policymakers seek to restore peace, rebuild an infrastructure, and end a humanitarian disaster. Large infantry forces and air surveillance assets are useful in peace operations that require troops to provide security and reassure the population. Military command and control, intelligence units, strategic and theater lift, and logistics assets play a useful role in humanitarian relief in general, particularly when combat is involved.[2]

Transitions are particularly important times for outside powers to play a role. As Barbara Walter argues, it is difficult for participants in a civil war to negotiate a settlement themselves, because both sides will fear laying down their arms. Thus, a credible outside power is often needed to guarantee security.[3] The discussion of democratization in Chapter 6 also suggests the value of outside intervention. Successfully establishing a democratic system is greatly aided when an outside power, such as a colonial power or benign neighbor, can establish the system and institutionalize it before groups become responsible for their own security. Without security, however, democratization is not likely to succeed. Similarly, as discussed in Chapter 7, to minimize the problems of partition outside management of a population transfer and assistance to the new state are often required.

Despite this potential, military intervention to bring about lasting peace in a communal conflict fails or even backfires far more often than it succeeds. Policymakers and military officials commonly ignore the characteristics that distinguish communal conflicts from other types of civil wars, even though they greatly affect an intervention's requirements and effectiveness.[4] The price is heavy. Short-term difficulties and long-term failures are the rule, not the exception, when the United States (or other countries) intervenes in a communal civil war. U.S. interventions in Lebanon in 1983 and Somalia in 1992–93 provide a few recent examples of the difficulties involved in intervening in a communal conflict. Despite promising initial results, all these conflicts later resumed, with the U.S. military either withdrawing completely, reducing its presence, or standing by ineffectively.[5]

This chapter relates the challenges inherent in military intervention in ethnic conflict for humanitarian reasons. Since the historical record is limited, this chapter focuses on identifying new ways to intervene that might prove more effective than the current approach. How well does the current U.S. and international approach to military intervention resolve communal conflict? What other strategies might help the military play a more constructive role? What are the conditions under which each strategy is most likely to succeed? What are the advantages and disadvantages of each strategy?

The current approach is to intervene militarily to halt the fighting and preserve peace for a short period of time while diplomats forge a political settlement and non-government organizations carry out humanitarian work. Communal civil wars, however, lead to lasting bitterness, making it extremely hard to establish a political settlement and carry out humanitarian operations. As noted in Chapter 2, the security dilemma is active, elites frequently compete for influence by stirring up ethnic antagonism, and all sides in general are preparing for the outbreak of future conflict. Moreover, long-term success means more than getting groups to the negotiating table: it requires a stable peace and a good, effective government. As a result, the standard humanitarian approach of applying short-term remedies to long-term problems often leads to failure.

The United States and other countries must rethink their approach to intervention in communal civil wars. To improve their track record, policymakers must consider a range of new types of missions instead of focusing solely on when to intervene and how to get out.[6] Specific missions worth examining include: (1) limiting an intervention to providing humanitarian relief to refugees; (2) quarantining the conflict to prevent it from spreading; (3) serving as an arsenal to create a local balance of power; (4) arming one side to help it win a complete victory; (5) transferring populations to reduce hostile ethnic commingling; and (6) deploying troops before a conflict begins in order to reduce local fears. All these forms of intervention have limits to their effectiveness and some are politically demanding. However, if the United States or other powers cannot meet the requirements of these missions and live within their limits, they should not intervene.

This chapter has five remaining sections. The first identifies several particularly troublesome characteristics of communal war that make effective intervention difficult. The second part reviews the current U.S. policy toward civil wars and problems with it. The third part—the heart of this chapter—proposes six alternative missions, the conditions conducive to their success, and the advantages and disadvantages of each one. The fourth section briefly considers what non-government organizations (NGOs) should, and should not, do when they operate after a communal civil war. The conclusion identifies limits to the ideas presented. Because the Middle East has witnessed few humanitarian interventions, almost all the examples in this chapter are drawn from U.S., UN, and other powers' experiences in other parts of the world.

Outside Intervention in Communal Civil Wars

Outside powers and non-state actors regularly become involved in communal civil wars. In the 1990s the United States intervened in Iraq after the Gulf War, Somalia, and the former Yugoslavia (twice), usually with the approval of the UN Security Council. Russia has intervened in Georgia, Tajikistan, and Moldova, in part to separate warring communal groups as well as to advance its own interests. France sent troops to Rwanda in 1994 to help restore stability, and Paris has long bolstered friendly governments in Francophone Africa by helping to police the region and ensure stability. Nigeria led the Economic Community of West African States Monitoring Group (ECOMOG) in an ongoing multilateral intervention that began in 1990 in Liberia and later migrated to Sierra Leone. The United Nations has sent troops to Angola, Georgia, Liberia, Rwanda, Somalia, and Bosnia, among other places. A wide variety of NGOs and UN relief agencies regularly carry out humanitarian relief, monitor human rights, and foster negotiations in communal civil wars.

Despite repeated interventions, statesmen, the military, and scholars alike often fail to recognize the unique demands of intervention in communal conflicts. Most military planners consider intervention in complex emergencies to be a lesser-included case of armed conflict, a challenge that can easily be met by preparing for other problems such as low-intensity conflict. Thus, the Department of Defense has rejected calls for specialized units specifically devoted to such interventions.[7] Many military observers consider interventions in communal civil wars as analogous to operations in Vietnam. In fact, such ideologically driven civil wars are increasingly rare today. The military is not alone in its misunderstanding of the nature of recent civil wars. Prominent literature and doctrine on humanitarian intervention tend to lump together all types of civil wars, not recognizing that the conflict in Haiti differs not just operationally but in fundamental ways from the conflict in Iraq.[8]

The Distinct Character of Communal Civil Wars

The nature of communal civil wars—as opposed to ideological civil wars or interstate conflicts—poses distinct problems for any power seeking to intervene. This section looks at several particularly troublesome legacies of communal civil wars relevant to intervention as a prelude to assessing the current approach to intervention and to presenting various alternatives.

One factor that distinguishes communal from ideological civil wars is the way in which the antagonistic groups define themselves. As Kaufmann notes, in ideological civil conflicts the division is permeable.[9] An individual can pass from one group to the other by embracing a new set of beliefs about desirable social, political, or economic relationships and how to achieve them. For instance, during the revolution in China in the late 1940s, nationalists were welcomed (as well as coerced) into the communist fold. In addition, the ideological group as a whole can modify its relationship with a rival group if the leaders reinterpret the ideology. The Communist Party in Italy survived by deciding to work within the liberal democratic system rather than trying to overthrow it. In communal civil conflicts, however, the division is less permeable. An individual cannot easily pass from one group to another because identity is defined by parentage and way of life, not by a set of beliefs. Although all social categories are malleable and change over time, after intense communal conflict, existing identities are both privileged and hardened. In 1990, it was difficult to determine who in Sarajevo was Muslim, Croat, or Serb. Now, alas, the lines are clear. Groups do not welcome each other's members as new converts, nor is it possible to be a Sarajevan.

The impermeability of communal groups in times of violent crisis has several consequences for intervening powers. Communal civil wars result in hardened identities, a high level of security sensitivity, extensive population displacement, and little potential for power-sharing agreements. These consequences make some military intervention strategies less likely to succeed and others more likely to succeed.

Most individuals have multiple identities that can be politically salient. As discussed in Chapter 5, however, communal identities are difficult to manipulate after a communal conflict because the violence tends to harden the identity of the individuals involved.[10] The irony is bitter: attempts to destroy a people make their objectionable identity stronger. Because of these hardened identities, nation-building becomes difficult if not impossible. It is hard to convince the victims of mass violence that they share an identity with its perpetrators.

As discussed in Chapter 2, communal conflict leads individuals to fear for their security even after the conflict ends. Once a group has suffered a mass killing or systematic oppression, it is far more likely to shoot first and ask questions later. The inability to distinguish combatants from noncombatants heightens security sensitivity. In communal conflicts, militia have an incentive to put young males and even children to the sword, as they are likely to be combatants in the future.[11] The Hutu who picks up his machete, kills his Tutsi neighbor, and returns to his field is both a combatant and a noncombatant. Reassuring Tutsis that this Hutu, or his son, will not kill again is almost impossible.

Internal conflicts of all stripes have the potential to displace large numbers of people, both across international borders and within their own country. However, the lack of the option to convert to the other group and the importance of land makes this potential particularly strong in communal conflicts.[12] The war in Bosnia has highlighted population displacement as an aim of violence. In Rwanda, population displacement was a logical consequence of the genocide and civil war. Large-scale population displacement contributes to economic breakdown and disintegration of local political structures. Farmers are unable to meet planting and harvesting seasons, and governing bodies do not convene, much less impose their authority. Displacement also imposes demands on neighboring states, which willingly or unwillingly host the refugees and consequently are more likely to become involved in the conflict.

Problems with the Current Peacemaker Policy

The current U.S. approach to intervention in communal conflict, labeled here as the *peacemaker approach*, has noble ambitions but suffers from several grave problems that often prevent it from achieving its objectives.

Typically, U.S. humanitarian interventions—and those of other powers as well—follow a rather disjointed process. The impetus to intervene comes from a confluence of elements (such as CNN images of starving children or of allies' fears of refugees) that are not necessarily in tune with U.S. abilities or interests. After policymakers decide to become militarily involved, they often fail to clearly articulate the goals of the intervention. Implicitly the goals are to bring about a political settlement, carry out humanitarian aid, or both. Unfortunately, the two are not always distinguished, even though they are entirely different sorts of undertakings.

The peacemaker military mission involves halting the violence temporarily, providing logistical support, or both. While the military keeps order, diplomats try to create power-sharing arrangements, organize elections, resettle displaced people, and otherwise restore peace and order. At the same time, humanitarian organizations try to alleviate the nightmares of displacement, disease, and hunger that often kill more people than the war itself.

In the short term, the peacemaker approach requires large forces to succeed; has burdensome rules of engagement; often requires counterproductive actions; and involves an unclear time commitment. In the long term, a peacemaker-style intervention often does little to foster a political settlement or nation-building. As a result, the United States and other countries have a dismal track record with regard to creating a stable peace by means of military intervention.

Short-term Difficulties

Because it is hard to distinguish combatants from noncombatants and because security sensitivity is particularly acute in communal conflicts, large numbers of troops are required to maintain peace when communal tension is high. One useful measure of this high level of military involvement is the security force to population ratio: the number of troops, police forces, and intelligence assets required to patrol the streets, protect the people from militia, and otherwise prevent or minimize conflict. The experiences of other countries suggest that high security force to population ratios are necessary to maintain peace. For example, the Israeli experience in the West Bank and the British experience in Northern Ireland indicate that roughly twenty security personnel are needed per thousand residents.[13]

Even when forces are deployed in sufficient numbers and have good intelligence, they often find themselves in the midst of a violent and confusing conflict without clear or appropriate rules of engagement (ROE). In humanitarian operations, it is difficult politically to justify rules of engagement that may lead to civilian casualties. Both domestic and international audiences might recoil if U.S. forces are perceived to be adding to, rather than ending, the violence—no one wants to save villages by destroying them. For similar reasons, U.S. forces are reluctant to interrogate, imprison, or otherwise interfere with the civil rights of the local populations.

Restrictive rules of engagement, while laudable in principle, often contribute to mission failure. In environments where it is hard to distinguish the combatants and where large numbers of the population are displaced and on the move, legalistic approaches to human rights often lead to a failure to collect intelligence on potential belligerents. They also allow war-prone leaders to organize freely. This is not to say that an intervention force should behave wantonly. Ideally the intervention force will be given permissive rules of engagement but will be disciplined enough to restrict their aggressive implementation. This requires training soldiers not only how to fight, but also how not to fight.

A particularly troubling aspect of the peacemaker approach is that it often involves operations that are unproductive or lead to further violence. Disarming groups and returning displaced persons are nearly always counterproductive tasks in environments characterized by hardened identities, high security sensitivity, little potential for power-sharing, and frequent outsider involvement.

Disarming groups relies on a heavy police presence that is willing to use intrusive measures to ensure that individuals surrender their weapons. However, it is easy for groups to hide small arms, which are the dominant type of weapon used in many communal conflicts. Weapons are also usually available from international arms markets. Peacemakers who try to force individuals to turn over their arms may encounter violent resistance, which will pose considerable dangers to the troops, raise force-protection concerns, and intensify the conflict that the intervention is meant to quell.

Even with a heavy police presence, disarming groups is difficult. Israel and Great Britain tried to disarm the inhabitants of the West Bank and Northern Ireland, respectively, with little success.[14] The individuals being disarmed faced, and may face again, a very real threat to their lives and well-being. Convincing a local fighter who was driven from his home, his brother butchered, and his sister raped that he does not need his weapon is foolish as well as naive. Kind-hearted humanitarians often naively assume that guns are inherently threatening. Yet in many parts of the world, weapons are considered necessary for security as well as desirable in general. In Somalia, for example, weapons are considered necessary for security and are traditional symbols of manhood.[15] A trip to Bosnia or the Sudan is not necessary to prove this point further: a trip to Texas will suffice.

Such risks might be worthwhile if disarming groups contributed to lasting peace, but in reality disarming groups often makes them more apprehensive about their security. Because it is easy to hide small arms, or to acquire them anew, groups are likely to believe that their former foes are still armed even after the intervening power declares an area free of weapons. Angola provides a depressing example of how militias can hide weapons successfully. Regardless of the truth, inevitable rumors will convince individuals that their enemies retain the means to harm them. Moreover, disarming groups increases the destabilizing impact of outside involvement: now a small shipment of arms can radically change the local balance of power. Not surprisingly, the individuals being disarmed perceive a very real threat to their lives and well-being and resent outsiders who campaign for disarmament.

Resettling people displaced by the conflict also can be a counterproductive mission. Many critics of the U.S. intervention in Bosnia contend that the United States and the international force in general should have done more to return the displaced to their original homes.[16] Such a policy, however, is frequently a mistake. Resettling refugees and internally displaced persons (IDPs) restores the population dispersion, which in turn raises security fears. When refugees return to their place of origin, concerns about enclaves, fifth column, and personal revenge reemerge. The returnees may also be physically isolated and vulnerable. If anything, security fears are even greater as the populations in question now have proof of other groups' hostile intentions. The number of killings in Rwanda increased from 10 to 20 per month to about 2,900 in May and June 1997, after refugees returned en masse from Zaire in late 1996.[17]

Another short-term problem with the peacemaker approach is that it leads to confusion between the end of military intervention and the successful completion of the mission. Some policymakers in the United States believe that if they do not specify a date by which the troops will return before the mission begins, they will lack public support. Such specificity bears no relation to the political mediation and the humanitarian relief programs being carried out by negotiators and NGOs. Equally worrisome is that belligerents may simply bide their time while intervening forces are in the country, gathering resources in preparation for a conflict after the foreigners depart.[18]

Long-term Difficulties

These short-term problems might be worth confronting if the peacemaker approach actually worked in the long term. However, the consequences of communal violence—a lack of trust, security fears, and population displacement—are inadequately addressed by a peacemaker-style intervention. The causes of conflict discussed in Chapter 2 often remain unaffected, or are exacerbated, by outside intervention. For this reason, U.S. and other foreign forces often endure (and at times inflict) short-term miseries for a mission that is likely to fail.

Policymakers and international organizations in the West suffer from a particularly acute delusion that compromise is always possible. Yet despite the repeated efforts of skilled and dedicated diplomats, communal conflicts regularly recur. A peacemaker-style intervention does not soften identities hardened by violence or reassure individuals about their security. Individuals in countries subject to recurring communal conflict are well aware that U.S. forces will eventually leave. Similarly, the mere presence of U.S. troops and the resulting hiatus in fighting neither gives former enemies a sense of common identity nor creates a cohort of moderate leaders who can guide the people to peaceful coexistence. The result is that little changes in the country's overall political dynamic. Elite-driven and status-focused causes of conflict are not ameliorated.

Diplomats are not the only ones who face problems: NGOs often materially underwrite the source of the suffering because they fail to recognize the dynamics of communal conflict. Since combatants and noncombatants extensively commingle, NGOs also provide material support to militias even as they aid noncombatants. Combatants exploit aid to sustain the fighting, and refugee camps become recruiting grounds for rival factions.[19]

The simplest humanitarian aid can make conflict worse. When economies are in chaos, food serves as currency. Whatever group controls food has access to wealth and power and can use this to bolster its position. In Ethiopia, the Eritrean Relief Association and the Relief Society of Tigray worked hand in hand with international relief efforts to feed their people. Because they were also the civic organizations attached to the Eritrean and Tigrayan Peoples Liberation Fronts, respectively, humanitarian aid actually increased local support for the separatist movements. Similarly, in Bosnia, local warlords used aid to dominate their regions and strengthen their positions.[20]

The most egregious example of disastrous good intentions was the United Nations High Commissioner for Refugees' (UNHCR) and dozens of NGOs' support to Hutu refugees in Zaire. Among those refugees were thousands of militiamen, soldiers, and government officials who committed acts of genocide against the Tutsis in Rwanda in 1994. Thanks to international aid efforts and the accommodation of the dictator Mobutu, they found a haven in Zaire from which to organize, arm, and launch raids into Rwanda. Hutu extremists in the camps also intensified ethnic animosities in eastern Zaire, precipitating a bloody civil war that toppled the decrepit Mobutu government.

Although peacekeepers and aid organizations enter a conflict claiming to be neutral, over the long term this attempt at neutrality crumbles.[21] Local actors usually perceive intervention as a partisan effort to aid particular parties. Because noncombatants are considered legitimate targets of violence and because they cannot be separated from combatants, aiding one communal group is perceived by its rival as succoring an enemy. Humanitarian organizations are fooling themselves (but not the belligerents) when they claim their actions have no political impact: it is simply naive to believe that the infusion of goods and services into a war zone has no effect on the war.

A Dismal Track Record

Not surprisingly, U.S. and other militaries have a dismal track record when it comes to achieving stable peace in communal conflict. In Lebanon and Somalia, communal fighting continued after U.S. forces departed, and today the two states display little internal cohesion. Communal conflict has continued in Iraq as well, although violence has been limited when compared to past degradations. None of these countries appear to be experiencing greater sentiments toward nation-building or power-sharing because of U.S. intervention.

The U.S. experience in Bosnia-Herzegovina illustrates many of the problems of intervention in communal conflicts. Combative nationalism is far more prevalent today than it was before the violence that began in 1991. Communal leaders, including those who won recent elections overseen by the international community, use their positions to foster hatred, not reconciliation. Attempts to make Bosnia a harmonious multinational state are failing, as each group confiscates the home of its rivals and pillages and murders those who resist. Refugees have not returned home and intercommunal institutions are weak. War has not returned to the area since U.S. forces were deployed, but after foreign troops withdraw the future of peace seems dismal.

Alternative Strategies

If intervention in communal conflict is to achieve lasting benefits—or at least avoid some common problems—the United States and other powers need to consider new strategies. Six alternative strategies are presented, each of which is referred to by a short label to reduce confusion: providing humanitarian relief without becoming involved in the larger conflict ("commissary"); trying to isolate a conflict to prevent outside meddling ("quarantine"); arming and training one side to create a local balance of power ("balance"); aiding one group in attaining outright victory ("pick a winner"); intervening to relocate groups into homogeneous, defensible areas ("transfer"); and using military force to ensure order and promote security before large-scale hostilities ("prophylaxis"). These strategies cover a wide range of possible options, from non-combat operations to full war fighting, from preventive deployment to reactive deployment, and from merely providing succor to resolving some of the toughest problems of communal conflict.

For each alternative, the strategy and the reasoning behind it are presented. The conditions most likely to lead to its successful implementation are identified, and its benefits and drawbacks are noted. In assessing the strategy, a range of factors, including terrain, the local parties' military strength, the level of interest of neighboring and intervening countries, and whether the war is a conventional conflict or a guerrilla struggle are noted.

Commissary

An important (although limited) mission that the military can carry out is to help deliver humanitarian aid and ensure its distribution. Due to their rapid mobility, military forces can often arrive in a disaster region days before NGOs arrive. Military forces can make it harder for local warlords to divert humanitarian aid by guarding warehouses and providing security escorts for food convoys. They can provide the necessary equipment and expertise to increase the logistical capacity to distribute supplies to a wider area. They can even provide a haven for internally displaced persons and noncombatants. Providing relief for a famine or other humanitarian disaster is an increasingly common mission for the U.S. military. Recent examples include operations in Somalia, northern Iraq, and Bangladesh.

Commissary is particularly valuable during the first few days of a crisis, when NGOs have not arrived or are overwhelmed. Under such circumstances, the tremendous U.S. logistical capability becomes highly useful. Thus, in contrast to conventional wisdom about when a military intervention is likely to be considered, a commissary strategy should be undertaken when the terrain is difficult—mountainous, swampy, heavily forested, without road access, or otherwise rough. When infrastructure is in place or the terrain is accessible, UN agencies and NGOs are equipped to transport relief supplies without military help. Operation Provide Comfort offered assistance to Kurds stranded in the rugged mountains of the Iraqi-Turkish border by air dropping food, providing shelter, and arranging transportation to bring hundreds of thousands of people out of the mountains to more sustainable locations. Operation Sea Angel—a U.S. response to the 1991 cyclone that inundated hundreds of square miles of Bangladesh's southeastern coast—succeeded because the military provided communications equipment and transportation assistance to locations where the entire infrastructure had been wiped out. The U.S. military can even make a lasting improvement in the local infrastructure. The Unified Task Force (UNITAF) succeeded in part because the U.S. military helped repair Somalia's infrastructure, which was necessary in order to distribute large quantities of humanitarian aid.

For a commissary mission to succeed, the military must work closely with the national government (if there is one), UN agencies, and the NGOs that run the camps and rehabilitate the local economy and society. UNITAF's initial success occurred because diplomats, military officials, and humanitarian aid organizations worked together to ensure the distribution of food. The various officials involved in Provide Comfort quickly recognized one another's expertise and dedication. Sea Angel worked well in part because the United States' task force, the Bangladeshi government, U.S. AID, and various NGOs all saw themselves as part of a larger team. Relief operations in Rwanda were less effective because relief agencies did not trust the French force that had created a safe zone in the southwest. When American forces arrived in response to the refugee situation in Zaire, their preoccupation with force protection and their formal contact procedures with the humanitarian community inhibited effective action.[22]

Commissary is far more difficult to implement in a hostile environment. Sea Angel required relatively few resources because both the government and the people of Bangladesh worked together in the wake of the disastrous cyclone. In a hostile environment, however, the provision of aid becomes a combat operation. Provide Comfort kept the conventional forces of the Ba'ath regime out of northern Iraq, but it required a huge military effort to do so. When the French deployed to Rwanda to limit the fighting during the Hutu-instigated genocide, their deployment inadvertently aided the *genocidaires,* enabling them to flee in safety to Zaire. Moreover, to carry out this disastrous mission, France had to deploy armored personnel carriers, combat aircraft, anti-tank missiles, and their elite infantry forces. In Bosnia, the safe havens of Srebrenica, Sara-jevo, Gorazde, Zepa, Tulza, and Bihac were created without the consent of the Bosnian Serbs who laid siege to the towns, restricted the flow of aid entering them, and eventually overran Gorazde and Srebrenica in conventional operations with horrible consequences.

Thus, the intervening power must consider the strength of military opposition and whether the war is being fought by conventional forces or guerrillas. Obviously, the weaker the party that is opposed to the commissary strategy, the easier it will be to implement the strategy. With regard to the character of the war, it is less difficult to protect convoys against guerrillas and bandits who are lightly armed and pursue hit-and-run tactics than it is to protect against conventional military operations that can confront convoys with heavily fortified roadblocks. On the other hand, safe areas are usually easier to defend against conventional attack (provided the defending force has greater military power), since guerrillas specialize in slipping through lines of defense and carrying out massacres and sabotage.

When successful, commissary allows NGOs to function properly. NGO workers can operate with less fear for their lives and will not be forced to cut as many deals with unsavory warlords in order to ensure the distribution of aid. UNITAF allowed large-scale humanitarian relief to resume in Somalia, saving perhaps tens of thousands of lives. Similarly, Provide Comfort enabled humanitarian organizations to move to the disaster region much more quickly and to concentrate on saving the lives of Kurds, rather than their own security. Even in Rwanda, aid organizations claimed they had greater access to the needy in the southwest after the French established the safe zone.

Commissary also requires relatively few resources when compared with the current U.S. approach and with other missions discussed in this book. Only small geographic areas need to be secured, and military forces will not become directly involved in the fighting unless these areas are threatened. In the refugee and IDP camps themselves, military police, civil engineers, and intelligence officers will play an important role, but they will not require large numbers of regular troops to support them.

As good as it may be in certain respects, commissary has many limits. First and most important, it does not end a conflict in either the short or the long term: thus, it is not a strategy for keeping the peace in an absolute sense, even though it does reduce overall suffering. The UNITAF mission sought only to provide humanitarian aid, not to resolve the conflict. The Hutu-Tutsi conflict rages on in Central Africa, although not at the same genocidal pace of the past. The provision of emergency assistance to the people of northern Iraq and Bosnia saved many lives, but it did nothing to resolve the political impasses underlying the conflicts. In fact, by providing sustenance to locals, commissary literally feeds the war, although on a more restricted diet than when military protection is not offered to aid operations.

Second, humanitarian aid is not neutral. Food is a weapon: those who control it have power. Local warlords who fear losing their control of the population and aid resources may try to block access to refugee camps, leading them to fight the intervening forces. In Sri Lanka, Tamil insurgents threatened refugees and tried to block their access to refugee camps to avoid losing their power base.

A third, related problem is that working with the locals often strengthens the hand of the most warlike leaders. UNITAF, for example, strengthened two of the more bellicose Somalia warlords, Aideed and Ali Mahdi, by giving them high-level military and diplomatic recognition. Aideed in particular gained, as UNITAF sent much of the food it distributed through his territory, allowing him to increase his overall resources. Intervening powers thus face a trade-off between strengthening corrupt warlords and fighting these same individuals in an effort to bypass them.

Fourth, a commissary mission has no clear withdrawal date if the source of the disaster is political rather than natural. Provide Comfort, initially a short-term humanitarian relief operation that became a balancing operation (under the name of Operation Northern Watch), has continued for years. If the United States withdrew, the Iraqi regime would probably massacre thousands of Kurds, as it has in the past. UNITAF and the Somali people suffered as the United States hurried to end the operation in Somalia for domestic political reasons, despite the shortcomings of the UN follow-on mission.

Finally, long-term humanitarian assistance frequently leads to distortions within the local economy. With free food available, farmers have no incentive to harvest and sell their crops. A large military and NGO presence also creates perverse economic incentives because aid organizations rent office and living space at rates that few within the country can match. Further, aid operations sometimes entail hiring local gunmen to provide auxiliary security, thus playing to those who seek to heighten the conflict.

Quarantine

In addition to helping provide humanitarian aid, military intervention can also reduce or prevent the outside meddling that often makes communal conflict more deadly. This intervention can involve interdicting outside aid to combatants, coercing outside powers to stay away, reassuring neighboring states, or all three of these. Such a mission potentially can decrease both the scope and scale of the conflict by reducing the total armaments available to combatants and by denying them access to secure rest, recruitment, and staging areas outside their own country. It also reduces the likelihood that the conflict will spread to neighboring states.

Quarantine is a strategy commonly attempted during wars of national interest, not during humanitarian interventions. During the Algerian War of Independence, France restricted the flow of arms and guerrillas from Tunisia into Algeria, creating the Morice Line along the border. During the Vietnam War, the United States interdicted supplies from North Vietnam to guerrillas in the South and to stop North Vietnamese army fighters from joining the fight directly. The Soviets tried to stop the infiltration of arms and fighters from Pakistan to Afghanistan, with little success. Thus, there is a precedent for military quarantine missions in general, but no specific instance of a humanitarian-oriented quarantine.

Successful interdiction is highly terrain-dependent. As the United States discovered in Vietnam and as the Soviets learned in Afghanistan, preventing cross-border infiltration is difficult in jungle or mountainous terrain. France, on the other hand, found the interdiction of supplies far easier in Algeria than it had in Vietnam. The barren Tunisia-Algeria border proved relatively simple to monitor, making it highly difficult for insurgents to receive supplies from compatriots outside Algeria.[23]

Neighboring state support for quarantine is useful because neighbors can provide rear bases and supplies. Neighboring state support for belligerents, in contrast, makes the mission far harder. Coercing area regimes to forego or end military involvement is difficult, however, because they usually have a far stronger interest in intervention than does the distant power in preventing it. Humanitarian interventions, almost by definition, do not involve the national interest of the United States or other possible intervening nations. This asymmetry of interest makes successful coercion far more difficult.[24] An alternative to coercion is to buy off the neighboring states by conditionally providing them with aid.

Demographics must also be considered. If some members of a community reside across an international border, it will be harder to quarantine the war because the diaspora will be a central source of recruits and resources. Further, if a cause of the conflict was to rescue the diaspora, significant combat capability would be required to stop groups from trying to gain territory across international borders.

Quarantine is particularly effective when the aid in question involves heavy weapons systems and direct military intervention with conventional forces. Guerrilla fighters usually have few logistical needs, since they work with and live off of the local populace, but larger conventional forces use trucks, tanks, and other large targets and have more demanding logistics requirements. In Vietnam, the Rolling Thunder operations were ineffective in cutting off North Vietnamese support for the Viet Cong guerrillas. The later Linebacker operations, however, proved highly effective in stopping the flow of North Vietnamese army forces to the south and led to several defeats of northern forces.[25]

Quarantine by itself does not end wars, but it does facilitate defeat of the weaker side. For this reason, when outside aid is important, quarantine can have a tremendous effect. French interdiction efforts devastated National Liberation Front (FLN) cadres in Algeria, making it difficult for them to sustain large-scale guerrilla operations.

Quarantine also diminishes, but hardly ends, the security dilemma. By regulating outside intervention, one source of potential instability is controlled. Thus, the belligerents need not fear that the local balance of power will be upset at some time in the future. Quarantine's impact can be large if a neighboring state is supporting guerrillas actively. If the conflict is entirely indigenous, it will have little effect.

Quarantine missions are attractive because they usually require relatively few resources, as long as the topography is friendly and the war does not involve international territorial expansion as a central goal. Air surveillance and some highly mobile ground forces can often survey a large area. Although such missions will not prevent all outside aid from reaching belligerents, they can significantly reduce the quantities of aid received. Recent advances in munitions and surveillance will make quarantine easier to implement than in the past.[26]

Even if quarantine succeeds, groups inside a country will still be able to fight with their own resources. Because the technologies involved in atrocities often are quite primitive, quarantine will not substantially reduce violence against civilians. Much of the killing in Rwanda in 1994, for example, was carried out by extremists armed only with machetes and stones. Quarantine missions are difficult to sustain politically. Because allies and regional powers may not share the U.S. view on which side is the aggressor, they may support local clients that seek to aid combatants. In Vietnam, the Soviets and the Chinese aided Hanoi, more than compensating for the damage done by U.S. interdiction.[27] Without allied support, efforts to embargo combatants will almost certainly fail. Even if an intervenor begins with regional support, in the time it takes for a quarantine strategy to work, that support often begins to erode.

Quarantine missions also lack a clear end date and require a long-term commitment. Although the Linebacker operations gained concessions from North Vietnam, and although the French devastated the FLN along the Morice Line, eventually popular disenchantment with the war led both the United States and France to accept defeat. In this way, the quarantine approach contributes to operational successes but offers no guarantee of political victory.

Balance

The balance strategy seeks to transform conflicts into stalemates by enabling groups to provide for their own security. To accomplish this, a balance mission builds up local police forces and militaries to create a balance of power. U.S. or international forces might also be used as a stopgap measure to prevent one side from winning while the new forces train. This approach operates on the theory that a "hurting stalemate" with a "precipice" (an impending deterioration of position) eventually will lead combatants to the peace table; that is, a stalemate with a sense of urgency will create a situation in which all combatants recognize that continued fighting will threaten their individual interests.[28] Arming and training local forces (governmental or other) in order to create a military balance was a common tactic for the superpowers during the Cold War and has been used subsequently with some success in both humanitarian and national interest interventions.

Balance requires local allies who are militarily competent and popularly supported. The central idea of the balance strategy is to build the client's strength. Communal conflicts are more likely to produce suitable allies than ideologically based conflicts;[29] however, at times a group may be too weak or have exceptionally poor leadership, either of which will prevent a balance approach from succeeding. In addition, if the balancing activity involves placing foreign troops on the ground, those troops will face far fewer difficulties if the local client retains popular support. As the United States learned in Vietnam, even massive resource transfers and troop deployments cannot save a leadership that is corrupt, unpopular, and weak. In contrast, popular support has played important roles in the successful U.S. efforts to balance against the Soviet military in Afghanistan by supporting the Mujahedin and against the Iraqi Ba'ath regime by providing air cover to the Kurds. In the years preceding and immediately following the collapse of the Soviet Union, Russia worked with minorities in Georgia against their central governments, giving them military aid that helped them resist central government control.[30] Russia also provided moderate assistance to Russian-speaking residents of the Transnistria, the small part of Moldova on the eastern side of the Dniester River, enabling them to resist the Moldovan government.[31] In these interventions, popular backing for the minorities' leadership made Russia's task far less difficult.

Balance is easier to implement when the terrain favors the defense. The mountains of Afghanistan, for example, are ideal for guerrillas, allowing small forces to hold off a much larger enemy. For this reason, U.S. aid to foes of the Soviet regime during the Cold War, and subsequent Russian assistance to anti-Taliban forces, proved extremely successful in preventing complete victory. Similarly, rivers, mountains, and other geographic obstacles helped minorities defend themselves in Moldova and Georgia. Open land, which is usually favorable for offensive forces, is also defense dominant when combined with advanced American airpower technology and total airspace dominance, so that any large military formations can be quickly identified and destroyed.

A necessary condition for the balance strategy to work is the agreement of neighboring states and other great powers. Support for a client will not bring about peace if other states provide arms and training to the other side, perpetuating the imbalance of power and raising hopes of an eventual triumph. ECOMOG in Liberia was stymied in part by support provided by dissenting regional states to Charles Taylor, against whom the Nigerian-led force was balancing.[32] The U.S. success in keeping Ba'ath government forces out of northern Iraq has been facilitated by the UN sanctions on Iraq, which keep the Iraqi military weak.

The balance strategy is easier to implement when opposing leaders have limited objectives such as autonomy or political inclusion than when they seek exclusive control over the state. A client with limited aims is easier to control; an opponent with limited aims is easier to deter. ECOMOG was ultimately unable to deter Charles Taylor, who desired to control the Liberian government, not just participate in it. Additionally, if either side has total war aims, then the outside power will find it difficult to extricate itself without upsetting the balance. It is for this reason, for example, that the United States cannot find a way out of Operation Northern Watch.

The balance strategy requires an extended military and political commitment, a willingness to escalate military involvement if necessary to preserve or achieve the balance, and constant diplomatic engagement by allies. For these reasons, the intervening power must see its own national interests to be at stake, at least in part. This criterion has usually held historically: for the United States in Afghanistan and Iraq; for Russia in Tajikistan, Afghanistan, Georgia, and Moldova; for Nigeria in Liberia; and for India in Sri Lanka.

A balance approach has several important advantages over the other strategies discussed so far. First, it actually addresses the security sensitivity legacy of a communal conflict; it reduces group perceptions of vulnerability by allowing groups to ensure their own security and to seal their own borders (if they are geographically separated). Balancing relies on power, not on common bonds, to ensure group security. Neither Georgia nor Moldova has witnessed a recurrence of the fighting that threatened to engulf these countries in civil war following the collapse of the Soviet Union, in part because the minorities in these countries are well-armed and confident in their ability to protect themselves. Sometimes, however, the feeling of security backfires. Freed from the immediate threat of Saddam, the Iraqi Kurds began fighting among themselves from 1994 to 1996, although with less carnage than Saddam's troops would have provoked.

A balance approach requires relatively few resources from the intervening power. Provide Comfort (and its successor Northern Watch), for example, relied almost entirely on air power; Russian operations in Afghanistan and the former Soviet Union consisted primarily of providing arms to local forces. Foreign military aid and air support enabled the Bosnian Muslims to better defend themselves against Serb attacks. In Croatia, foreign military purchases and advisers strengthened the Croat army, allowing it to reverse previous losses in western Slavonia and in the Krajina. Blood was spilled in these operations, but little of it from personnel of the intervening power.

Third, sometimes there is an end date to a balancing mission: outside forces can leave when adversaries accept that they cannot gain a military victory or when local forces are prepared to assume their own defense. Indian troops departed from Sri Lanka after the Sri Lankan government, recognizing that Indian support would make the Tamils impossible to defeat, approved a peace plan that sought to ensure Tamil security and provided a real devolution of power. Russia no longer has troops poised to help the Abkhaz and the South Ossetians to fight the Georgians. Northern Watch, however, suggests the importance of making the balance less dependent on the intervening power. If the United States withdraws its air umbrella from northern Iraq, many Kurds will quickly be killed by the Ba'ath because they lack a strong military force of their own.

Balance is a tool that recognizes groups as governments and ignores the apparatus of the failed state, creating the potential for a de facto partition.[33] Indeed, it is likely to increase short-term fighting as groups press to seize their advantage before a local power balance is restored. Indian support of the Sri Lankan Tamils led the Sinhalese-dominated government to compromise, but it did not lead Tamil radicals to do so. Instead, they exploited the resources given to them by India to make themselves more autonomous. Similarly, as Pakistan, the United States, and other powers began aiding the Mujahedin, they became more intransigent, not less. In the former Soviet Union, Soviet and Russian arms encouraged the Abkhaz and the Ossetians in their opposition to Tblisi, preventing the Georgian government from attaining a quick victory.

Balance often creates a non-hurting stalemate: military forces cannot prevail over their enemies, but the leaders all prefer war to peace. In the Balkans, some warlords depend on continued conflict to stay in power and thus prefer war to peace. Similarly, the conflict in Afghanistan has produced over a million casualties and 5 million refugees, yet the combatants have not reached the "hurting" stalemate stage.[34]

Balancing creates the danger that the troops who receive arms and training will conduct offensives even after a balance of power is restored, seeking to tip the scales in their favor. Under these circumstances, the intervening power often cannot control its supposed proxies. The factions in Afghanistan were not simply superpower surrogates: they had local goals and did not hesitate to ignore their superpower and regional masters when necessary. Ideally, local forces would have defensive equipment and doctrine to minimize their chances of going on the offensive. Such fine-grained intervention, however, is often beyond the means of most interested parties.

Because a balance mission initially favors war over peace, it involves tremendous political difficulties internationally and in the region. A balance of power approach is vulnerable to critics who promise more peaceful solutions, regardless of the viability of these solutions. British officials, for example, criticized efforts to arm the Bosnian Muslims as a policy that would level the killing fields without spelling out a vision of their own as to how other forms of intervention would foster lasting peace. Turkey opposed the U.S. support of the Iraqi Kurds and would vociferously object to any attempt to make them more militarily capable. Moreover, local parties are highly opposed to outside efforts to arm their foes and thus will turn against the intervening power.

Finally, attempts at balancing can often lead to increased fighting. For example, Pakistan's support for Afghan insurgents led the Soviets to attack Pakistan directly. After the Sri Lankan government agreed to political compromises for the Tamil population, the Indian government began to work with the government rather than with Tamil groups. Tamil radicals of the Liberation Tigers of Tamil Eelam (LTTE), enraged by the cutoff of Indian support for their cause, assassinated former Indian prime minister Rajiv Gandhi. He resigned in 1989 and was killed in 1991.

Pick a Winner

At times the international community may prefer the victory of one side to the creation of a balance of power or to supporting secession. Most civil wars are resolved by the outright victory of one party. Roy Licklider contends that only 25 percent of post–Cold War civil wars that have ended have been resolved by negotiation.[35] Helping one side win an outright victory allows members of the international community to play the troubling but important role of Kingmaker. After all, if war is inevitable, then a shorter war is better than a longer one. This strategy assumes that the side chosen to win is the most just or, more cynically and realistically, at least favors the intervening states' interests. The situation in Rwanda in 1994 would have been a good time to pick a winner. If countries other than Uganda had materially supported the Rwandan Patriotic Front (and had the French not actively interfered with the Front's attempt to remove the *genocidaires* from power), the conflict in Rwanda might have been less bloody. (By the time outside governments figured out what was happening, much of the killing had already occurred; by the time they admitted what they knew, it was almost over.)[36]

The pick-a-winner strategy is highly variable in its operationalization. At one end of the spectrum, it involves supplying arms and other materiel to give the client a military advantage—a more muscular version of the balance approach. Further along the spectrum, depending on the strength of the various forces on the ground, U.S. forces may have to equip allied units, enforce a selective no-fly zone, insert and extract allied troops, and conduct raids against high-value targets. If the opposing group is strong, a large ground contingent may be required to defeat them militarily. The goal is to install a government that eventually will be strong enough to implement other strategies discussed in this book.

The pick-a-winner approach is a common strategy for intervention, especially when the intervention implicates national interests. During the Cold War, the Soviet Union and Cuba worked with the Popular Movement for the Liberation of Angola (MPLA) in Angola, providing it with arms and training and sending Cuban troops to assist it. South Africa and the United States unsuccessfully backed the rival UNITA force. Russia regularly tried to install local allies in power in its former empire, helping out former apparatchiks in Tajikistan, working with Eduard Shevardnadze over Zviad Gamsakhurdia in Georgia, and backing the Najibullah regime in Afghanistan after departing. India successfully picked a winner in the 1971 Pakistan civil war, aiding the Bangladeshis over the forces of the West Pakistan government. Tanzania successfully invaded Uganda in 1979 on behalf of former president Milton Obote against Idi Amin. In 1994, the United States used the threat of imminent invasion to force Raoul Cedras to make way for Jean Bertrand Aristide. In 1996 and 1997, Uganda, Rwanda, and Angola provided extensive military assistance to Laurant Kabila's successful attempt to overthrown Mobutu Sese Seko of Zaire.

The NATO intervention in Kosovo represents an attempt to use a pick-a-winner strategy for humanitarian purposes. In the seventy-eight-day air campaign against Serbia, NATO helped the Kosovar Albanians gain de facto autonomy from Serbia. NATO forces did not directly coordinate with Kosovar resistance fighters, but in essence they acted as the military of the Albanian people. NATO, however, hesitated to create a separate state after its victory, maintaining the pretense of Serbian sovereignty over the disputed territory.

Picking a winner is easier when the client enjoys widespread popular support. Popular support facilitates a guerrilla campaign and increases the effectiveness of counterinsurgent operations. India aided the widely popular Awami League in Bangladesh, which had proven its popular support by winning elections there. The United States reinstalled wildly popular President Aristide in Haiti. Conversely, popular disaffection, if not hatred, of Pol Pot in Cambodia, Amin in Uganda, and Mobutu in Zaire facilitated their overthrows. The Soviets in Afghanistan failed in part because they worked with the much-maligned Najibullah.

Military competence should complement popular support. The Allied Democratic Forces for the liberation of Congo-Zaire (ADFL) under Laurent Kabila were, when bolstered by Rwandan and Ugandan troops, more capable, more motivated, and better led than the Armed Forces of Zaire, who were intent on looting and raping rather than standing and fighting. Conversely, the strategy is facilitated when the opposing military is weak. The supporters of Aristide in Haiti had no military capability, but the U.S. army acted as Aristide's army, presidential guard, and police force. It was opposed by a Haitian military that collapsed before the first armed confrontation. Soviet efforts in Afghanistan and American efforts in Vietnam failed in part because the opposition was more militarily capable than were the superpowers' clients.

Picking a winner is far easier when neighboring states and other powers do not balance. The MPLA won control of Angola in large part because South Africa and the United States withdrew their support for UNITA; when UNITA had outside support, Angola's civil war was bloody and unending. In Afghanistan, however, far more massive Soviet assistance to the Najibullah regime failed to keep him in power, as Pakistan, Saudi Arabia, Iran, and the United States aided rival factions, thus preventing him from gaining military superiority. Tajikistan represents a mixed case. Although Emomali Rahmanov took power with Russian and Uzbek support, various Afghan militia and Arab and Muslim donors supported some opposition groups.[37] The United States and its NATO allies devoted considerable energy in the Kosovo conflict to ensuring that Russia did not actively champion Belgrade's cause.

Picking a winner is more difficult when terrain and geography favor the defense. Afghanistan, of course, is difficult for any force to dominate given its mountainous terrain. In Bangladesh, on the other hand, the West Pakistan government had to conduct operations across 1,600 miles of Indian territory, making it relatively easy for the already superior Indian army to defeat them. However, as successful efforts to oust the governments of Cambodia, Uganda, and Zaire show, jungles and mountains alone do not prevent pick a winner from succeeding.

If using the pick-a-winner strategy, the intervening state(s) would do well to have at least some national interests at stake. National interest arguments are easier than others for diplomats to sell to other states and for politicians to sell to domestic constituencies. The strategy may also involve significant military engagement. This condition is somewhat autogenic, since a government would not be inclined to commit to picking a winner unless it felt strongly about the consequences of the conflict. India's interests in ensuring a friendly government in Bangladesh and returning some 8 million refugees were obvious to all concerned; thus, it was willing to provide rear bases, training, and materiel to Awami League and other insurgents. When its Bangladeshi allies were losing the conflict, India launched a full-scale invasion in December 1971. Uzbekistan and Russia, fearing that fighting in Tajikistan would lead to regional instability and refugee flows, decided to sustain operations there.[38] If such a strong commitment is lacking, the intervening power may either not provide enough aid or not sustain the aid for a sufficient period of time.

Picking a winner's greatest advantage is that it brings about an end to a civil war through direct military means. The end of a war offers substantial humanitarian benefits even when peace is bitter: the conflict stops; NGOs can operate in relative safety; and refugees can return to their homes. Russian assistance to Shevardnadze allowed him to defeat Gamsakhurdia's forces quickly. India's intervention helped the Awami League triumph, ending a brutal civil war. Similarly, Russia's and Uzbekistan's support helped Rahmanov win a quicker victory (indeed, without this support Rahmanov might not have triumphed). In situations such as Cambodia under the Khmer Rouge, Uganda under Amin, and (potentially) Rwanda just after the death of President Juvenal Habyarimana, pick a winner can remove a regime that is killing its own people in droves. As these cases illustrate, the strategy also has the potential advantage (depending on the players involved) of bringing to power a government more respectful of human and civil rights.

If the government is strong enough, it can then implement other strategies that can help it keep the peace over the long term. In 1948, the new Israeli government won the international and civil wars with its Arab neighbors; it then used control policies, co-optation, and eventually power-sharing to help prevent a renewal of civil conflict. If outside intervention can foster the victory of a government that intends to maintain social peace, it can serve a benign purpose over time—even if the victory itself poses the danger that one group will dominate politics in the short term.

The greatest problem with pick a winner is that victory comes with the agonies of an unjust peace. Picking a winner is a euphemism for supporting a war: ideally the war is quick and involves few casualties, but such wars are rare. Mass killing, rape, repression, and other human rights abuses often go hand in hand with military victory. Intervening powers can condition their support on the good behavior of their proxy, but these conditions will have little effect as war rolls through every village. Even when victory is not accompanied by widespread depredation, the likely result is that one group dominates politics, society, and the economy. Status problems for losers in the war are of course likely.

Picking a winner is particularly difficult to implement in humanitarian interventions. Humanitarian interventions seek good government as well as an end to the killing. Good government, however, depends on including rival groups in the same political structure. Because picking a winner often requires working with one group to the exclusion of others, it fosters an exclusive government. The Kosovar Albanians have, through rampant discrimination and occasional brutalization, encouraged Serbs to leave Kosovo for Serbia proper.

Picking a winner often trades short-term peace for long-term unrest. Although they do not suffer the all-out civil wars that plagued them earlier, the people of many areas (Cambodia, Tajikistan, and Uganda) continue to experience sporadic violence. Fundamental causes of conflict, such as belligerent elites, communal security fears, and discrimination may be exacerbated by victory, sowing the seeds of future violence.

Picking a winner also shares many of the problems of a balance strategy. The ally to be armed must be competent, regardless of the supplies and training received. Picking a winner often is difficult politically both in the region and internationally, since other powers may prefer to back the rival side. The strategy also is highly likely to result in a short-term increase in the fighting as arms flow into the country and the receiving party develops a new incentive to fight.

Transfer

Population transfers are another powerful tool that outside governments can use to foster peace, particularly when combined with efforts to create a military balance. The strategy of population transfer recognizes and tries to work around the hardened identity and security sensitivity legacies of communal conflicts by giving warring groups control over their own states or regions. As discussed in Chapter 7, transfer is often necessary to achieve a successful partition. Myron Weiner argues that population transfers are called for after a partition has occurred, to relocate the minorities who remain on both sides.[39]

In practice, a transfer policy involves creating homogeneous geographic areas to encourage population displacement. The process can be horrific.

Members of the international community, however, can make it more humane by providing humanitarian assistance and security for the refugees, by identifying borders that are defensible, and by trying to make the populations as homogeneous as possible. Moreover, the military can guard the refugees against local thugs, organize the flow of refugees, and in doing so, calm the security fears of the local population. The international community can also help settle the liquidation of property and otherwise succor refugees.

Successful transfer requires the consent of the authorities in question (recognized governments and others) and the support of the peoples involved. Most of the Greeks and Turks exchanged under the 1923 Lausanne Convention suffered relatively little during the transfer compared with others who fled without official government support.[40] Thousands of people died in Bengal before independence, but millions of people passed between India and East Pakistan in the years following independence with relatively little violence. The demarcation of the border and the establishment of order both prevented violence. When transfer is not agreed upon by the governments in question, the strategy can quickly become one of ethnic cleansing. The transfer of Greek and Turkish populations in Cyprus transformed an intermixed country into two nations, one a homogeneous Greek area and the other a homogeneous Turkish area. This transfer took place amid terror and violence directed against both Greek and Turkish civilians. Out of a total Cypriot population of 631,000, roughly 200,000 were displaced.[41]

The local population must consent to a transfer because an outside power intervening for humanitarian purposes is not likely to sanction the use of violence against civilians. However, people seldom leave their homes voluntarily, and many individuals will remain even in the face of great danger. Ironically, this conundrum of a lack of popular support can be solved by strong local military or paramilitary forces. When at least one of the local parties has a strong military that threatens people who do not leave their homes, "voluntary" transfer is more likely. The Serbs remaining in Kosovo after the NATO victory, for example, found themselves threatened by Albanian paramilitary forces. The intervening state, however, is then in the uncomfortable position of having its strategy benefit from threatened massacres. The trick is to move people before the massacres take place, but such precise timing is often difficult.

Defensible terrain can both aid and impede a transfer. Land that lends itself to defense is desirable in the end, for it helps the segregated groups overcome their security sensitivity. However, if the population of a defensible location does not want to move, it will be difficult to make them do so. The result may be isolated and vulnerable pockets of threatened people. Cyprus presented such a situation after fierce communal conflict broke out in December 1963 and before the Turkish intervention in July 1964.[42] Bosnia likewise exhibited a similar pattern in recent years.

The demographic picture is also an important consideration. Obviously, the more separated the antagonistic communities are to begin with, the easier it will be to create distinct homogeneous groups. Some degree of separation before the transfer strategy is considered is necessary, because transfer will become a tenable choice only after the sides have shown themselves unwilling to live together.

The final condition for successfully implementing transfer is a high degree of coordination among political, military, and humanitarian actors. Transfer requires extraordinary logistical expertise. Uprooting hundreds of thousands, and perhaps millions, of people requires providing them with food, water, medical care, and transportation. In past transfers, much of the death and suffering occurred because of the haphazard nature of the transfer rather than factors inherent in the transfer itself.

Transfer can offer several distinct advantages over other missions. Most important, transfer allows many of the benefits of partition (see Chapter 7) to accrue while reducing some of the costs of this wrenching policy. Thus, transfer allows for long-term solutions not available to states that remain intact but highly divided. Democracy, nation-building, and other relatively mild methods that help people live together in peace are far easier in homogeneous states with no history of bloodshed. Greece and Turkey are democratic nations today, as is India. Although communal tensions certainly remain in these three countries, they are probably less fierce than they would be had the population transfers not have occurred.[43]

Transfer also increases perceptions of security. Groups living in homogeneous, defensible areas have fewer concerns about fifth columns or rescuing beleaguered compatriots. Although Turkish-Kurdish questions plague Turkey today, the Greek Question has disappeared, in part due to population transfers.

Inevitably, transfer creates problems. It requires the international community to forcibly move individuals who, in many cases, will resist leaving the homes and lands they have occupied for generations. To carry out transfer, the international community must at times punish the innocent and reward the guilty. Transferring Muslims, Serbs, and Croats to homogeneous enclaves in the former Yugoslavia, for example, would require moving people whose families resided in mixed areas for centuries and who were not involved in the fighting directly. People leave their homes only under extreme duress and usually return quickly. The brutality used by the Greek and Turkish governments in the 1920s to "encourage" people to move would not be condoned by the international community today.

Another difficulty is that the new states are likely to be weak and unstable, their leadership may be uncertain, and their social fabric has been torn apart by war and population shifts. Further, a displaced population may generate a "myth of return," a central tenet of which is to reclaim a homeland by force. A concurrent balance strategy is probably necessary to make transferred people militarily viable. Economic aid will be required to restart their economies, and civic programs must be organized to help cope with the trauma inherent in a sudden move away from the people's historic homes.

Transfer missions are also a contentious political issue. Many of the problems inherent in partition are also present when populations are transferred. Not surprisingly, the international community has shown little enthusiasm for tampering with borders. Although the transfer of populations was proposed during civil conflicts in Cyprus and the former Yugoslavia, the international community in general did not favor these solutions. States that have their own boundary problems are especially likely to resist creating a precedent of partition.

Prophylaxis

Given the difficulties involved in many of these strategies, outside powers should consider deploying military forces prior to the outbreak of large-scale communal violence in the hope of deterring communal civil war. Predicting where and when a communal civil war will occur is difficult in some cases; however, at times the potential for horrendous violence is painfully obvious to outside observers.[44]

Prophylaxis missions are rare. The United Nations deployed forces to Macedonia to keep conflict in the former Yugoslavia from spreading and to prevent violence against Albanians in the republic. In fact, this was perhaps the first purely humanitarian preventive deployment.[45] Preemptive deployments for the national interest, such as the U.S. deployment of forces to Lebanon in 1958, at times also prevented a communal conflict from spreading.[46]

The option of whether or not to employ prophylaxis depends on superb intelligence assessments on the likelihood of conflict in a particular region. Governments must know both where and when a conflict will break out and whether outside troops will excite or calm passions. The Rwanda genocide caught governments in the West by surprise (and also surprised the UN, NGOs, and the media), thus making a preemptive deployment impossible. Indeed, the impetus for a humanitarian intervention often only exists after the suffering begins. CNN pictures of healthy Africans who are about to become starving refugees hardly make compelling footage.

Prophylaxis also requires the consent of the parties in question, which is often difficult when no violence has occurred. Government cooperation is difficult to obtain, because the existing government is often a party to the conflict and is likely to resist any perceived encroachment on its sovereignty. In Albania, for example, the government rejected outside intervention in 1997, when chaos threatened to engulf the country. For consent to occur, the government in question must fear conflict and be militarily weak, or else it would seek to end the violence itself.

For prophylaxis to succeed, the immediate source of the violence must be related to the security dilemma rather than to other causes of ethnic violence, such as status concerns. The solution—deploying outside forces—does not foster a common identity, promote good government, or otherwise address non-security sources of ethnic conflict. It affects only the immediate fears of violence, preventing the security dilemma from spiraling out of control. The U.S. deployment to Lebanon, for example, calmed an excitable situation and restored order to Lebanon before the violence became widespread.[47] Unfortunately, the calm did not last.

A prophylactic intervention also depends heavily on successful diplomacy. The 1958 intervention in Lebanon smoothly replaced the Camille Chamoun government with that of Fuad Chehab, who commanded far more support from other Lebanese communal groups and was willing to work with potential insurgents. Without an agreement that satisfies all parties, potential belligerents can simply use the interlude of talks to prepare for war.

Prophylaxis has the potential to reduce or preclude fighting, saving lives and preventing the general carnage that accompanies war. A prophylactic intervention can preempt many of the bitter legacies of communal conflict, particularly hardened identities. Demagogues will find it harder to stir up fears if communities believe that outsiders will protect their security. In this way, prophylaxis can make a lasting political settlement and nation-building far easier to accomplish, assuming it does not have the perverse effect of decreasing the incentive of local parties to reach a compromise by shielding them from the ravages of war.

Prophylactic intervention is easier than other forms of action, because the antagonists have not completely mobilized for war. The UN mission in Macedonia involved only a few hundred troops, requiring relatively little support. Similarly, the United States deployed roughly 14,000 troops quickly to Lebanon and withdrew them shortly thereafter.

A prophylactic approach, like other intervention missions, has several drawbacks. Sending troops to a country is difficult to justify, both at home and internationally. When little blood has been shed, other demands, both economic and military, will inevitably seem more important than preventing a war that might never occur. A prophylactic approach often has no clear end date, which may make it difficult for U.S. and other outside forces to withdraw. For prophylaxis to end, the government or another party must be able to replace the intervening power. The Lebanese government never grew strong after the 1958 U.S. intervention, and thus could not prevent the collapse into civil war that occurred in 1975. Only when the government is fully capable can UN forces or other peacekeepers withdraw without fear of violence breaking out.

The six mission types examined here are ideal types, not exclusive options. Some missions should be combined: transfer often requires balancing, and balance may create de facto states that would benefit from a transfer policy. Distinctions between other missions are blurry. Where balancing ends and pick a winner begins is often difficult to discern. It is useful for purposes of planning and analysis, however, to assess these missions as ideal types, while recognizing that reality is often far more complex.

Political Feasibility and Intervention

Although the purpose of this book is to explore how best to intervene, leaving the question of feasibility to others, it is important to note that not all strategies will garner the same degree of domestic political and diplomatic support. Humanitarian intervention in general attracts at best limited domestic support.[48] Casualty sensitivity is high, and policymakers seek to avoid any lengthy embroilment in a conflict that has little to do with the national interest. Not surprisingly, it is difficult to gather political support for more muscular types of intervention that require large numbers of military forces, such as "pick a winner" and "transfer." Ironically, it is also difficult to muster the political will for prophylactic missions even though it requires relatively few resources. For many interventions, the will to intervene comes from the existence of mass suffering. Intervening before suffering occurs, while sensible (if difficult), is thus politically impossible.[49]

How humanitarian operations are sold to the public also affects the feasibility of different types of missions. Humans, not nature, cause many crises. When portraying intervention publicly, however, policymakers stress the damage done by famine and flood, not by warlords and despots. Even though addressing the human roots of conflict often requires fighting, violence appears at odds with the public rationalization of these operations. Explaining that killing warlords and defeating their militias is often necessary to feed people is difficult and at odds with the peaceful image that policymakers like to convey about the mission in general. Killing, after all, is not the acme of humanitarianism. Even though they are less effective at getting at the roots of a conflict, commissary, and to a lesser extent quarantine, operations are often chosen as a result because these operations involve little force. On the other hand, balance and transfer operations—although feasible and, in the case of balance, involving limited risks for intervening force—are difficult to rationalize politically.

The Role of Non-governmental Actors

This book has focused on the role of governments, both inside and outside a country, in preserving peace. But governments are hardly the only actors in today's world. International organizations, religious institutions, human rights groups, and other organizations whose activities cross borders can greatly affect communal conflict. Although scholars' pens are seldom mightier than combatants' swords, their scribbling also shapes communal dynamics. The role of these actors, while usually less important than that of nation-states, also affects efforts to keep the peace.

Aid organizations, like outside governments, must rethink their approach to intervention. Intervention is not neutral. It often strengthens groups vis-à-vis their rivals or the central government, and it invariably changes communal dynamics. Even the most basic and humane forms of assistance, such as succoring refugees and providing food to starving children, changes the balance of power within a country. When aid organizations and other important actors pretend that their intervention is neutral, they are more likely to blunder, perhaps worsening the conflict.

Efforts by international organizations and scholars to preserve language, chronicle cultures, and otherwise study, preserve, and strengthen communal identities often have a tremendous influence on successful assimilation and nation-building.[50] Preserving the culture of peoples whose language and traditions are dying is a laudable attempt to promote cultural diversity, but its impact on nation-building should not be ignored. At times, we are faced with the choice of communal peace through assimilation and communal tension (or even war) through continued diversity. This sentiment, of course, can easily be taken too far. When the dominant culture or identity is hegemonic, it often will both denigrate rival cultures and set limits to assimilation. In such circumstances, individuals of subordinate groups face the ugly choice of hiding their cultures with no reward for that sacrifice. Again, this is not to say that we should refrain from preserving cultures, but rather that we should recognize that such efforts have a broader impact.

As noted above, resettling refugees and disarming combatants are often particularly dangerous ideas if implemented without recognizing their impact on security. Resettlement, often strongly supported by the United Nations High Commissioner on Refugees, can irritate newly healed wounds and rekindle communal fears of other groups. Apparently, mediators have forgotten that these refugees fled communal rivals who were bent on rape and murder—not a flood, fire, or other natural disaster. When refugees return to their homes, they are not greeted with open arms: the men who threatened them in the past still live there. At best, relations will be as strained as they were before fighting broke out. More commonly, the returning refugees are greeted with hatred and suspicion by the new inhabitants of their former homes and will be the next victims if international forces relax their vigilance. While helping people return to their homes seems just, such a policy in reality represents the height of cynicism if the returnees' security is overlooked or cannot be ensured in the future. Similarly, relief agencies must recognize that disarming combatants can exacerbate rather than calm security fears.

NGOs, international organizations, and scholars all must recognize their responsibilities.[51] Calls for human rights, preserving cultural diversity, and other interventions are not simple goods. If they are not backed up with resources, and often by force, they may simply aggravate tensions, harming the very people who need their help the most.

A Delicate Balance

As this discussion of potential military missions suggests, outside intervention can help alleviate suffering in a civil war, bring about a cease-fire, and even foster a lasting peace. Outside intervention, however, must be carried out with great care or else it may backfire. Most important, outside intervention can interfere with many of the strategies that governments use to foster peace. As noted in other chapters, outside powers can make control less effective, prevent identity manipulation, undermine consociational democracy, and otherwise throw a wrench into a government's good work. When intervening, outside powers must make sure that they are not interfering with another, perhaps more effective, means of keeping the peace.

Another problem is that outside intervention often leads to a spiral of violence. One group, usually the weaker one, may call on outsiders for assistance. Such assistance, in turn, alarms the government and leads it to avoid compromise. The government then mobilizes its supporters (and perhaps calls for outside support of its own), making the conflict bloodier. Outside intervention to protect or to aid a minority can lead to the perception that it is even more of an enemy. Foreign attention often creates doubt about a communal group's loyalty, thus increasing resentment and discrimination.

When weighing intervention, the question of political feasibility remains paramount. In every conflict, one or two alternative strategies will be more likely to succeed than the rest. Yet the strategy that appears most probable for bringing a stable peace might be objectionable for other reasons. Getting allies on board will often be difficult, particularly with the more aggressive strategies. Some of the suggested strategies could be costly to carry out. When soldiers are deployed, some may die. No matter what, money will be spent and political capital will be expended. The higher the potential cost of the mission, the stronger the leadership that is needed.

Outside involvement also brings with it a heavy moral burden. Intervening powers disregard the sovereignty of the government in question, recognizing that continued war can justify interference, particularly when the regime in question is exacerbating the problem. Intervention, however, is both difficult and costly, and its impact is often limited. Outside powers may find themselves in the morally troubling position of becoming involved a conflict without actually helping end it. If the conditions for successful intervention are not present, leaders must instead discourage intervention. As we have discovered in the past, half-measures are often the worst measures of all.

9 Dilemmas and Choices

Creating a lasting peace is difficult under the most propitious conditions and impossible when fate and circumstances conspire to keep a conflict going. As this book makes clear, however, keeping the peace after a bitter ethnic conflict is not impossible. Arabs and Berbers in Morocco, Israeli Arabs and Jews, Bahraini Shi'a and Sunnis, the Persians and Bakhtiyaris of Iran, and other Middle Eastern groups live side by side with their former (or current) communal rivals, yet conflict has not recurred in these countries on a large scale. Although the memory of conflict left a legacy of fear and suspicion, over time the groups embraced peace, if not always each other.

This concluding chapter compares the various options for keeping the peace. How can analysts and policymakers determine which policy is best? What are the trade-offs and dilemmas inherent in keeping the peace in highly divided societies? While hardly offering a definitive answer to these questions, this chapter outlines ways to think about these issues.

Choosing among the Strategies

Under the right circumstances, all the strategies discussed in this book can help keep the peace. The true question is not which of these strategies is best, but under what circumstances each strategy has the strongest chance of succeeding. Selecting the best strategy requires discerning the cause of the conflict. Each cause discussed in Chapter 2 poses its own challenges and demands a different set of solutions. Increasing a university admissions quota might help satisfy a group's status concerns, for example, but this would do little to reassure a group that feared for its security. Similarly, hegemonic ambitions and elite competition demand their own set of solutions. Each of the four causes, and the appropriate remedies, are discussed below.

Because the potential for a security dilemma is always high after a communal conflict, governments seeking to prevent conflict from recurring must quickly (and seriously) address the issue of security. The immediacy of the past conflict makes all groups fearful of their neighbors and suspicious of compromises that require them to relax their guard. Governments must take this fear into account and impose a degree of control. Control is not the only strategy that reduces the security dilemma. Co-optation decreases a group's ability to mobilize by shifting the allegiance of the group's leadership from the community to the government. Identity manipulation and participation strategies over time can encourage trust and give groups and individuals means to influence politics. In contrast to co-optation and control, however, these measures take years if not generations to affect group attitudes, making them less useful for solving security fears in the immediate aftermath of a conflict.

In addition to decreasing the potential for a security dilemma, control is often necessary to satisfy or subdue hegemonic groups. However, finding the right balance between reassurance and repression is difficult. It is not enough to reassure hegemonic groups of their security: governments must either repress the non-dominant groups to such a degree that the majority achieves its hegemonic goals or use its power to deter the hegemonic group from seeking to dominate the state and society. Either alternative is difficult. In Iraq, the Ba'ath regime's attempt to enforce Sunni Arab hegemony provoked repeated Kurdish revolts that spiraled into truly massive violence; in Syria, Asad failed to stop Sunni militants from opposing his regime despite his demonstrated willingness to torture, jail, and kill.

Compromise measures and hegemony are anathema. Co-optation, which entails granting rival groups at least nominal positions, often fails because the hegemonic group will not share power even in a token way. Power-sharing is particularly difficult to institutionalize, since the hegemonic group will seek a skewed distribution of power while rival groups will resist being given less representation than their numbers warrant. Basic elements and premises of human rights and democracy—that all individuals are equal under the law and have the same voice in the political system—are undermined when trying to structure an electoral system that satisfies hegemonic groups. Fair solutions, whether measured in terms of proportionality, set-asides for minorities, symbolic gestures of respect for all cultures, or other efforts to guarantee a place for everyone, are derided by the hegemonic group. Unfair solutions that placate hegemonic groups, in contrast, raise status concerns for their rivals. This circle cannot be squared. When one group demands that its members and institutions dominate, other groups must accept a subordinate status or else conflict is likely. This delicate situation becomes impossible when more than one group is hegemonic. In situations such as Palestine on the eve of the British withdrawal an acceptable compromise is impossible.

The task of preventing hegemonic groups from triggering a conflict is not always hopeless. Hegemonic groups can become more inclusive over time. In Israel, the military government's high degree of control reassured the Israeli Jews that they controlled the state and, over several decades, this level of control declined considerably and true democracy that embraced Israeli Arabs even took root. Today, Israeli Jews have relented in their determinedly hostile attitudes toward their Arab neighbors, and are now willing to permit them a greater voice in decision-making. We must remember, however, that this gentling process, when it occurs, can take generations.

Status-motivated conflicts demand a different set of solutions. Co-optation, identity manipulation, and power-sharing are powerful strategies for meeting groups' status goals. Co-optation can convince groups, and particularly their leaders, that they are represented. Berbers who are members of the Throne Council in Morocco or Bahraini Shi'a who are part of an enlarged National Assembly do not necessarily have influence commensurate with their nominal position. Nevertheless, their very presence among the country's elite suggests that the regimes in question respect their communities. Identity manipulation strategies appeal to individuals, offering them greater status if they assimilate or embrace a new national identity. Thus, Bakhtiyaris in Iran can, in essence, become Persians and achieve a high rank in society. Power-sharing offers perhaps the best way to assure groups of their status. Israeli Arabs became supportive of the Israeli system and opposed to violence as the political system provided them with a true voice in the selection of the political elite and helped them gain access to a greater share of resources.

Control policies, useful in solving the security dilemma and preventing hegemonic conflict, are of little use and can even backfire when groups fear for their status. The heavy hand of the state convinced Iraqi Kurds and Israeli Arabs (during the period of the military government) that they did not have a true place in their state, making them more likely to support radical causes. When control measures inhibit free organization and suppress a group's ability to express itself peacefully—measures that are often necessary to mollify security concerns—the use of control will raise status concerns, thus negating its usefulness.

When elite competition threatens to provoke conflict, several strategies are helpful. Co-optation can win elite goodwill, even when the elites' newfound conciliatory rhetoric does not reflect the sentiment of their followers. Control policies work in an opposite, but complementary manner by threatening leaders with imprisonment, censorship, or worse if they do not refrain from stirring up communal passions. Divide-and-rule efforts can also hinder elite efforts to foment conflict, since the divisions strengthen a rival set of elites, who often prefer to work with the government rather than risk losing their positions by cooperating with potential rivals.

Power-sharing offers perhaps the best solution, since it gives elites an opportunity to realize their ambitions peacefully. Less influential elites may still preach war, but if a community can gain status and influence through peaceful politics it is more likely to choose leaders who will support such a system. Most important, leaders become wedded to a system that gives them positions among the country's elites and will resist efforts to topple it. When Lebanon's system was at its peak, elites worked together to preserve the system, often ignoring the immediate wishes of their community to do so.

Yet power-sharing is also a poor solution to elite competition if it is not properly implemented. When institutions are weak and tensions are high, elites will exploit democratic freedoms to rabble rouse and stir up hatred. If security is lacking, extremist rhetoric can excite latent fears, and small bands of thugs can spark much larger conflicts. At best, communal cooperation will be limited; at worst, power-sharing will foster civil war.

Trying to change a community's identity spawns conflict as ethnic elites will lose power and thus become likely to incite violence. Attempts by the Ba'ath in Iraq and by the Istiqlal government in Morocco to promote a new identity that disempowered local elites led to immediate revolts. In short, elites can be wooed or cowed, but threatening to displace them is a recipe for disaster.

Policymakers and scholars must not forget that the composition of elites is subject to change. Elites can always be replaced, whether by newly emerging leaders, by rival traditional ones, or both. Thus, governments must constantly anticipate the emergence of new elites. As the Israeli Arabs became more educated and their traditional patterns of life decayed, newly educated nationalists and other emerging elites assumed more influence, making the co-optation of traditional leaders less effective. Similarly, in Lebanon the co-opted Shi'a families that ruled their community for decades gradually lost influence to new leaders who appealed to the migrants and modernizing elements of the community. New elites are not the only danger. If the government co-opts elites too effectively, the chosen elites will simply lose influence, being seen as little more than puppets of the government.

The above review indicates that no single strategy is sufficient to keep the peace. Only the optimal combination of multiple strategies has a chance of succeeding. A variety of strategies should be used in combination or at different points in time to maximize the possibility of preserving peace.

Several obvious combinations suggest themselves. Co-optation goes well with almost all the strategies addressed in this book: it takes the bitter edge out of control, helps satisfy political leaders with their place in a hegemonic democracy, and otherwise mollifies elites. Control and identity manipulation also work well together. Identity manipulation efforts involve rewards for assimilating or otherwise accepting a new identity; control reinforces these efforts by punishing, or at least limiting, expressions of a traditional identity and raising the costs of refusing assimilation. Thus, Bakhtiyaris who assimilated could ascend to a high social status, while those who clung to their traditional identity faced discrimination and were not able to organize as a collective group for political purposes. The choice for many Bakhtiyaris was painful but obvious.

Some strategies must be implemented in the proper sequence. Identity manipulation, for example, requires the exercise of control for many years to be effective. Because elites will resist attempts to reduce their group's cohesion and importance, they must often be coerced into cooperation, or at least deterred from supporting violence. Co-optation, too, helps smooth the path for identity manipulation, reducing elite fears or at least satisfying them with an array of inducements. Democratization is more likely to succeed when control and co-optation have already kept the peace for a significant time period. Cooperation and trust, necessary for the success of any democracy, are more likely to take hold when groups are no longer frightened of one another and when elites recognize that inciting violence will lead to punishment. As democratization becomes institutionalized or a new identity takes hold, the need for control and cooptation declines.

Of course, some strategies are incompatible and not meant to be employed simultaneously. The structure of consociational democracy and the requirements of effective control are often at odds. Consociational democracy promotes strong groups and reassures them by keeping the government weak. When control is applied under such circumstances, it is likely to fail. Identity manipulation also does not work well with consociational systems. The consociational structure strengthens and rewards particularist identities, reducing incentives to change individual identities. Even before the civil war, there was no reward for being Lebanese, while membership in a community promised security and at least a modicum of social status. Partition, of course, entails the recognition that other strategies, even in combination, will not keep the peace.

The Unfortunate Necessity of Control

Fostering strong governments that can initiate effective control measures is a vital step toward preserving ethnic peace and preventing conflict from recurring. Effective control proved itself invaluable in such strife-torn countries as Morocco and Israel, preventing bitter security fears from becoming realities. If control can help such groups remain at peace, it may also end the nightmare of recurring communal conflicts in other lands.

The international community, however, shies away from promoting effective control, preferring to concentrate its energies on more benign aspects of ethnic harmony, such as building civil society or encouraging elections. When the government in question cannot implement control, however, other forms of communal cooperation break down. The price of these failures is readily apparent. Cease-fires in conflicts often do not last.[1] Civic organizations that might otherwise bring communities together become power bases of ethnic chauvinists. Because of a lack of control, democratization often founders during the transition.[2] Minority mistrust, dominant group resentment, and the elite exploitation of freedoms all contribute to ethnic tension and, frequently, to ethnic conflict. However unpleasant it is to admit, benign measures often depend on coercive ones to succeed. This picture is not completely bleak, however. Over time, as security fears diminish, ethnic cooperation can increase.

Understanding the Context

Recognizing the underlying causes of a conflict and how to combine strategies is necessary for peace, but by itself this knowledge is not enough. We must also understand the context of the conflict in order to determine which strategy is best and when to employ it. Several variables are particularly important, including the impact of the strategy on fundamental versus precipitating causes of conflict, the time needed for the strategy to work, the strength of a government, the level of past conflict, the type of social change, and the neighborhood of a state.

The experience of the various Middle East states suggests that some strategies to keep the peace affect fundamental causes of conflict, while others influence proximate factors. Some strategies try to solve the core problem itself, be it security, status, hegemony, or elite goals. For example, by offering groups a voice in politics, power-sharing eliminates or reduces a group's status concerns, a fundamental cause of ethnic conflict. Solutions also work at a more immediate and superficial level as well. Control and co-optation inhibit ethnic organization and mobilization, making conflict less deadly and less prevalent, even when fundamental sources of conflict remain. Like medicines that treat symptoms rather than the disease, strategies that inhibit mobilization do not solve any fundamental grievances. They may, however, ameliorate the most troubling characteristics of communal rivalry that most often lead to violence. We should not dismiss these apparently superficial effects. At times, kicking the can down the road can provide a breathing space. As time begins to heal wounds, strategies such as power-sharing and identity change that address fundamental causes can begin to take effect.

Strategies also differ in the time required for their impact to be felt. Control, for example, can calm a group's security fears and deter radicals once its power is felt—a process that can be quick if the force demonstrated is impressive enough. The impact of some strategies becomes stronger over time. Successful power-sharing instills trust, which increases the likelihood that power-sharing will succeed in the future. Similarly, successful control reduces security fears, not only making further efforts at control easier, but ultimately requiring a lower level of control.

Some strategies, however, are of little use during the initial years of the peace while others become less effective over time. When the security dilemma is intense, democratization becomes difficult to carry out. Groups fear for their security, and their leaders often play on these fears rather than trying to minimize them. As a result, democratization should not be attempted in the immediate aftermath of a civil war unless an outside power is willing to provide security. Partition poses similar problems for the transition period. Giving each group involved in violence its own state may mitigate the causes of conflict in the long term; however, the actual transfer of populations, demarcation and defense of boundaries, and other troublesome issues must be managed immediately or else tremendous violence will result. Co-optation, in contrast, can become weaker over time. New elites emerge, and co-opted elites can lose touch with the community at large.

The effectiveness of identity manipulation also varies greatly with time. Because the measures threaten the status of groups in general and the position of elites in particular, the initial response to attempts at assimilation and nation-building is usually hostile. Thus, identity actually becomes stronger. Kurds became more "Kurdish" in response to Arabization efforts in Iraq. However, over time, if assimilation occurs, it can foster peace among individuals. The group as a whole may remain hostile to the dominant group or the state, but many of its members define themselves in new ways, which makes conflict less likely.

The strength of the state is another key variable. To implement control policies, a strong state is necessary—particularly in the immediate aftermath of a conflict when communal fear is prevalent. Other strategies, such as democratization and identity change, also benefit initially from a state that is strong enough to implement a difficult transition to a new constitution or national identity. Co-optation is a strategy available to almost all governments and is often more effective in poorer societies, where the relative advantages of ties to the government often make a tremendous difference in people's daily lives.

The previous degree of bloodletting also affects whether strategies succeed or fail. All conflict is not alike. When many are killed, and when the memories of bloodshed are well-preserved, transcending past conflict becomes more difficult. Groups like the Bakhtiyaris and the Berbers, for example, did not suffer tremendous bloodshed at the hands of their communal rivals, and, in any event, memories of conflict were not determinedly preserved by cultural elites. As a result, accepting the protection of a government controlled by former rivals is acceptable, and assimilating may even be considered. This experience stands in contrast today to such groups as the Armenians, Tutsis, Kurds, and Jews, which have experienced exceptionally bloody periods in their histories, searing their distinct identity into the groups' political consciousnesses and making them less likely to accept new identities.

Social change can alter the effectiveness of various policies over time. As education and modernization spread, policies that affect group status concerns become more important. On the other hand, migration and modernization may break up communal concentrations and foster assimilation, both of which make it harder for groups to take up arms. Various peacemaking strategies themselves often foster changes that, in turn, affect the success of the policy. Control fosters tremendous social changes in traditional societies, decreasing the importance of organizations such as the tribe, which is no longer necessary for personal security. Increased individual security, in turn, makes migration more likely, allows nomadic or transhumant groups to settle and become farmers, and otherwise changes the ethos of warrior tribes. These changes may lead to new sources of conflict—individuals in towns might become caught up in political movements appealing to them as poor workers, for example—but they also make communal security concerns less of an issue over time.

The neighborhood of the state in question also greatly affects efforts to keep the peace. As noted in Chapter 2, outside powers also can exacerbate the security dilemma, heighten status concerns, shelter bellicose elites, or otherwise foster conflict. When outside powers meddle, preserving a consociational democracy or other delicate means of keeping the peace becomes far more difficult. Lebanon's sorry history suggests how the presence of outside powers can cause even a carefully calibrated power-sharing system to quickly collapse into brutal civil war. Although consociational democracy is perhaps the strategy most vulnerable to outside meddling, all the other solutions discussed in this book can also be foiled or hindered by outside opposition.

The Israeli experience offers perhaps the best example of a government that effectively countered outside pressure. Israel faced neighbors that sponsored guerrillas, conducted terrorist attacks, and even warred on the new state, to say nothing of more mundane interference such as promoting Arab culture and harboring anti-Israeli Arab leaders. Through strong control and co-optation measures, the Israeli state successfully prevented Israeli Arabs from mobilizing while simultaneously reassuring Israeli Jews that their Arab neighbors would not prove to be a fifth column. Even in this instance, however, outside hostility delayed true democratization and has otherwise kept communal tension high.

Trade-offs

Even when they save thousands of lives, strategies to keep the peace can take a toll in human rights, cultural diversity, and equality. No strategy is perfect, and even the best often suffer from severe problems.

Control is the most problematic strategy. In all the instances examined in this book, the level of control used to prevent violence exceeded the level that would be acceptable in most Western democracies. Israel, Morocco, Bahrain, and other ethnic relations successes used a considerable degree of force: governments in these countries suppressed ethnic organization, arrested activists, and otherwise interfered with activities that are part and parcel of a democratic society. At times, the level of force went beyond even this high level. The Bahraini government jailed and exiled activists, and opposition groups claimed that torture was widespread. Those seeking to keep the peace often must choose between two evils: a repressive government or continued communal violence. To pretend that violent activists will be deterred by more gentle means is as foolish as it is dangerous. The price of stability is often repression. But peace, while the focus of this book, is not the only virtue. Any acceptable long-term solution to ethnic conflict must not come at the price of brutalization and regular human rights violations.

Strategies that emphasize nation-building and assimilation into a common identity also demand a price in cultural diversity. The nation-building done by Iran, Morocco, and other states has both contributed to the destruction of tribal and national identities and, to varying degrees, fostered peace. As assimilation occurs, however, there will be fewer languages and fewer distinct cultures. The human mosaic will become less colorful as a result.

Another dilemma involves the tension between individual equity and the ethnic group rights. Even limited measures to promote communal equity, such as education quotas for race in the United States, are a highly contentious issue, and no one advocates hiring, promoting, or simply bribing leaders of various U.S. communities to keep them loyal to the existing order. Consociational democracy and co-optation, however, involve just such actions—communal equity demands limits to a merit-based system. Needless to say, these efforts to satisfy communities often anger individuals of rival groups who believe they are more qualified for leadership positions.

A related trade-off involves balancing the tensions raised by social and demographic change and the difficulties in maintaining a stable democracy. Power-sharing often requires quotas that allot each group a specified share of power and resources. In Lebanon, for example, the 1943 National Pact carefully divided power among Lebanon's many ethnic and religious groups. However, Lebanon's changing demographics and the gradual politicization of the Shi'a community made the compromise untenable. The dominant Maronite Christian community, which had the most to lose from any reallocation of power, resisted change, laying the foundation for the ensuing civil war. Such dilemmas are not easily solved. Guarantees of a group's share of power and status work best when they are concrete, but the price of this surety is an inability to accommodate change.

Measures to foster peace also can inhibit economic efficiency. Co-optation and control, for example, are both more effective when the government dominates the economy. In such circumstances, governments have more resources to gain elite goodwill, and groups have fewer resources with which to engage in violence. A high degree of government control over the economy, however, may contribute to stagnation, high unemployment, and other economic ills that are themselves a source of unrest. Moreover, co-opted elites often make poor administrators: their membership in an ethnic group and their support for the government usually count for far more than their administrative skills.[3]

Many scholars have argued that a strong civil society—formal and informal associations of citizens that include unions, religious groups, clubs, and other organizations that are distinct from the state—helps democracy succeed, fosters economic development, and promotes stability.

Civil society supposedly leads individuals to learn the habits of cooperation and public-spiritedness and provides a network to carry out related tasks.[4]

This book suggests, however, that civil society is not an unalloyed good. In the Middle East, civil society often is weak, including in countries where there is ethnic harmony. Moreover, the institutions that do exist often do little to help citizens learn public-spiritedness or cooperation.[5] Control and co-optation are more difficult when civil society is strong. Informal institutions that individuals employ to strengthen their communities also enable the group to organize more effectively when they seek to use violence. Not surprisingly, almost every government in the Middle East that has prevented conflict from recurring has made a strong effort to suborn civil society by making it dependent on the state. Weakening civil institutions makes society in general poorer, but it can help prevent violence.

Even development is often a mixed blessing for keeping the peace. Social and economic development raise standards of living and life expectancy, in addition to providing a host of personal benefits and intellectual enrichment. However, education and modernization can foster new elites, make groups dissatisfied with their subordinate status, or otherwise upset the communal balance.

These problems with civil society and development, by themselves, do not justify opposing autonomous organizations or stunting growth. But the doctrinaire and cavalier manner in which the West advocates such destabilizing blessings should change. Even the most beneficial changes can produce unanticipated consequences. We must recognize that ostensibly nonpolitical activities such as economic development and social organization can have tremendous political consequences.

Finally, this book focuses on ethnic peace, but often peace is not the most desirable outcome for a country or for a people. Submitting to repression, having your culture destroyed, or other measures can, at times, foster peace among communal groups. Yet the price is high, and it is often more than individuals, groups, or societies should pay. The price of peace should not be eternal repression or discrimination. In the first chapter the definition of "ethnic conflict" focused on violence—this emphasis, however, should not blind us to other injustices. Weighing such trade-offs is beyond the scope of this book, but they remain vital to a comprehensive evaluation of the solutions for understanding how to best foster ethnic harmony in the long term.

Final Words

Crafting peace is difficult. It requires understanding both the causes of conflict and how, and when, it can be ended for good. Unfortunately, the causes of conflict are myriad and run deep, while solutions often have only a limited impact and carry their own sets of trade-offs. If scholars, international organizations, and others are to help statesmen in the difficult task of putting an ethnic war to rest, we must begin the process of accumulating knowledge about a complex and often confusing subject. This book is dedicated to that effort.

NOTES

Preface

1. Readers familiar with the Middle East, and with Middle Eastern languages, will note that my renderings of common names and places are often not exact. In general, I have followed several principles: First, if a name, place, or term has a conventional and widely used spelling in English, I continue to employ it even though it may have a more accurate Arabic, Hebrew, or Persian rendering. For less familiar place names, where no English equivalent is commonly used, I try to follow the U.S. government transliteration. If this is not available, I rely on that of area experts who write in English. Second, for place names that vary in time, whenever possible I follow the term used at the time in question. Thus, when discussing Israel I refer to it as "the area in what was to become Palestine" when discussing the Ottoman empire; as "the Palestine Mandate area" when discussing the 1917–48 period; and as "Israel" when discussing the post-1948 era. Third, whenever an author writes in English I use his or her preferred spelling of the name. This results in anomalies (Mohammed, for example, has several different spellings), but I prefer these differences in order to preserve the citation intact and respect the preferences of the author.

Chapter 1. Ethnic Conflict in Today's World

1. Many new conflicts began with the breakup of the Soviet Union and Yugoslavia at the beginning of the decade. By the middle of the decade, the incidence of conflict had peaked, and it declined toward the decade's end. See Gurr, "Ethnic Conflict on the Wane."

2. Kaufmann, "Possible and Impossible Solutions to Ethnic Civil Wars," and Walter, "Introduction." T. David Mason and Patrick J. Fett, however, argue that ethnic civil wars are no more difficult to end than other types of civil wars. See "How Civil Wars End."

3. A devastating critique of the Western mediation effort before the genocide can be found in Kuperman, "The Other Lesson of Rwanda."

4. For an account of the international aid fiasco that helped the perpetrators of genocide, see Gourevitch, *We Wish to Inform You that Tomorrow We Will Be Killed with All Our Families,* 155–205.

5. This definition is loosely based on that of Max Weber, who defines ethnic groups as "human groups that entertain a subjective belief in their common descent because of similarities of physical type or of customs or both, or because of memories of colonization and migration . . . it does not matter whether or not an objective blood relationship exists." Weber, *Economy and Society,* 389. Weber astutely notes that ethnic membership does not constitute a group in any politically meaningful way; membership only facilitates group formation.

6. What the particular manifestations of conflict are also varies widely. Pogroms, riots, rebellions, terrorism, insurgencies, and civil wars all fall into the category of violence—although the causes of these varied phenomena often differ markedly. Brubaker and Laitin, "Ethnic and Nationalist Violence," 423–52, especially 428.

7. I am also deliberately excluding "structural violence," such as discrimination and poverty, that often result from ethnic rivalries and divisions. See Galtung, "Violence, Peace, and Peace Research." Such problems are clearly deserving of attention, but their inclusion would shift the emphasis of this work from violence, which is my focus.

8. Wippman, "Introduction." For an example of a work that tries to justify secession as part of a broader philosophical framework, see Beran, "A Liberal Theory of Secession."

9. Etzioni, "The Evils of Self-Determination," 34.

10. Teson, "Ethnicity, Human Rights, and Self-Determination," 87.

11. Ergil, "The Kurdish Question in Turkey," 123.

12. For a discussion, see Orentlicher, "Citizenship and National Identity."

13. Beran, "A Liberal Theory," 22–27.

14. See Van Evera, *Guide to Methods for Students of Political Science,* for more on the merits of single case studies and their limits. Lijphart, "Comparative Politics and the Comparative Method," 691. For additional works on the case study method, see George and McKeown, "Case Studies and Theories of Organizational Decision Making," 21–58, and Eckstein, "Case Study and Theory in Political Science."

15. This volume seeks to compare a wide range of solutions and, given the relative paucity of work on this subject, is taking the initial steps of organizing the

debate and fleshing out the solutions. More cases focused on only one solution would provide us greater knowledge of that particular solution, and I hope that these more narrow questions will be explored in future scholarship.

16. Sammy Smooha and Theodor Hanf define a deeply divided society as one where "the constituent ethnic or racial groups are different in culture, separate in institutions, unequal in power and privilege, or disagreeing on fundamental issues. The potentiality for conflict among them is high and eruptions of disputes and violence are quite common, especially following shifts in power relations and rises in levels of relative deprivation." See "The Diverse Modes of Conflict-Regulation in Deeply Divided Societies," 26.

Chapter 2. Causes of Ethnic Conflict

1. Barry Posen's arguments flesh out the security dilemma approach to ethnic conflict. "The Security Dilemma and Ethnic Conflict." See also Lake and Rothchild, "Containing Fear," Rose, "The Security Dilemma and Ethnic Conflict," and Fearon, "Rationalist Explanations for War." These works draw on, but do not follow exactly, the security dilemma concept as defined by Jervis in "Cooperation under the Security Dilemma." See also Snyder, "Perceptions of the Security Dilemma in 1914." Donald Horowitz also notes that "unranked ethnic systems resemble the international system," but does not develop this analogy directly. *Ethnic Groups in Conflict,* 187. He does, however, develop the importance of ethnic domination and suppression as a motivating force for groups to seek power.

My description below draws on Posen and other international relations scholars who have explored the security dilemma. However, as it applies this dilemma to ethnic conflict—a quite different phenomenon from the competition among states in an anarchic environment—the description provided below often varies considerably from the classic international relations concept.

2. Walter, "Introduction," 4.

3. Drawing this distinction is Kaufman, "An 'International' Theory of Inter-Ethnic War."

4. Kaufman, "An 'International' Theory of Inter-Ethnic War," 151. Posen uses the example of the former Yugoslavia in examining how scattered ethnic enclaves create a situation of high vulnerability, while the technology and operational concepts common in ethnic conflict create a situation where offense is dominant. Posen, "The Security Dilemma and Ethnic Conflict," 32.

5. Jervis, *Perception and Misperception in International Politics,* 67.

6. Van Evera, "Primed for Peace." See also Kaufman, "An 'International' Theory of Inter-Ethnic War," 155, and Snyder and Jervis, "Civil War and the Security Dilemma," 16.

7. Snyder, *From Voting to Violence,* 53–67.

8. Kaufman, "An 'International' Theory of Inter-Ethnic War," 152.

9. For a description of this phenomenon, see Kaufman and Bowers, "Transnational Dimensions of Transnistrian Conflict."

10. Brubaker and Laitin, "Ethnic and Nationalist Violence," 423–52, especially 424.

11. De Figueiredo Jr. and Weingast, "The Rationality of Fear," 263.

12. The importance of offense dominance is drawn from the work of Barry Posen. See also Van Evera, "The Cult of the Offensive and the Origins of the First World War," 58–107, and *Causes of War* for more information on this concept.

13. Laitin, *Identity in Formation,* 328.

14. Andrew Bell-Fialkoff defines ethnic cleansing as "The expulsion of an 'undesirable' population from a given territory due to religious or ethnic discrimination, political, strategic or ideological considerations, or a combination of these." Bell-Fialkoff, "A Brief History of Ethnic Cleansing," 110.

15. See Laitin, *Identity in Formation,* 34 for a discussion of this process of ensuring in-group solidarity.

16. Status should not be confused with a quest for equality. Many groups do not seek an even playing field, but rather seek one tilted in their favor. As Horowitz and Weiner note, backward groups feel weak vis-à-vis advanced groups and often deride their own groups' intelligence, initiative, or labor ethic. Thus, backward groups, particularly ones whose dominant position may be threatened, may seek "protection" against advanced groups or a guaranteed share of resources and status positions. See Horowitz, *Ethnic Groups in Conflict,* 167, and Weiner, *Sons of the Soil,* 47, 113, 167.

17. Berlin, "Two Concepts of Liberty," 156.

18. Horowitz, *Ethnic Groups in Conflict,* 176.

19. Ibid., 24–25.

20. Weiner, *Sons of the Soil,* 7.

21. Ibid., 353–54.

22. Ibid., 293.

23. Ibid., 9–10.

24. Ganguly, "Ethno-Religious Conflict in South Asia."

25. Weiner, *Sons of the Soil,* 3.

26. Horowitz, *Ethnic Groups in Conflict,* 150–54.

27. Ibid., 149–66. As Walker Connor points out, these advances also make the ethnic group member more aware of ethnic brethren formerly separated by distance. See "Nation Building or Nation Destroying?" 329.

28. Weiner, *Sons of the Soil,* 9.

29. Ibid., 285.

30. See Byman and Van Evera, "Why They Fight."

31. Solonar, "Hatred and Fear on Both Banks of the Dniester," and Crowther,

"Moldova after Independence." The Gagauzi, a Turkic-speaking, Orthodox Christian people from Bulgaria, also resisted incorporation into the new state and proclaimed their independence.

32. At the conference, German Chancellor Otto von Bismarck "continually warned the representatives of the Great Powers that their principal business was to reach a settlement among themselves and not to worry unduly about the happiness of lesser breeds without the law." Craig, *Germany,* 112. For more on the European role in the creation of borders in Africa, see Pakenham, *The Scramble for Africa.*

33. Horowitz, *Ethnic Groups in Conflict,* 148. Horowitz defines advanced groups as those groups distinguishable by being disproportionately educated, represented in the civil service, or wealthy. The term *backward* is used by Horowitz to contrast less educated or wealthy groups and is not intended as a normative judgment on their condition.

34. Ibid., 188.

35. Language is a particularly important factor in many modern nationalist movements, since it contains a culture's memories and it is a key part of economic and political success. Sagarin and Moneymaker, "Language and Nationalist, Separatist, and Secessionist Movements," 19–20.

36. For a best discussion of the role of sacred symbols and identity, see two essays by Clifford Geertz, "Religion as a Cultural System" and "Ideology as a Cultural System." For a description of the interplay among art, poetry, and national feeling, see Schama, *Landscape and Memory.*

37. For a good description of the hegemonic problem, see Brubaker, "National Minorities, Nationalizing States, and External National Homelands in the New Europe."

38. Brubaker, "Nationalizing States in the Old 'New Europe'—and the New," 410–37, especially 416.

39. Both the Rwanda and the Turkey cases illustrate the lethal nature of what Rogers Brubaker has labeled "nationalizing states"—states that are ethnically heterogeneous but are conceived by their elites as nation-states. Moreover, nationalizing states are particularly dangerous because elites see the country as in transition. They believe the country should be a nation-state that is dominated by one group but that further measures must be taken to ensure this is so. Brubaker, "National Minorities, Nationalizing States, and External National Homelands in the New Europe," 107–32, especially 114–17.

40. For this argument, see Fukuyama, "Second Thoughts," 27.

41. Berlin, "Kant as an Unfamiliar Source of Nationalism," 232.

42. For more on this source of nationalism, see Greenfeld, *Nationalism.*

43. Volkan, "Psychoanalytic Aspects of Ethnic Conflicts," 85.

44. See Arfi, "Ethnic Fear." Arfi argues that the construction of identities is a

key factor in creating ethnic fear, a precondition to conflict.

45. Berlin, "Kant as an Unfamiliar Source of Nationalism," 244, 248.

46. Geertz, "The Integrative Revolution," 259.

47. For example, Ismet Inonu, president from 1938 to 1950, was said to be a Kurd, as was Admiral Fehmi Koruturk, who also became president. McDowall, *A Modern History of the Kurds,* 405–6.

48. Kaufmann, "Possible and Impossible Solutions to Ethnic Civil Wars," 153–54.

49. O'Leary and McGarry, *The Politics of Antagonism,* 160.

50. One of the major initial works on this subject is Snyder, "Nationalism and the Crisis of the Post-Soviet State," 17–19. This concept of outbidding is taken from Kaufman, "Spiraling to Ethnic War." The to and fro of ethnic elites using outbidding to mobilize their followers is described in Rabushka and Shepsle, *Politics in Plural Societies.* Gagnon expands this concept considerably in "Ethnic Nation-alism and International Conflict," 130–66.

51. Horowitz notes that many groups are content to accept their backward status, consoling themselves that another group's success requires morally disreputable behavior. Their elites, however, often push the group to change their behavior. Thus, group members receive two different messages: early socialization that endorses a certain ethos, and criticism from their elite that rejects this ethos. Horowitz, *Ethnic Groups in Conflict,* 174–75. This contention suggests that stopping elite efforts to push change can head off status as a source of ethnic conflict.

52. Laitin, *Identity in Formation,* 22.

53. See Snyder, "The New Nationalism," and Gagnon, "Ethnic Nationalism and International Conflict," 131, 140.

54. Gagnon, "Ethnic Nationalism and International Conflict," 137.

55. There are several commonly cited hypotheses on the causes of ethnic conflict, including the belief that groups fight because of irreconcilable differences among cultures; that ethnic conflict is a function of modernization; and that economic interest is at the heart of ethnic conflict. Although other scholars have shown them to be unsatisfying or of narrow applicability, these causes may be correct in part, and indeed both the security dilemma and the status theory draw on parts of these theories. Proponents of the view that cultural differences lead to conflict include Parsons, "Racial and Religious Differences," and Smith, *The Plural Society.* For an assessment of the importance of economic factors and modernization in ethnic competition (although not necessarily conflict), see Bates, "Modernization, Ethnic Competition, and the Rationality of Politics in Contemporary Africa." Horowitz explores these theories and their faults on pages 134–35 in *Ethnic Groups in Conflict.* Walker Connor provides a detailed analysis of modernization's impact on nation-building in "Nation-Building or Nation-Destroying?"

56. Snyder, *From Voting to Violence,* 57.

57. Ibid., 50, 67; Kaufman, “An ‘International’ Theory of Inter-Ethnic War,” 158; Kaufman, “The Irresistible Force and the Imperceptible Object,” 282.

58. Mueller, “The Banality of ‘Ethnic War,’ ” 42–46.

59. Ibid., 53.

60. See Gagnon, “Ethnic Nationalism and International Conflict,” 140–64, for an account of this.

61. Hopf, “The Promise of Constructivism in International Relations Theory,” 173.

62. Organization is particularly important if groups are going to act as another state or movement’s proxy. In such cases, well-timed operations are essential if the operational or political effect of the local group’s action is to serve the particular needs of the outside group.

63. Ashkenasi, “Socio-Ethnic Conflict and Paramilitary Organization in the Near East,” 314.

64. Kaufman, “Spiraling to Ethnic War,” 129–32.

Chapter 3. Control Policies

1. The term *control* is drawn from the work of Lustick, “Stability in Deeply Divided Societies.” Lustick’s work is the foundational basis of control as a theory of conflict mitigation.

2. Making this argument is Ganguly, “Explaining the Kashmir Insurgency,” 78.

3. This description of Israeli policies and Israeli Arab attitudes relies on Lustick, *Arabs in the Jewish State;* Smooha, *Arabs and Jews in Israel;* the collection of essays in *Palestinians under Israeli Rule;* Jiryis, *The Arabs in Israel, 1948–1966;* Kimmerling and Migdal, *Palestinians;* and Ashkenasi, *Palestinian Identities and Preferences.* For more personalized views of Israeli Arab sentiment, I have drawn on three works: El-Asmar, *To Be an Arab in Israel;* Gorkin, *Days of Honey, Days of Onion;* and Shammas, “Diary.” These sources were supplemented by interviews I conducted in Israel in September 1996 and other interviews conducted in 1996 by phone or by electronic mail. One of the conditions for the interviews was a promise of anonymity.

4. These Arabs represent a large segment of Israel’s population—today Jews are roughly 82 percent of the total population. *Statistical Abstract of Israel 1993,* 3.

5. I use the term *Israeli Arab* to distinguish those Arabs living within Israel from their brethren across the Green Line in the West Bank and Gaza Strip. Such a use may be objectionable to those who espouse Palestinian solidarity regardless of national boundaries, but it is useful for analytic purposes to be able to distinguish within a community.

6. Smooha and Hofman, “Some Problems of Arab-Jewish Coexistence in Israel,” 7.

7. Israel tried to settle Jews in predominantly Arab areas to offset any threat

they might pose. This effort, the "Judaization of the Galilee" (*Yehud ha-Galil*), provoked considerable resentment.

8. Interview with Israeli Arab community leader, September 1996.

9. Kretzmer, *The Legal Status of the Arabs in Israel,* 83.

10. Kanaana, *Socio-Cultural and Psychological Adjustment of the Arab Minority in Israel,* 61–62.

11. Ben-Dor, *The Druzes in Israel,* 101.

12. Lustick, *Arabs in the Jewish State,* 133, 210.

13. Shammas, "Diary," 33.

14. Interview with Israeli academic, September 1996.

15. Jiryis, *The Arabs in Israel, 1948–1966,* 130–40; Lustick, *Arabs in the Jewish State,* 128.

16. Lustick, *Arabs in the Jewish State,* 128.

17. Ibid., 115.

18. Interview with Israeli government official, September 1996.

19. Lustick, *Arabs in the Jewish State,* 68.

20. Shammas, "Diary," 30.

21. Kanaana, *Socio-Cultural and Psychological Adjustment of the Arab Minority in Israel,* 69.

22. Jiryis, *The Arabs in Israel, 1948–1966,* 101–10.

23. This description of Iraq draws on Marr, *The Modern History of Iraq;* Batatu, *The Old Social Classes and the Revolutionary Movements of Iraq;* and Farouk-Sluglett and Sluglett, *Iraq since 1958.* Amatzia Baram provides an excellent account of elite politics in Iraq in "The Ruling Political Elite in Ba'thi Iraq, 1968–1986." For information on the Kurds, McDowall, *A Modern History of the Kurds,* is the primary source of information. A good overview of the Shi'a in Iraq can be found in Nakash, *The Shi'is of Iraq.*

24. The Ba'ath briefly took power in 1963, but soon lost it in a coup to other Arab nationalist forces. The Ba'ath regained power in a coup on July 17, 1968, and have ruled Iraq ever since. This second Ba'ath period is the focus of this section.

25. Batatu, basing his figures on Iraqi government figures, gives the following communal breakdown for 1947 Iraq: Arab Shi'as at 51.4 percent of the population; Arab Sunnis at 19.7 percent; Kurdish Sunnis at 18.4 percent; Persian Shi'as at 1.2 percent; Turkoman Sunnis and Shi'as at 1.1 and 0.9 percent, respectively; Christians at 3.1 percent; and Jews at 2.6 percent. Iraq's Christian community is quite diverse. Catholic Nestorians represented the largest community, Assyrians (Nestorians who did not unite with Rome) the second largest, with Syrian Catholics and Armenians also present. Most of Iraq's Jewish population fled in the late 1940s. Sunni Muslims occupied the religious pinnacle, followed by Shi'a Muslims, Christians, and Jews. Batatu, *The Old Social Classes and the Revolutionary Movements of Iraq,* 9–13, 40.

26. See Smooha, *Arabs and Jews in Israel: Change and Continuity in Mutual Intolerance*, 51, and Smooha, *Arabs and Jews in Israel: Conflicting and Shared Attitudes in a Divided Society*, 89.

27. Although this chapter does not discuss the impact of colonialism in the Middle East, the presence of a strong government, even a foreign one, forever changed the daily rhythms of many individuals in the Middle East. In Morocco, for example, the French imposition of control enabled individual tribesmen to leave their tribal home or to settle down to farm without fear for their lives. Thus, the strength of the tribal identity decayed as the colonial power consolidated its position.

28. Such a situation is not a security dilemma in the classic sense in that groups are operating under hegemony, not anarchy. Nevertheless, group members have no means of protection from the government and must consider using their own resources to defend themselves.

29. At times a regime may be able to co-opt significant numbers of individuals from a group, or select members of a subgroup such as a particular tribe, and use them against the group as a whole. In such circumstances, however, the security forces are hardly representative of the people in general and thus do not represent a true form of inclusion. This argument, of course, borders on the tautological.

30. Wolf, *Peasant Wars of the Twentieth Century*, 290.

31. Carnegie Commission on Preventing Deadly Conflict, *Preventing Deadly Conflict*, 16.

32. O'Neill, "Introduction," 16–17.

33. Byman, "The Logic of Ethnic Terrorism," 157–58.

34. This finding is not unique to ethnic organizations. For a broader analysis of how disrupting organization works for political movements in general, see Pye, *Guerrilla Communism in Malaya*, 189, 334, and O'Neill, "Introduction," 12–13.

35. In essence, working with moderates encourages in-group policing, as described in Fearon and Laitin, "Explaining Interethnic Cooperation."

36. For a non-ethnic example of this, see Della Porta, "Left Wing Terrorism in Italy," 126–27.

37. O'Neill, "Introduction," 20.

38. Byman, "The Logic of Ethnic Terrorism," 162; O'Neill, "Introduction," 25.

39. Shulsky, *Silent Warfare*, 148–51.

40. Ibid., 155.

Chapter 4. Co-optation

1. The best work on the use of co-optation as a form of social control remains Zonis, *The Political Elite of Iran*.

2. Richards and Waterbury, *A Political Economy of the Middle East*, 331. Further-

more, families will often place offspring in several domains—business, the clergy, the military—in order to ensure that they are protected in all eventualities.

3. For a more comprehensive review of Morocco's experience, see Byman, "Explaining Ethnic Peace in Morocco."

4. Most scholars note the perpetual division between the areas controlled by the *makhzan,* or royal court, and the areas that resisted the *makhzan* encroachment, which took its name from the Arabic word for dissidence, *siba.* The neatness of this division is a subject of considerable debate.

5. Munson, *The House of Si Abd Allah,* 61.

6. Hart, *The Aith Waryaghar of the Moroccan Rif,* 351. At times, sultans such as Mulay Sulaiman in the early nineteenth century sent out expeditions to punish and tax gather in Berber areas, but these areas never were consolidated under the sultan's control.

7. This review of co-optation in Morocco under the French is drawn from Perkins, *Qaids, Captains, and Colons;* Hoisington Jr., *Lyautey and the French Conquest of Morocco;* Hoisington, *The Casablanca Connection;* Hart, "The Tribe in Modern Morocco"; Scham, *Lyautey in Morocco;* Cohen, *Rulers of Empire;* and Bidwell, *Morocco under Colonial Rule.* Overviews of Berber society are from Gellner, *The Saints of the Atlas,* and Montagne, *The Berbers,* 131–57.

8. Violence did erupt toward the end of the colonial period, but it was political violence directed against the French occupiers, not conflict along ethnic lines, and the level of bloodshed was limited.

9. Quoted in Hoisington, *Lyautey and the French Conquest of Morocco,* 6.

10. French efforts helped offset a nationalist backlash. As a result of indirect rule, much of the resentment that might have arisen from French control efforts was transferred to the co-ethnics who enforced French laws. When force was required—such as during an early campaign to put down a pretender to the sultan's throne, Lyautey tried to use rival tribes rather than French forces. Local administrators also shared the blame for unpopular measures such as taxes or punishments.

11. David Hart notes that among the Rifian Berber group, no colonial Rifi leaders survived the transfer of power. Hart, *The Aith Waryaghar of the Moroccan Rif,* 427. See also Marais, "The Political Evolution of the Berbers in Independent Morocco," 277.

12. A program for the Rif area submitted to King Muhammad V in 1958 as the Rifian revolt was in progress included calls for local Rifian judges, Rifian representation in the central government, the development of Rif agriculture, and the creation of rural schools. These issues suggest the Berbers wanted more co-optation and resources, not autonomy from the central government as in the past. The revolt was neither a simple rebellion of a people long suppressed by colonialism nor the same sort of revolt as the ones that had plagued pre-colonial Moroccan

governments. Rather, the protests were in tune with the Berbers' desire for more co-optation and recognition of their status. Hart, "The Tribe in Modern Morocco," 46.

13. Ibid., 49.

14. For a bleak but intriguing description of this type of corruption, see Ben Jelloun, *Corruption.*

15. This account of Syria is drawn from Hopwood, *Syria 1945–1986;* Hinnebusch, "State and Civil Society in Syria"; Hinnebusch, "Class and State in Ba'athist Syria"; Drysdale, "The Syrian Political Elite, 1966–1976"; and Van Dam, *The Struggle for Power in Syria.*

16. Seale, "Asad," 103.

17. Hinnebusch, "State and Civil Society in Syria," 252.

18. Bahrain's experience falls outside the strict boundaries of this book in that it did not suffer widespread communal conflict in the past. In addition, many of the techniques used to prevent communal violence were part of a more general strategy to help the monarchy keep itself in control of Bahrain in general. Communal tension between Sunnis and Shi'a, however, has been high since the 1970s at least, making Bahrain's experience useful in illuminating how co-optation can reduce the propensity for communal violence. This narrative is drawn from Bahry, "The Opposition in Bahrain"; Gause, *Oil Monarchies;* and Fakhro, "The Uprising in Bahrain."

19. For a description of Bahrain's security services, see Cordesman, *Bahrain, Oman, Qatar, and the UAE,* 107–14.

20. The Al Khalifa, however, have tried to blame the violence exclusively on Iranian meddling. "Bahrain: Defendants' Confessions Reported," and "Bahrain: Interior Ministry on Arrest of 'Hizballah of Bahrain' Group."

21. For more on *rentier* economies and their impact on government-society relationships and civil society in the Gulf, see Crystal, *Oil and Politics in the Gulf.*

Chapter 5. Manipulating Ethnic Identities

1. Parts of this chapter appeared in Byman, "Forever Enemies?"

2. Kaufmann contends that ethnic violence hardens identities, making communal cooperation impossible. "Possible and Impossible Solutions to Ethnic Civil Wars," 136–75. Van Evera argues that past crimes make a renewal of ethnonationalist wars far more likely. "Hypotheses on Nationalism and War," 23–36.

3. For leading academic works on themes of assimilation and nation-building, see Deutsch, *Nationalism and Social Communication; Nation-Building,* ed. Deutsch and Foltz; Deutsch, *Nationalism and Its Alternatives;* Smith, *The Ethnic Origins of Nations;* Greenfeld, *Nationalism;* and *The Formation of National States in Western Europe,* ed. Tilly.

4. A range of actors can manipulate identities. Although this book focuses on government attempts to do so, neighboring states, diaspora communities, and even international organizations all can manipulate identities, or interfere with state efforts to do so.

5. Kaufmann, "Possible and Impossible Solutions to Ethnic Civil Wars," 137.

6. Divide-and-rule policies, discussed in Chapter 3, also represent a form of identity manipulation. Divide-and-rule efforts promote cleavages within an ethnic group, creating more identities that are salient in an effort to weaken the group's cohesion.

7. Barth, "Ethnic Groups and Boundaries"; Blumer and Duster, "Theories of Race and Social Action," 220; and Isaacs, *Idols of the Tribe,* 39–45.

8. Examples of this school include Greenfeld, *Nationalism,* and Weber, *Peasants into Frenchmen.*

9. Two leading perennialist scholars are Walker Connor and Anthony Smith. See, in particular, Connor, *Ethnonationalism,* and Smith, *The Ethnic Origins of Nations.* Superb empirical support for the perennialist position can be found in Ascherson, *Black Sea.*

10. Kaufmann, "Possible and Impossible Solutions to Ethnic Civil Wars," 140–46.

11. As David Laitin notes in his works on Nigeria and on the former Soviet Union, governments and ethnic elites can alter ethnic identity by providing individuals with incentives to organize along new lines. Laitin, *Identity in Formation* and "Hegemony and Religious Conflict." Laitin argues that identities are both constructed and reconstructed as opportunities change, but individual identities are built on real foundations. *Identity in Formation,* 20.

12. For a general statement of the constructivist point of view and research agenda, see Hopf, "The Promise of Constructivism in International Relations Theory."

13. Snyder, *From Voting to Violence,* 49.

14. See Gagnon, "Ethnic Nationalism and International Conflict," 131–32.

15. See Bates, "Ethnic Competition and Modernization in Contemporary Africa"; Kasfir, "Explaining Ethnic Political Participation"; and Young, *Ideology and Development in Africa.*

16. See, for example, Laitin, "What Is a Language Community?"

17. See Weber, *Peasants into Frenchmen,* for a riveting account of this transformation.

18. As quoted in Welsh, "Domestic Politics and Ethnic Conflict," 44.

19. As quoted in Gourevitch, *We Wish to Inform You that Tomorrow We Will Be Killed with All Our Families,* 240. He also notes (233) that, "In the aftermath of the genocide, the ethnic categories had become more meaningful and more charged than ever before."

20. Weber, *Peasants into Frenchmen*, 100.

21. See Horowitz, *Ethnic Groups in Conflict*, 167; and Weiner, *Sons of the Soil*, 293.

22. Weber, *Peasants into Frenchmen*, 485–96.

23. Immigration poses a particularly promising model of identity change—one that is not examined in this book.

24. For information on the Bakhtiyaris, I have relied heavily on the works of Gene Garthwaite. See in particular, *Khans and Shahs;* "Tribes, Confederation, and the State;" and "The Bakhtiyari Khans, the Government of Iran, and the British, 1846–1915." For information on Iranian politics more broadly, I have drawn on Fuller, *The "Center of the Universe";* Ghods, *Iran in the Twentieth Century;* Abrahamian, *Iran between Two Revolutions;* Akhavi, "State Formation and Consolidation in 20th Century Iran"; and Upton, *The History of Modern Iran.*

25. Iran is 51 percent Persian; 25 percent Azerbaijani; 9 percent Kurdish; 8 percent Gilaki and Mazandarani; 2 percent Lur; 1 percent Baluch; 1 percent Arab; and contains small pockets of other ethnic and tribal groups. Although 95 percent of Iran's citizens are Shi'a Muslims, Sunni Muslims comprise 4 percent of the population. Despite this demographic diversity, Persian language and culture dominate Iran's schools, and Persian Shi'a fill most leading positions in society.

26. The Pahlavi effort was built on literally thousands of years of attempts to distinguish Persian culture from others around it. Persians have long regarded themselves as a superior people: in their writings, they divided their region into Iranian and Turanian (Turkic) peoples, a division comparable to the Greek and Barbarian distinction of Periclean Athens. Neighboring Arabs are considered uncultured nomads; Turks are described as crass and boorish.

27. Abrahamian reports that the number of Bakhtiyaris in 1979, 250,000, is the same as in 1851. The figure I use—drawn from the Iran yearbook based on the 1986 Iran census—is 200,000. Abrahamian, *Iran between Two Revolutions*, 12, 25. According to his figures, in 1956 the Bakhtiyaris had 400,000 members, suggesting a precipitous decline through assimilation in the past few decades.

28. Garthwaite, *Khans and Shahs*, 97–98, 114, 121; and Garthwaite, "The Bakhtiyari Khans, the Government of Iran, and the British, 1846–1915," 30–36.

29. As quoted in Brooks, "The Enemy Within," 340.

30. The implementation of education, however, was much slower in rural and tribal areas. Menashri, *Education and the Making of Modern Iran*, 91–92, 98, 102, 110, 121, 178.

31. Ibid., 186; and Ghods, *Iran in the Twentieth Century*, 198.

32. Menashri, *Iran*, 141–42, 236.

33. McDowall, *A Modern History of the Kurds*, 231–87.

34. Garthwaite, *Khans and Shahs*, 21, notes that this is a ritualistic act for many Bakhtiyaris that reaffirms group identity but is not a way of life anymore.

35. For information on the Berbers and identity change, I have relied heavily on

the works of David Hart. See "The Tribe in Modern Morocco," *The Aith Waryaghar of the Moroccan Rif*, *Daddy 'Atta and His Forty Grandsons*, and *The Ait 'Atta of Southern Morocco*. For information on Morocco today, I have drawn on Waterbury, *Commander of the Faithful;* Waterbury, "Tribalism, Trade, and Politics"; and Waterbury, "Bargaining for Segmentarity." I have also relied on Marais, "The Political Evolution of the Berbers in Independent Morocco." These sources were supplemented heavily by interviews I conducted in Morocco in May and June 1996.

36. The French colonial regime had tried to encourage a separate Berber identity. In 1930, the French promulgated the so-called Berber *zahir*, which enshrined Berber autonomy at the expense of Arab and traditional Islamic authority—a move that provoked a nationalist backlash. See Hart, "The Berber Dahir of 1930 in Colonial Morocco."

37. "Human Rights in Morocco," *Human Rights Watch*, 8.

38. "Human Rights in Morocco," *United States Department of State Human Rights Report*, 3.

39. Author's interview, June 1996.

40. Author's interview, May 1996.

41. "Morocco bans Berber cultural show."

42. Author's interview, June 1996.

43. Author's interview, June 1996.

44. For information on identity change in Iraq, I have drawn on McDowall, *A Modern History of the Kurds;* Marr, *The Modern History of Iraq;* Baram, "The Ruling Political Elite in Ba'thi Iraq, 1968–1986"; and Farouk-Sluglett and Sluglett, *Iraq since 1958*.

45. Histories of atrocities can solidify boundaries between groups, but they do not necessarily increase internal unity on any other issue besides rejecting identification with an ethnic enemy. Thus the Kurds reject calls to become Arabs, but they have remained split among themselves despite facing many threats and a shared brutalization that might lead them to unite.

46. Laitin notes that this tendency is true for the Russian-speaking minorities in the titular republics of the former Soviet Union. *Identity in Formation*, 29.

47. See Alterman, *New Media, New Politics?* for a review of the information revolution on the Middle East.

48. See Laitin, *Identity in Formation*, 29, for more on this concept.

Chapter 6. Participatory Systems

1. Smooha and Hanf, "The Diverse Modes of Conflict-Regulation in Deeply Divided Societies," 33.

2. Dahl, *Democracy and Its Critics*, 254; Horowitz, *Ethnic Groups in Conflict*, 681.

3. For the best description of this process, see Horowitz, *Ethnic Groups in Conflict*,

395–440; Horowitz, "Making Moderation Pay"; and Stubbs, "Malaysia," 287. The example these authors draw on is Malaysia, which has successfully overcome tension among Malays, ethnic Chinese, and ethnic Indians. Malaysia uses an integrative model that relies on electoral incentives to foster cooperation.

4. Lijphart, *Democracies,* 22–29; and Lijphart, "Majority Rule in Theory and Practice."

5. For a description of the relationship between democratization and interstate war, see Mansfield and Snyder, "Democratization and the Danger of War."

6. *State Failure Task Force Report,* 19–22.

7. An account is Brogan, *The Fighting Never Stopped,* 227–34.

8. Gourevitch, *We Wish to Inform You that Tomorrow We Will Be Killed with All Our Families,* 82–83.

9. Snyder and Jervis, "Civil War and the Security Dilemma," 19.

10. Walter, "The Critical Barrier to Civil War Settlement."

11. Smooha and Hanf use the term *ethnic democracy* in their overview of government types in divided societies instead of *hegemonic democracy* to describe the same type of system. See Smooha and Hanf, "The Diverse Modes of Conflict-Regulation in Deeply Divided Societies," 31–32. I believe the term *hegemonic* is more descriptive.

12. This review of Israel's democracy and Israeli Arabs from 1966 on comes primarily from Smooha, *Arabs and Jews in Israel: Change and Continuity in Mutual Intolerance;* Smooha, *Arabs and Jews in Israel: Conflicting and Shared Attitudes in a Divided Society;* Smooha, *The Orientation and Politicization of the Arab Minority in Israel;* Lustick, "The Changing Political Role of Israeli Arabs;" Lustick, *Arabs in the Jewish State;* Jiryis, *The Arabs in Israel, 1948–1966;* Kimmerling and Migdal, *Palestinians;* Lustick, "Creeping Binationalism within the Green Line"; Rekhess, "Israeli Arab Intelligentsia"; Rekhess, "Red Lines and Realities"; McDowall, *The Palestinians;* Ashkenasi, *Palestinian Identities and Preferences;* Rekhess, "Israel's Arab Citizens and the Peace Process"; and Zureik, *The Palestinians in Israel.*

13. Lustick, *Arabs in the Jewish State,* 228.

14. Zureik, *The Palestinians in Israel,* 135.

15. Israeli Arab areas also faced regular discrimination in basic services such as water, electricity, health, and sport centers. Arab areas were often given a tenth of what Jewish areas received from the central government. See Alonia, "Discrimination against Arab Settlements."

16. Burg, "A Statistical Portrait," 20.

17. Kimmerling and Migdal, *Palestinians,* 177.

18. Ben-Rafael and Sharot, *Ethnicity, Religion and Class in Israeli Society,* 16.

19. This shift in Israeli Arab voting was recognized by those opposed to Israeli Arab causes. Because Israeli Arab participation as pragmatists hurts overall conservative strength, they have tried to brand Israeli Arabs as dangerous enemies in

order to discredit their Jewish allies. Ariel Sharon, for example, claimed that Israeli Arabs were a strong force in the *intifada.* See Lustick, "The Changing Political Role of Israeli Arabs," 126.

20. Jiryis, *The Arabs in Israel, 1948–1966,* 35.

21. Interview with Israeli Arab political party official, September 1996.

22. As quoted in Rekhess, "Red Lines and Realities."

23. Minns and Hijab, *Citizens Apart,* 58. Examples of such associations include the Arab Association for Human Rights, the Galilee Society for Health Research and Services, and the Galilee Center for Social Research. See McDowall, *The Palestinians,* 60.

24. Smooha, *Arabs and Jews in Israel: Change and Continuity in Mutual Intolerance,* 117; Smooha, *Arabs and Jews in Israel: Conflicting and Shared Attitudes in a Divided Society,* 114. The National Committee of Arab Mayors and Local Council Chairmen also includes Israeli Arab members of the Knesset, Histadrut members, and other important Israeli Arab officials.

25. Smooha, *Arabs and Jews in Israel: Conflicting and Shared Attitudes in a Divided Society,* 18.

26. Ibid., 139–40.

27. McDowall, *The Palestinians,* 59.

28. Smooha, *Arabs and Jews in Israel: Change and Continuity in Mutual Intolerance,* 137.

29. Lustick, "Creeping Binationalism within the Green Line," 18; Rudge, "Rabin Campaigns in Arab Village."

30. Smooha, *Arabs and Jews in Israel: Change and Continuity in Mutual Intolerance,* 132–33; and Smooha, *Arabs and Jews in Israel: Conflicting and Shared Attitudes in a Divided Society,* 126–27.

31. Dunsky, "Standing on the Green Line."

32. Ashkenasi, *Palestinian Identities and Preferences,* 50.

33. Gorkin, *Days of Honey, Days of Onion,* 97.

34. Harven, "The Arabs of Israel," 10–11; Smooha, *The Orientation and Politicization of the Arab Minority in Israel,* 78; Smooha, *Arabs and Jews in Israel: Conflicting and Shared Attitudes in a Divided Society,* 79.

35. Interview with Israeli academic expert, August 1996.

36. Goell, "Israel's Arabs"; Smooha, *Arabs and Jews in Israel: Change and Continuity in Mutual Intolerance,* 5. Israeli Arab demonstrations in support of the Palestinian leadership's position in 2000 as part of the "Al Aqsa" *intifada* also raised tensions. These demonstrations increased Jewish concerns about the loyalty of the Israeli Arabs and their willingness to coexist peacefully within a Jewish state.

37. As quoted in Rekhess, "Israeli Arab Intelligentsia," 56.

38. Smooha, *Arabs and Jews in Israel: Change and Continuity in Mutual Intolerance,*

89, 112, 240; Smooha, *Arabs and Jews in Israel: Conflicting and Shared Attitudes in a Divided Society,* 214.

39. Interview with Israeli government official, August 1996.

40. See Lijphart, *Democracy in Plural Societies,* 25–44, and Lijphart, "The Power Sharing Approach," 494. For a critique of Lijphart's work on consociational democracy, see Lustick, "Lijphart, Lakatos, and Consociationalism."

41. This account of Lebanon relies heavily on the following sources: Brynen, *Sanctuary and Survival;* Hiro, *Lebanon;* Norton, *Amal and the Shi'a;* Hudson, "The Breakdown of Democracy in Lebanon"; and Rabinovich, *The War for Lebanon, 1970–1985.*

42. These factors fulfill criteria identified by Arend Lijphart as helpful to the success of power-sharing. Lebanon lacked overarching loyalties, geographic concentration to make federalism easier, and internal unity in response to external dangers—other criteria identified as helpful by Lijphart. See Lijphart, "The Power Sharing Approach," 498.

43. See Fawaz, *An Occasion for War.*

44. Lebanon almost certainly was victim to shoddy census work that was politicized for the purposes of the census takers.

45. Hudson, "The Breakdown of Democracy in Lebanon," 280.

46. Lijphart, *Democracy in Plural Societies,* 149–50.

47. By 1975, Muslims probably represented 60 percent of Lebanon's population, and Shi'a had become the largest sect. By 1983, this shift in favor of Lebanon's Muslim population, and Shi'a in particular, became even more dramatic. Hudson, "The Breakdown of Democracy in Lebanon," 281.

48. As quoted in Brynen, *Sanctuary and Survival,* 29.

49. As quoted in Brynen, ibid., 136.

50. Ibid., 61–67; Hiro, *Lebanon,*18.

51. Hiro, *Lebanon,* 23.

52. Ibid., 12–16.

53. For example, Syria has tacitly supported Shaykh Subhi al-Tufayli's 1997 "Revolution of the Hungry" and propped up the Shi'a Amal, both in an effort to undercut Hezbollah's strength among Shi'a in general. Zisser, "Hizballah."

54. Syria's control, however, is not absolute. Although no politician will openly defy Syria, not all Lebanese leaders are in Damascus's pocket. Rafiq Hariri won the 2000 election for prime minister despite not being Damascus's choice.

55. Zisser, "Hizballah."

56. Eisenberg, "Do Good Fences Make Good Neighbors?"

57. Hudson, "From Consociationalism to the Public Sphere," 106.

58. Norton, "Lebanon's Malaise,"45.

59. Ibid., 35–36.

60. Hudson, "From Consociationalism to the Public Sphere," 106.
61. Ibid., 100–105.
62. Norton, "Lebanon's Malaise," 35.
63. As quoted in Hudson, "From Consociationalism to the Public Sphere," 101.
64. Fiske, *Pity the Nation*, 26.
65. Snyder and Jervis, "Civil War and the Security Dilemma," 19.

Chapter 7. The Promise and Perils of Partition

1. For my additional thoughts on the complexities of partition, see "Rethinking Partition."

2. Many arguments for partition focus on the legal and moral question of whether a people have a right to self-determination. Although this question is important, the focus of this chapter is on partition as a solution to conflict, not as the fulfillment of a people's right to self-determination.

3. Because of this problem, some scholars even go so far as to claim that partition is almost always the best solution after a bloody conflict. Chaim Kaufmann is the leading champion of this point of view. See Kaufmann, "Possible and Impossible Solutions to Ethnic Civil Wars"; Kaufmann, "Intervention in Ethnic and Ideological Civil Wars"; and Kaufmann, "When All Else Fails." Kaufmann focuses on the question of how best to separate warring populations, with partition being the natural outcome of his analysis. Other authors focus more on the question of the political viability of ethnically divided states. Conor Cruise O'Brien implicitly makes an argument for partition in his eloquent analysis of how nationalism can lead to recurring conflict. See "The Wrath of Ages." Michael Lind goes so far as to argue that democracy never works where a state is highly divided along linguistic and cultural lines. See "In Defense of Liberal Nationalism," 95.

4. Works that address both legal and practical problems with partition include Hannum, "Rethinking Self-Determination"; Etzioni, "The Evils of Self-Determination"; Buchanan, "Self-Determination and the Right to Secede." Robert Schaeffer argues strongly that partition tends to lead to interstate war. See *Warpaths.* Other works discussing divided states and the problems they face include Henderson, Lebow, and Stroessinger, *Divided Nations in a Divided World;* and Buchheit, *Secession.* For a work assessing the moral dimensions of secession, see Buchanan, *Secession.*

5. In a rigorous challenge to partition advocates, Nicholas Sambanis argues that most tenets of partition theorists regarding war recurrence, democratization, and violence prevention at best hold weakly. See "Partition as a Solution to Ethnic War."

6. Kaufmann, "When All Else Fails, 126.

7. This account of partition and its aftermath draws on the following sources: Kimmerling and Migdal, *Palestinians;* Lesch, *Arab Politics in Palestine, 1917–1939; Pal-*

estine Royal Commission Report; Palestine Partition Commission Report; Hurewitz, *The Struggle for Palestine;* Lachman, "Arab Rebellion and Terrorism in Palestine, 1929–1939"; Benvenisti, *Intimate Enemies;* Morris, *1948 and After;* Rabinovich, *The War for Lebanon, 1970–1985;* and Schiff and Ya'ari, *Israel's Lebanon War.* Dupuy, *Elusive Victory,* provides perhaps the best military history of the Arab-Israeli conflicts through 1973. An excellent analysis of Israel's strategy in the border conflicts can be found in Shimshoni, *Israel and Conventional Deterrence.*

8. Benvenisti, *Intimate Enemies,* 78–80. As this book went to press in early 2001, the "Al Aqsa" *intifada* appeared far from ending. Thus complete information on its impact, both in terms of lives and on ethnic relations, is not available.

9. Dupuy, *Elusive Victory,* 12–13.

10. Morris, *Israel's Border Wars, 1948–1956,* 435.

11. Ibid., 100–110.

12. As quoted in Bar-Joseph, "Variations on a Theme," 152.

13. Morris, *Israel's Border Wars, 1948–1956,* 340–418, 429–31.

14. Dupuy, *Elusive Victory,* 379.

15. See ibid., 378–81, for information on the Palestinian guerrillas and the crisis in Jordan in 1968–70.

16. Benvenisti, *Intimate Enemies,* 84.

17. Ibid., 88–89.

18. Kaufmann, "When All Else Fails," 122.

19. McDowall, *A Modern History of the Kurds,* 371–91.

20. Turkey faced a brutal insurgency among its Kurdish population in the 1990s, and Kurdish rebels of the Kurdish Workers' Party (PKK) took shelter on Iraqi soil. Ankara feared that an independent Kurdish state would aid the insurgents materially and inspire them to demand a state in Turkey too. Iran, which had won its own brutal war against the Kurds only in 1984, also feared the precedent of a Kurdish state. Syria, where 8.5 percent of the population is Kurdish, also opposed the emergence of a Kurdish state. Van Dam, *The Struggle for Power in Syria,* 1.

21. The Kurds have tens of thousands of men under arms, but they are lightly armed, poorly trained, and not integrated into a common force. As a result, they are no match for the heavy Iraqi conventional forces, even though the terrain in the north favors defensive operations.

22. Gunter, *The Kurdish Predicament in Iraq,* 67.

23. McDowall, *A Modern History of the Kurds,* 379–82.

24. Lawrence, "Iraqi Kurds Enjoy a De Facto State"; Ricciardone, "An American Diplomat's Perspectives on Kurds in the Global Arena."

25. McDowall, *A Modern History of the Kurds,* 380–82.

26. McAllester, "Rebuilding on Ruins," 6.

27. See Baram, *Building toward Crises,* 51, 55.

28. McDowall, *A Modern History of the Kurds,* 378–79.

29. See Byman and Waxman, *Confronting Iraq*, 43–60.

30. Gunter, *The Kurdish Predicament*, 135.

31. McDowall, *A Modern History of the Kurds*, 385.

32. Gunter, *The Kurdish Predicament*, 74–98.

33. McDowall, *A Modern History of the Kurds*, 386; Baram, *Building toward Crises*, 53–55.

34. Lawrence, "Iraqi Kurds Enjoy a De Facto State."

35. For a review, see Baram, "The Effects of Iraqi Sanctions."

36. See Segev, *One Palestine, Complete*, for an argument on the importance of the Arab revolt in the British decision to abandon the Mandate.

37. The deliberate transfer of populations is a rare historical event, but massive refugee flows have occurred frequently in response to ethnic or political violence. In the early part of the twentieth century, Turkey and Greece exchanged populations—sometimes peacefully, sometimes due to appalling massacres and repression. Before and during World War I, several hundred thousands of Christians in Turkish lands fled to Greece, while Muslims living in Greece fled to Turkey. After the Turkish army defeated the Greeks in 1922, over one million Greeks fled to Greece from western Asia Minor. Under the 1923 Convention of Lausanne, Greece and Turkey arranged the transfer—by compulsion—of perhaps 2 million Greeks and Turks. (The transfer actually occurred along religious, not linguistic, lines as the Christian Turkish-speaking residents went to Greece while the Greek-speaking Muslims went to Turkey.) Following independence, India and Pakistan also exchanged populations as did the Greek and Turkish populations of Cyprus. Far more common is transfer resulting from conflict, such as that in the former Yugoslavia, where ethnic cleansing operations have led to refugee flows. Lewis, *The Emergence of Modern Turkey*, 354–55. See also *Refugees in the Age of Total War*, 17–19.

38. See Rai, *Partition of the Punjab*, 74–75.

39. Morris, *Israel's Border Wars, 1948–1956*, 12, notes that Moshe Dayan found the borders "ridiculous" and that the relatively dovish Foreign Minister Sharett, while opposed to an Israeli attack to gain territory, explicitly noted that he might support an expansion in a defensive war. In private, Ben-Gurion proposed conquering parts of the West Bank to stop infiltration.

40. Horowitz, *Ethnic Groups in Conflict*, 589.

41. Sambanis, "Partition as a Solution to Ethnic War," 461.

42. Laitin, for example, argues that appeasing national groups by giving them political recognition simply creates more national actors who seek similar recognition for themselves. *Identity in Formation*, 340.

43. See Byman and Van Evera, "Why They Fight," for the war-causing effects of empire collapse.

44. See Dupuy, *Elusive Victory*, 12. For a superb description of Abdullah's ambitions and the regional rivalry in general, see Shlaim, *Collusion across the Jordan*.

45. Kaufmann, "When All Else Fails," 147.

46. See, for example, de Nevers, "Democratization and Ethnic Conflict," 34.

47. Levine, "Political Accommodation and the Prevention of Secessionist Violence," 332, and Horowitz, *Ethnic Groups in Conflict*, 613–21.

Chapter 8. Military Intervention in Ethnic Conflict

1. Stuart Kaufman, for example, argues that elite-led conflict is difficult for outside powers to deter or affect in general. Kaufman, "The Irresistible Force and the Imperceptible Object," 318–19.

2. Taw and Vick, "From Sideshow to Center Stage," 189.

3. Walter, "The Critical Barrier to Civil War Settlement," 339–40.

4. The term *ideology* refers to a set of beliefs about proper political, social, and economic goals and how to achieve them. An ideological group is bound together by a shared set of such beliefs. I adopt the communal-ideological bifurcation of Kaufmann, "Intervention in Ethnic and Ideological Civil Wars." Myron Weiner separates internal conflicts into ethnic and non-ethnic. Non-ethnic civil conflicts include "those based upon class, regional, or ideological differences or an armed struggle for political power by the military or by political factions." Weiner, "Bad Neighbors, Bad Neighborhoods," 10.

5. The definition of a humanitarian intervention is contentious. For this chapter I define a humanitarian intervention as one where the intervening power is acting primarily out of a concern for the local population. In practice, such definitions are difficult, as often the most brutal aggression is justified on humanitarian grounds, while some wars of national interest—such as the Indian intervention in East Pakistan, the Tanzanian intervention in Uganda, and the Vietnamese intervention in Cambodia—had clear humanitarian benefits. To judge whether a mission is humanitarian, I assess the mission objectives, the history of the intervening power in the region, and the support of the international community, all of which are imperfect measures at best. By my count, humanitarian interventions include the following: the U.S. and British intervention in northern Iraq in 1991; the U.S. relief of Bangladesh in 1991; the ECOMOG intervention in Liberia from 1990 to 1997; the UN and U.S. interventions in Somalia (UNOSOM I, UNOSOM II, and UNITAF); various UN operations in Bosnia since 1991; UN and French operations in Rwanda in 1994; U.S. and French operations in the Goma region of Zaire in 1994; U.S. operations in Haiti in 1994 and 1995; Italy's intervention in Albania in 1997; and NATO's war against Serbia over Kosovo in 1999. Some of these instances (e.g., the U.S. interventions in Iraq) had strong national interest and humanitarian elements in them.

6. For works of value related to intervention in communal civil wars, see Posen, "Military Responses to Refugee Disasters"; Gurr and Harff, *Ethnic Conflict in World*

Politics; Stopping the Killing, ed. Licklider; Kaufmann, "Possible and Impossible Solutions to Ethnic Civil Wars"; and Stedman, "Spoiler Problems in Peace Processes."

7. Taw and Vick, "From Sideshow to Center Stage," 180. A complex emergency is a violent conflict that results in disruption of the political, economic, and social systems of the state. The term is most commonly used by humanitarians who are concerned primarily with the welfare of the population. Dworkin, "What's So Special about Humanitarian Operations?"

8. For the official U.S. Army doctrine, see *Field Manual 100–23, Peace Operations.*

9. Kaufmann, "Intervention in Ethnic and Ideological Civil Wars," 66. Kaufmann believes the distinction leads to different dynamics: ideological civil wars are primarily political contests and ethnic ones are primarily military contests (70–80).

10. Ibid., 74–75.

11. Posen, "The Security Dilemma and Ethnic Conflict," 27–35, and Kaufmann, "Intervention in Ethnic and Ideological Civil Wars," 78.

12. Weiner, "Bad Neighbors, Bad Neighborhoods," 21.

13. Because of the general problems distinguishing between combatants and noncombatants in communal wars, and a general focus in peace operations on the population rather than the guerrilla, the true size of a deployment depends in large part on the total size of a population, not on the total size of the guerrilla movement. It is the population, after all, that must be made to feel secure. In situations of high communal tension, the ratio of police force to total population becomes quite high. In Punjab, for example, the Indian government had a security force of about 115,000 in a territory of roughly 20.2 million—a force ratio of 5.7 per thousand. The British reached a level of 20 per 1,000 in the Malay insurgency in the 1950s, and in Northern Ireland this level reached around 20 per 1,000 as well. Quinlivan, "Force Requirements in Stability Operations," 59–69, especially 60–64. In Somalia, two infantry divisions would provide approximately a 5.3:1,000 ratio (32,000 troops/6,000,000 population). In Bosnia, one infantry division would yield a troop to citizen ratio of about 6 to 1,000 (16,000/2,650,000 population). John Mueller, however, argues that intervention is often far easier in many conflicts because the rival "armies" are in fact gangs of thugs who lack organization, discipline, or broad popular support. Mueller, "The Banality of 'Ethnic War,' " 64–65.

14. The difficult tasks these countries faced will be even more challenging to the United States. While many Israelis know Arabic and the British and Irish speak the same language (despite claims to the contrary by wags in both countries), few U.S. or allied forces know the local language or customs of Bosnia, Somalia, or other sites of recent interventions.

15. Natsios, "Humanitarian Relief Intervention in Somalia," 84.

16. O'Connor, "Bosnians Back Home, with Quiet U.S. Help," A3.

17. United Nations Human Rights Field Operation Report, cited in UN Department of Humanitarian Affairs Integrated Regional Information Network for the Great Lakes, "IRIN Weekly Roundup 24–97 of Main Events in the Great Lakes Region (26 Sept.–2 Oct. 1997)."

18. See Rose, "The Exit Strategy Delusion."

19. On the use of refugee camps as military assets, see Barber, "Feeding Refugees, or War?"

20. Duffield and Prendergast, *Without Troops and Tanks,* 9, 23–24, and Woodward, *Balkan Tragedy,* 363–67.

21. For a critique, see Betts, "The Delusion of Impartial Intervention."

22. For a review of military-NGO relations, see Byman et al., *Strengthening the Partnership.*

23. Horne, *A Savage War of Peace,* 263–67.

24. George and Simons, "Findings and Conclusions," 281–82.

25. See Pape, *Bombing to Win,* for a comparison of the two campaigns in Vietnam.

26. See Lambeth, *The Transformation of American Air Power.*

27. Clodfelter, *The Limits of Air Power,* 111, 135.

28. A balance approach thus tries to create the conditions that will make a conflict more likely to be resolved. Zartman, *Ripe for Resolution.*

29. In communal conflicts, groups in general have a tremendous motivation to fight. Communal conflicts involve "us" versus "them"—no quarter or good treatment can be expected from the hostile enemy. Thus, even a corrupt leadership will gain a following if the alternative is domination by a rival communal group. See Kaufmann, "Intervention in Ethnic and Ideological Civil Wars," for more on this point.

30. Information on Russian involvement in the conflicts in Georgia and Moldova is sparse. See "Georgia: Against the Odds" and "Georgia: Tricked and Abandoned" for reporting on Russian involvement in the fighting in Abkhazia and South Ossetia.

31. See Laitin, *Identity in Formation,* 330; Solonar, "Hatred and Fear on Both Banks of the Dniester," 8–9; and Crowther, "Moldova after Independence." Information on the conflict in Abkhazia (Georgia) is extremely scarce. A description of the issues and the region's politics can be found in Ascherson, *Black Sea,* 244–56.

32. Howe, "Lessons of Liberia," 163, 171.

33. Because of this, a balance approach may not be appropriate unless accompanied by a transfer mission as well.

34. Roy, *The Lessons of the Soviet-Afghan War,* 21.

35. Licklider, "The Consequences of Negotiated Settlements in Civil Wars, 1945–1993," 684. Exact figures very tremendously by how conflicts are coded. Nevertheless, figures drawn from Licklider (686) suggest roughly 40 percent of con-

flicts recur, so 15 percent of conflicts have been terminated through negotiation (one-quarter of 60 percent). Kaufmann reports a larger but also underwhelming figure (under 30 percent) for communal conflicts, noting that only 8 of 27 post-1944 conflicts that have ended were resolved by a negotiated settlement that did not involve partition. Kaufmann, "Possible and Impossible Solutions to Ethnic Civil Wars," 159.

36. See Kuperman, "Rwanda in Retrospect" for a review.

37. For overviews, see Rubin, "The Fragmentation of Tajikistan"; Tadjbakhsh, "Tajikistan"; and Roy, *The Civil War in Tajikistan.*

38. Tadjbakhsh, "Tajikistan," 175.

39. "Ethnic unmixing through organized population transfers is clearly preferable to killings and refugee flights." Weiner, "Bad Neighbors, Bad Neighborhoods," 37–38.

40. Bellaigue, "Turkey's Hidden Past," 38.

41. Hoover, "The Society and Its Environment," 65.

42. Ibid., 61–65.

43. One transfer and partition that did not occur was the creation of a Kurdish state that included Turkey's Kurdish minority. The one active conflict in Turkey today involves the Kurdish quest for autonomy. Conflicts between Turks and Greeks and Turks and Armenians, however, are quiescent even though tension is high.

44. Miskel and Norton, "The Paradox of Early Warning."

45. In November 1992, Macedonian President Kiro Gligorov asked for a UNPROFOR presence in Bosnia. The initial goal was to monitor border areas and to strengthen the country's stability. Initially, this was named the UNPROFOR's Macedonia Command, which was changed in 1995 to the United Nations Preventive Deployment Force (UNPREDEP). For information on the concerns of violence against ethnic Albanians, see Woodward, *Balkan Tragedy,* 393–94.

46. Although the primary purpose of the U.S. deployment to Lebanon in 1958 was to prevent the spread of left-leaning pan-Arabism in the Middle East, it did stabilize the political situation in Lebanon and help end the civil war. See Hiro, *Lebanon,* 8; and Quandt, "Lebanon, 1958, and Jordan, 1970," 239.

47. Quandt, "Lebanon, 1958, and Jordan, 1970," 255.

48. Gow, *Triumph of the Lack of Will,* 299–300.

49. See Menkhaus, "Complex Emergencies, Humanitarianism, and National Security."

50. Ascherson, *Black Sea,* 199–209, details an account of the Lazi people and efforts to save their distinct identity.

51. Outsiders also must focus analytic attention on the majority community, not just minorities within a country. Understandably, many analysts focus on the condition of minorities and try to gauge whether they are dissatisfied with their lot.

This emphasis, however, ignores that majorities and dominant groups often are the true drivers of conflict. Whether the dominant community seeks an exclusive political system, will accept assimilation, understands the need for co-optation, or otherwise is willing to cooperate often means the difference between peace and war.

Chapter 9. Dilemmas and Choices

1. Walter, "The Critical Barrier to Civil War Settlement," passim.

2. See Byman and Van Evera, "Why They Fight," 33–34, 49.

3. Milton J. Esman has documented how economically disadvantaged groups can use the state to redress their economic subordination. Common measures include expanding higher education, using a language policy that favors the economically subordinate group, expanding state-owned enterprises and bureaucracies to increase employment, fostering entrepreneurs among particular ethnic groups, and compelling private firms to increase subordinate group hiring. Esman, "Ethnic Politics and Economic Power," 410–12.

4. For proponents of civil society, see Putnam, *Making Democracy Work*, and Fukuyama, *Trust*. A review of civil society in the Middle East can be found in *Civil Society in the Middle East*, ed. Augustus Richard Norton and Farhad Kazemi, and Abootalebi, "Civil Society, Democracy, and the Middle East." For a review of the positive role that civil society can play in reducing conflict, see Carnegie Commission on Preventing Deadly Violence, *Preventing Deadly Conflict*, 109–27. Sheri Berman offers a superb critique of the more breathless arguments for the benefits of civil society in "Civil Society and the Collapse of the Weimar Republic."

5. Abootalebi, "Civil Society, Democracy, and the Middle East."

BIBLIOGRAPHY

Abootalebi, Ali R. "Civil Society, Democracy, and the Middle East." *Middle East Review of International Affairs* 2, no. 3 (September 1998), electronic version.

Abrahamian, Ervand. *Iran between Two Revolutions.* Princeton: Princeton University Press, 1982.

Akhavi, Shahrough. "State Formation and Consolidation in 20th Century Iran." In *The State, Religion, and Ethnic Politics,* edited by Ali Banuazizi and Myron Weiner. Syracuse, N.Y.: Syracuse University Press, 1986.

Alonia, Shulamit. "Discrimination against Arab Settlements." *Yediot Ahronot,* October 10, 1975.

Alterman, Jon B. *New Media, New Politics? From Satellite Television to the Internet in the Arab World.* Washington, D.C.: Washington Institute for Near East Policy, 1998.

Arfi, Bedredine. "Ethnic Fear: The Social Construction of Insecurity." *Security Studies* 8, no. 1 (Autumn 1998): 151–203.

Ascherson, Neal. *Black Sea.* New York: Hill and Wang, 1995.

Ashkenasi, Abraham. *Palestinian Identities and Preferences.* New York: Praeger, 1992.

———. "Socio-Ethnic Conflict and Paramilitary Organization in the Near East." In *Political Violence and Terror: Motifs and Motivations,* edited by Peter H. Merkl. Berkeley: University of California Press, 1986.

"Bahrain: Defendants' Confessions Reported." Manama WAKH, FBIS-NES-96-110, June 5, 1996.

"Bahrain: Interior Ministry on Arrest of 'Hizballah of Bahrain' Group." Manama WAKH, FBIS-NES-96-107, June 3, 1996.

Bahry, Louay. "The Opposition in Bahrain: A Bellwether for the Gulf?" *Middle East Policy* 5, no. 2 (May 1997): 42–57.

Baram, Amatzia. *Building toward Crises: Saddam Husayn's Strategy for Survival.* Washington, D.C.: Washington Institute for Near East Policy, 1998.

———. "The Effect of Iraqi Sanctions: Statistical Pitfalls and Responsibility." *The Middle East Journal* 54, no. 2 (Spring 2000): 194–223.

———. "The Ruling Political Elite in Ba'thi Iraq, 1968–1986: The Changing Features of a Collective Profile." *International Journal of Middle East Studies* 21 (1989).

Barber, Ben. "Feeding Refugees, or War?" *Foreign Affairs* 76, no. 4 (July–August 1997): 8–14.

Bar-Joseph, Uri. "Variations on a Theme: The Conceptualization of Deterrence in Israeli Strategic Thinking." *Security Studies* 7, no. 3 (Spring 1998): 145–81.

Barth, Frederik. "Ethnic Groups and Boundaries." In *Process and Form in Social Life: Selected Essays,* edited by Frederik Barth, 198–227. London: Routledge & Kegan Paul, 1981.

Batatu, Hanna. *The Old Social Classes and the Revolutionary Movements of Iraq.* Princeton: Princeton University Press, 1978.

Bates, Robert. "Ethnic Competition and Modernization in Contemporary Africa." *Comparative Political Studies* 6, no. 4 (1974): 457–84.

———. "Modernization, Ethnic Competition, and the Rationality of Politics in Contemporary Africa." In *State Versus Ethnic Claims: African Policy Dilemmas,* edited by D. Rothchild and V. Olorunsola, 457–84. Boulder, Colo.: Westview, 1985.

Bellaigue, Christopher de. "Turkey's Hidden Past." *New York Review of Books,* March 8, 2001, 37–40.

Bell-Fialkoff, Andrew. "A Brief History of Ethnic Cleansing." *Foreign Affairs* 72, no. 3 (Summer 1993): 110–21.

Ben Jelloun, Tahar. *Corruption.* New York: The Free Press, 1990.

Ben-Dor, Gabriel. *The Druzes in Israel.* Boulder, Colo.: Westview, 1979.

Ben-Rafael, Eliezer, and Stephen Sharot. *Ethnicity, Religion and Class in Israeli Society.* Cambridge: Cambridge University Press, 1991.

Benvenisti, Meron. *Intimate Enemies: Jews and Arabs in a Shared Land.* Berkeley: University of California Press, 1995.

Beran, Harry. "A Liberal Theory of Secession." *Political Studies* 32 (1984): 21–31.

Berlin, Isaiah. "Kant as an Unfamiliar Source of Nationalism." In *The Sense of Reality.* New York: Farrar, Straus, and Giroux, 1996.

———. "Two Concepts of Liberty." In *Four Essays on Liberty.* New York: Oxford University Press, 1969.

Berman, Sheri. "Civil Society and the Collapse of the Weimar Republic." *World Politics* 49 (April 1997): 401–29.

Betts, Richard K. "The Delusion of Impartial Intervention." *Foreign Affairs* 73, no. 6 (November–December 1994): 20–33.

Bidwell, Robin. *Morocco under Colonial Rule.* London: Frank Cass, 1973.

Blumer, H., and T. Duster. "Theories of Race and Social Action." In *Sociological Theories: Race and Colonialism.* Paris: UNESCO, 1980.

Bramwell, Anna C., ed. *Refugees in the Age of Total War.* London: Unwin Hyman, 1988.

Brogan, Patrick. *The Fighting Never Stopped: A Comprehensive Guide to World Conflicts since 1945.* New York: Vintage, 1990.

Brooks, David. "The Enemy Within: Limitations on Leadership in the Bakhtiyari." In *The Conflict of Tribe and State in Iran and Afghanistan,* edited by Richard Tapper. New York: St. Martin's, 1983.

Brubaker, Rogers. "National Minorities, Nationalizing States, and External National Homelands in the New Europe." *Daedalus* 124, no. 2 (Spring 1995): 107–32.

———. "Nationalizing States in the Old 'New Europe'—and the New." *Ethnic and Racial Studies* 19, no. 2 (April 1996): 410–37.

Brubaker, Rogers, and David D. Laitin. "Ethnic and Nationalist Violence." *Annual Review of Sociology* 24 (1998): 423–52.

Brynen, Don. *Sanctuary and Survival: The PLO in Lebanon.* London: Westview, 1990.

Buchanan, Allen. *Secession: The Morality of Political Divorce from Fort Sumter to Lithuania and Quebec.* Boulder, Colo.: Westview, 1991.

———. "Self-Determination and the Right to Secede." *Journal of International Affairs* 45, no. 2 (Winter 1992): 347–65.

Buchheit, Lee C. *Secession: The Legitimacy of Self-Determination.* New Haven: Yale University Press, 1978.

Burg, Avraham. "A Statistical Portrait." In *Every Sixth Israeli: Relations between the Jewish Majority and the Arab Minority in Israel,* edited by Alouph Hareven. Jerusalem: Daf-Chen, 1983.

Byman, Daniel. "Explaining Ethnic Peace in Morocco." *Harvard Middle East and Islamic Review* 4, nos. 1–2 (1997–98): 1–29.

———. "Forever Enemies? The Manipulation of Ethnic Identities to End Ethnic Wars." *Security Studies* 9, no. 3 (Spring 2000): 149–90.

———. "The Logic of Ethnic Terrorism." *Studies in Conflict and Terrorism* 21, no. 2 (April–June 1998): 149–69.

———. "Rethinking Partition: Lessons from Iraq and Lebanon." *Security Studies* 7, no. 1 (Autumn 1997): 1–32.

Byman, Daniel, Ian Lesser, Bruce Pirnie, Cheryl Bernard, and Matthew Waxman. *Strengthening the Partnership: Improving Military Coordination with Relief Agencies and Allies in Humanitarian Operations.* Santa Monica, Calif.: RAND, 2000.

Byman, Daniel, and Stephen Van Evera. "Why They Fight: Hypotheses on the Causes of Contemporary Deadly Violence." *Security Studies* 7 (Spring 1998): 1–50.

Byman, Daniel, and Matthew Waxman. *Confronting Iraq: U.S. Policy and the Use of Force since the End of the Gulf War.* Santa Monica, Calif.: RAND, 2000.

Carnegie Commission on Preventing Deadly Conflict. *Preventing Deadly Conflict.* New York: Carnegie Corporation, December 1997.

Clodfelter, Mark. *The Limits of Air Power: The American Bombing of North Vietnam.* New York: The Free Press, 1989.

Cohen, William B. *Rulers of Empire: The French Colonial Service in Africa.* Stanford, Calif.: Hoover Institution Press, 1971.

Connor, Walker. *Ethnonationalism: The Quest for Understanding.* Princeton: Princeton University Press, 1994.

———. "Nation Building or Nation Destroying?" *World Politics* 24, no. 3 (April 1972): 319–55.

Cordesman, Anthony. *Bahrain, Oman, Qatar, and the UAE.* Boulder, Colo.: Westview, 1997.

Craig, Gordon A. *Germany: 1866–1945.* New York: Oxford University Press, 1978.

Crowther, William. "Moldova after Independence." *Current History* 93, no. 585 (October 1994): 342–47.

Crystal, Jill. *Oil and Politics in the Gulf: Rulers and Merchants in Kuwait and Qatar.* New York: Cambridge University Press, 1995.

Dahl, Robert. *Democracy and Its Critics.* New Haven: Yale University Press, 1989.

Della Porta, Donatella. "Left Wing Terrorism in Italy." In *Terrorism in Context,* edited by Martha Crenshaw, 126–27. University Park: Pennsylvania State University Press, 1995.

Deutsch, Karl. *Nationalism and Its Alternatives.* New York: Knopf, 1969.

———. *Nationalism and Social Communication.* Cambridge, Mass.: MIT Press, 1953.

Deutsch, Karl W., and William J. Foltz, eds. *Nation-Building.* New York: Atherton, 1963.

Drysdale, Alasdair. "The Syrian Political Elite, 1966–1976: A Spatial and Social Analysis." *Middle Eastern Studies* 17, no. 1 (1981).

Duffield, Mark, and John Prendergast. *Without Troops and Tanks: Humanitarian Intervention in Ethiopia and Eritrea.* Lawrenceville, N.J.: Red Sea, 1994.

Dunsky, Marda. "Standing on the Green Line." *The Jerusalem Post,* June 16, 1989.

Dupuy, Trevor. *Elusive Victory: The Arab-Israeli Wars, 1947–1974.* Dubuque, Iowa: Kendall/Hunt, 1992.

Dworkin, Jonathan. "What's So Special about Humanitarian Operations?" *Comparative Strategy* 13, no. 4 (October 1994): 391–99.

Eckstein, Harry. "Case Study and Theory in Political Science." In *Handbook of Political Science,* vol. 7, *Strategies of Inquiry,* edited by Fred I. Greenstein and Nelson W. Polsby, 79–137. Reading, Mass.: Addison-Wesley, 1975.

Eisenberg, Laura Zittrain. "Do Good Fences Make Good Neighbors? Israel and Lebanon after the Withdrawal." *Middle East Review of International Affairs* 4, no. 3 (September 2000), electronic version

El-Asmar, Fouzi. *To Be an Arab in Israel.* Beirut: Institute for Palestine Studies, 1978.

Ergil, Dogu. "The Kurdish Question in Turkey." *Journal of Democracy* 11, no. 3 (July 2000): 122–35.

Esman, Milton J. "Ethnic Politics and Economic Power." *Comparative Politics* 19, no. 4 (July 1987): 395–418.

Etzioni, Amitai. "The Evils of Self-Determination." *Foreign Policy* 89 (Winter 1992–93): 21–35.

Fakhro, Munira A. "The Uprising in Bahrain: An Assessment." In *The Persian Gulf at the Millennium: Essays in Politics, Economy, Security, and Religion,* edited by Gary Sick and Lawrence G. Potter, 167–88. New York: St. Martin's, 1997.

Farouk-Sluglett, Marion, and Peter Sluglett. *Iraq since 1958: From Revolution to Dictatorship.* London: KPI Limited, 1987.

Fawaz, Leila Tarazi. *An Occasion for War: Civil Conflict in Lebanon and Damascus in 1860.* Berkeley: University of California Press, 1994.

Fearon, James. "Rationalist Explanations for War." *International Organization* 49, no. 3 (Summer 1995): 379–444.

Fearon, James D., and David D. Laitin. "Explaining Interethnic Cooperation." *American Political Science Review* 90, no. 4 (December 1996): 715–35.

Field Manual 100–23, Peace Operations. Washington, D.C.: Headquarters, U.S. Department of the Army, December 1994.

De Figueiredo, Rui J. P., Jr., and Barry R. Weingast. "The Rationality of Fear: Political Opportunism and Ethnic Conflict." In *Civil Wars, Insecurity, and Intervention,* edited by Barbara F. Walter and Jack Snyder, 261–302. New York: Columbia University Press, 1999.

Fiske, Robert. *Pity the Nation: Lebanon at War.* London: Andre Deutch, 1990.

Fukuyama, Francis. "Second Thoughts." *The National Interest* 56 (Summer 1999): 16–33.

———. *Trust: Social Virtues and the Creation of Prosperity.* New York: The Free Press, 1995.

Fuller, Graham. *The "Center of the Universe": The Geopolitics of Iran.* Boulder, Colo.: Westview, 1991.

Gagnon, V. P., Jr. "Ethnic Nationalism and International Conflict: The Case of Serbia." *International Security* 19, no. 3 (Winter 1994–95): 130–66.

Galtung, Johan. "Violence, Peace, and Peace Research." *Journal of Peace Research* 6, no. 3 (1969): 167–91.

Ganguly, Sumit. "Ethno-Religious Conflict in South Asia." *Survival* 35, no. 2 (Summer 1993): 88–109.

———. "Explaining the Kashmir Insurgency: Political Mobilization and Institutional Decay." *International Security* 21, no. 2 (Fall 1996): 76–107.

Garthwaite, Gene. "The Bakhtiyari Khans, the Government of Iran, and the British, 1846–1915." *International Journal of Middle East Studies* 3 (1977): 30–36.

———. *Khans and Shahs: A Documentary Analysis of the Bakhtiyari in Iran.* Cambridge: Cambridge University Press, 1983.

———. "Tribes, Confederation, and the State: An Historical Overview of the Bakhtiari and Iran." In *The Conflict of Tribe and State in Iran and Afghanistan,* edited by Richard Tapper. New York: St. Martin's, 1983.

Gause, F. Gregory, III. *Oil Monarchies: Domestic and Security Challenges in the Arab Gulf States.* New York: Council on Foreign Relations Press, 1994.

Geertz, Clifford. "Ideology as a Cultural System." In *The Interpretation of Cultures.* New York: Basic, 1973.

———. "The Integrative Revolution." In *The Interpretation of Cultures.* New York: Basic, 1973.

———. "Religion as a Cultural System." In *The Interpretation of Cultures.* New York: Basic, 1973.

Gellner, Ernest. *The Saints of the Atlas.* Chicago: University of Chicago Press, 1969.

George, Alexander L., and Timothy J. McKeown. "Case Studies and Theories of Organizational Decision Making." In *Advances in Information Processing in Organizations,* vol. 2, 21–58. Greenwich, Conn.: JAI, 1985.

George, Alexander L., and William E. Simons. "Findings and Conclusions." In *The Limits of Coercive Diplomacy,* edited by Alexander L. George and William E. Simons, 281–82. Boulder, Colo.: Westview, 1994.

"Georgia: Against the Odds." *The Economist,* August 14, 1993, 48.

"Georgia: Tricked and Abandoned." *The Economist,* October 2, 1993, 56.

Ghods, M. Reza. *Iran in the Twentieth Century: A Political History.* Boulder, Colo.: Lynne Rienner, 1989.

Goell, Yosef. "Israel's Arabs: A Linking of Fates." *The Jerusalem Post,* October 4, 1991.

Gorkin, Michael. *Days of Honey, Days of Onion: The Story of a Palestinian Family in Israel.* Boston: Beacon, 1991.

Gourevitch, Philip. *We Wish to Inform You that Tomorrow We Will Be Killed with All Our Families: Stories from Rwanda.* New York: Farrar Straus and Giroux, 1998.

Gow, James. *Triumph of the Lack of Will: International Diplomacy and the Yugoslav War.* New York: Columbia University Press, 1997.

Greenfeld, Liah. *Nationalism.* Cambridge, Mass.: Harvard University Press, 1992.

Gunter, Michael M. *The Kurdish Predicament in Iraq: A Political Analysis.* New York: St. Martin's, 1999.

Gurr, Ted Robert. "Ethnic Conflict on the Wane." *Foreign Affairs* 79, no. 3 (May–June 2000): 52–64.

Gurr, Ted Robert, and Barbara Harff. *Ethnic Conflict in World Politics.* Boulder, Colo.: Westview, 1994.

Hannum, Hurst. "Rethinking Self-Determination." *Virginia Journal of International Law* 34, no. 1 (1993): 1–69.

Hareven, Alouph. "The Arabs of Israel: A Jewish Problem." In *Every Sixth Israeli: Relations between the Jewish Majority and the Arab Minority in Israel,* edited by Alouph Hareven. Jerusalem: Daf-Chen, 1983.

Hart, David. *The Ait 'Atta of Southern Morocco: Daily Life and Recent History.* Cambridge, Mass.: Middle East and North African Studies Press, 1984.

———. *The Aith Waryaghar of the Moroccan Rif: An Ethnography and History.* Tucson: University of Arizona Press, 1976.

———. "The Berber Dahir of 1930 in Colonial Morocco: Then and Now (1930–1996)." *Journal of North African Studies* 2, no. 2 (Autumn 1997): 11–33.

———. *Daddy 'Atta and His Forty Grandsons: The Sociopolitical Organization of the Ait 'Atta of Southern Morocco.* Boulder, Colo.: Westview, 1981.

———. "The Tribe in Modern Morocco: Two Case Studies." In *Arabs and Berbers,* edited by E. Gellner and C. Micaud. London: Gerald Duckworth, 1972.

Henderson, Gregory, R. N. Lebow, and J. G. Stroessinger. *Divided Nations in a Divided World.* New York: David McKay, 1974.

Hinnebusch, Raymond. "Class and State in Ba'athist Syria." In *Syria: Society, Culture, and Politics,* edited by Richard T. Antoun and Donald Quartaert. Albany: State University of New York Press, 1991.

———. "State and Civil Society in Syria." *Middle East Journal* 47, no. 2 (Spring 1993): 243–57.

Hiro, Dilip. *Lebanon: Fire and Embers.* New York: St. Martin's, 1992.

Hoisington, William A., Jr. *The Casablanca Connection: French Colonial Policy, 1936–1943.* Chapel Hill: University of North Carolina Press, 1984.

———. *Lyautey and the French Conquest of Morocco.* New York: St. Martin's, 1995.

Hoover, J. Jeffery. "The Society and Its Environment." In *Cyprus: A Country Study,* edited by Frederica M. Bunge. Washington, D.C.: U.S. Government Printing Office, 1980.

Hopf, Ted. "The Promise of Constructivism in International Relations Theory." *International Security* 23, no. 1 (Summer 1998): 171–200.

Hopwood, Derek. *Syria 1945–1986: Politics and Society.* Boston: Unwin Hyman, 1988.

Horne, Alistair. *A Savage War of Peace.* New York: Penguin, 1987.

Horowitz, Donald. *Ethnic Groups in Conflict.* Berkeley: University of California Press, 1985.

———. "Making Moderation Pay: The Comparative Politics of Ethnic Conflict Management." In *Conflict and Peacemaking in Multiethnic Societies,* edited by Joseph Montville, 451–76. New York: Lexington, 1991.

Howe, Herbert. "Lessons of Liberia: ECOMOG and Regional Peacekeeping." *International Security* 21, no. 3 (Winter 1996–97): 145–76.

Hudson, Michael C. "The Breakdown of Democracy in Lebanon." *Journal of International Affairs* 38 (Winter 1985): 277–92.

———. "From Consociationalism to the Public Sphere: Recent Evidence from Lebanon." In *Ethnic Conflict and International Politics in the Middle East*, edited by Leonard Binder, 92–109. Gainesville: University Press of Florida, 1999.

"Human Rights in Morocco." *Human Rights Watch* 7, no. 6 (October 1995).

"Human Rights in Morocco." *United States Department of State Human Rights Report.* Washington, D.C.: U.S. Department of State, 1994.

Hurewitz, J. C. *The Struggle for Palestine.* New York: Schocken, 1976.

Isaacs, Harold. *Idols of the Tribe: Group Identity and Political Change.* New York: Harper & Row, 1975.

Jervis, Robert. "Cooperation under the Security Dilemma." *World Politics* 30, no. 2 (January 1978): 167–213.

———. *Perception and Misperception in International Politics.* Princeton: Princeton University Press, 1976.

Jiryis, Sabri. *The Arabs in Israel, 1948–1966.* Beirut: The Institute for Palestine Studies, 1969.

Kanaana, Sharif. *Socio-Cultural and Psychological Adjustment of the Arab Minority in Israel.* San Francisco: R and E Research Associates, 1976.

Kasfir, Nelson. "Explaining Ethnic Political Participation." *World Politics* 31, no. 3 (April 1979): 365–88.

Kaufman, Stuart. "An 'International' Theory of Inter-Ethnic War." *Review of International Studies* 22, no. 2 (1996): 149–71.

———. "The Irresistible Force and the Imperceptible Object: The Yugoslav Breakup and Western Policy." *Security Studies* 4, no. 2 (Winter 1994–95): 281–329.

———. "Spiraling to Ethnic War: Elites, Masses, and Moscow in Moldova's Civil War." *International Security* 21, no. 2 (Fall 1996): 108–38.

Kaufman, Stuart J., and Stephen R. Bowers. "Transnational Dimensions of Transnistrian Conflict." *Nationalities Papers* 26, no. 1 (1998): 129–46.

Kaufmann, Chaim. "Intervention in Ethnic and Ideological Civil Wars: Why One Can Be Done and the Other Can't." *Security Studies* 6, no. 1 (Autumn 1996): 62–100.

———. "Possible and Impossible Solutions to Ethnic Civil Wars." *International Security* 20, no. 4 (Spring 1996): 136–75.

———. "When All Else Fails: Ethnic Population Transfers and Partitions in the Twentieth Century." *International Security* 23, no. 2 (Fall 1998): 120–56.

Kimmerling, Baruch, and Joel S. Migdal. *Palestinians: The Making of a People.* Cambridge: Cambridge University Press, 1993.

Kretzmer, David. *The Legal Status of the Arabs in Israel.* Boulder, Colo.: Westview, 1990.

Kuperman, Alan. "The Other Lesson of Rwanda: Mediators Sometimes Do More Damage than Good." *SAIS Review* 16, no. 1 (Winter–Spring 1996): 221–40.

———. "Rwanda in Retrospect." *Foreign Affairs* 79, no. 1 (January–February 2000): 94–118.

Lachman, Shai. "Arab Rebellion and Terrorism in Palestine, 1929–1939." In *Zionism and Arabism in Palestine and Israel*, edited by Philip G. Kreyenbroek and Stefan Sperl. New York: Routledge, 1992.

Laitin, David. "Hegemony and Religious Conflict." In *Bringing the State Back In*, edited by D. Rueschemeyer, P. Evans, and T. Skocpol, 285–316. New York: Cambridge University Press, 1985.

———. *Identity in Formation: The Russian-Speaking Populations in the Near Abroad.* Ithaca, N.Y.: Cornell University Press, 1998.

———. "What Is a Language Community?" *American Journal of Political Science* 44, no. 1 (January 2000): 142–55.

Lake, David A., and Donald Rothchild. "Containing Fear: The Origins and Management of Ethnic Conflict." *International Security* 21, no. 2 (Fall 1996): 41–75.

Lambeth, Benjamin S. *The Transformation of American Air Power*. Ithaca, N.Y.: Cornell University Press, 2000.

Lawrence, David Aquila. "Iraqi Kurds Enjoy a De Facto State." *Christian Science Monitor*, May 3, 2000, 6.

Lesch, Ann Mosely. *Arab Politics in Palestine, 1917–1939: The Frustrations of a Nationalist Movement.* Ithaca, N.Y.: Cornell University Press, 1979.

Levine, Alicia. "Political Accommodation and the Prevention of Secessionist Violence." In *The International Dimensions of Internal Conflict*, edited by Michael E. Brown. Cambridge, Mass.: MIT Press, 1996.

Lewis, Bernard. *The Emergence of Modern Turkey.* New York: Oxford University Press, 1968.

Licklider, Roy. "The Consequences of Negotiated Settlements in Civil Wars, 1945–1993." *American Political Science Review* 89, no. 3 (September 1995): 681–90.

Licklider, Roy, ed., *Stopping the Killing: How Civil Wars End.* New York: New York University Press, 1993.

Lijphart, Arend. "Comparative Politics and the Comparative Method." *American Political Science Review* 65, no. 3 (September 1971): 682–93.

———. *Democracies: Patterns of Majoritarian and Consensus Government in Twenty-One Countries.* New Haven: Yale University Press, 1994.

———. *Democracy in Plural Societies.* New Haven: Yale University Press, 1977.

———. "Majority Rule in Theory and Practice: The Tenacity of a Flawed Paradigm." *International Social Science Journal* 129 (August 1991): 482–93.

———. "The Power Sharing Approach." In *Conflict and Peacemaking in Multiethnic Societies*, edited by Joseph Montville. New York: Lexington, 1991.

Lind, Michael. "In Defense of Liberal Nationalism." *Foreign Affairs* 73, no. 3 (May–June 1994): 87–99.

Lustick, Ian. *Arabs in the Jewish State: Israel's Control of a National Minority.* Austin: University of Texas Press, 1980.

———. "The Changing Political Role of Israeli Arabs." In *Elections in Israel—1988*, edited by Asher Arian and Michal Shamir. Boulder, Colo.: Westview, 1990.

———. "Creeping Binationalism within the Green Line." *New Outlook* 31, no. 7 (July 1988).

———. "Lijphart, Lakatos, and Consociationalism." *World Politics* 50 (October 1997): 88–117.

———, ed. *Palestinians under Israeli Rule.* New York: Garland, 1994.

———. "Stability in Deeply Divided Societies: Consociationalism versus Control." *World Politics* 31, no. 3 (April 1979): 325–44.

Mansfield, Edward D., and Jack Snyder. "Democratization and the Danger of War." *International Security* 20, no. 1 (Summer 1995): 5–38.

Marais, Octave. "The Political Evolution of the Berbers in Independent Morocco." In *Arabs and Berbers*, edited by E. Gellner and C. Micaud. London: Gerald Duckworth, 1972.

Marr, Phebe. *The Modern History of Iraq.* Boulder, Colo.: Westview, 1985.

Mason, T. David, and Patrick J. Fett. "How Civil Wars End: A Rational Choice Approach." *Journal of Conflict Resolution* 40, no. 4 (December 1996): 546–68.

McAllester, Matthew. "Rebuilding on Ruins." *Long Island Newsday,* June 21, 2000, 6.

McDowall, David. *A Modern History of the Kurds.* New York: I. B. Tauris, 1996.

———. *The Palestinians: The Road to Nationhood.* London: Minority Rights, 1994.

McGarry, John, and Brendan O'Leary. *The Politics of Antagonism: Understanding Northern Ireland.* Atlantic Highlands, N.J.: Athlone, 1993.

Menashri, David. *Education and the Making of Modern Iran.* Ithaca, N.Y.: Cornell University Press, 1992.

———. *Iran: A Decade of War and Revolution.* New York: Holmes & Meier, 1990.

Menkhaus, Ken. "Complex Emergencies, Humanitarianism, and National Security." *National Security Studies Quarterly* 4, no. 4 (Autumn 1998): 53–61.

Minns, Amina, and Nadia Hijab. *Citizens Apart: A Portrait of Palestinians in Israel.* New York: St. Martin's, 1990.

Miskel, James F., and Richard J. Norton. "The Paradox of Early Warning." *Journal of Humanitarian Assistance* (electronic journal), available at http://www.jha.sps.cam.ac.uk/a/a014.htm. Posted July 4, 1997.

Montagne, Robert. *The Berbers: Their Social and Political Organization.* London: Frank Cass, 1931.

"Morocco bans Berber cultural show." *Reuters,* February 5, 1996.

Morris, Benny. *1948 and After.* New York: Oxford University Press, 1994.

———. *Israel's Border Wars, 1948–1956.* New York: Oxford University Press, 1997.

Mueller, John. "The Banality of 'Ethnic War.'" *International Security* 25, no. 1 (Summer 2000): 42–70.

Munson, Henry, Jr. *The House of Si Abd Allah.* New Haven: Yale University Press, 1983.

Nakash, Yitzhak. *The Shi'is of Iraq.* Princeton: Princeton University Press, 1994.

Natsios, Andrew S. "Humanitarian Relief Intervention in Somalia: The Economics of Chaos." In *Learning from Somalia: The Lessons of Armed Humanitarian Intervention,* edited by Walter Clarke and Jeffrey Herbst. Boulder, Colo.: Westview, 1997.

Nevers, Renee de. "Democratization and Ethnic Conflict." *Survival* 35, no. 2 (Summer 1993): 31–48.

Norton, Augustus Richard. *Amal and the Shi'a.* Austin: University of Texas Press, 1987.

———. "Lebanon's Malaise." *Survival* 42, no. 2 (Winter 2000–2001): 35–50.

Norton, Augustus Richard, and Farhad Kazemi, eds. *Civil Society in the Middle East.* New York: Brill, 1994.

O'Brien, Conor Cruise. "The Wrath of Ages: Nationalism's Primordial Roots." *Foreign Affairs* 72, no. 5 (November–December 1993): 142–49.

O'Connor, Mike. "Bosnians Back Home, with Quiet U.S. Help." *New York Times,* July 29, 1997, A3.

O'Leary, John, and Brendan McGarry. *The Politics of Antagonism: Understanding Northern Ireland.* London: Athlone, 1993.

O'Neill, Bard. "Introduction." In *Insurgency in the Modern World,* edited by Bard E. O'Neill, William R. Heaton, and Donald J. Alberts. Boulder, Colo.: Westview, 1980.

Orentlicher, Diane F. "Citizenship and National Identity." In *International Law and Ethnic Conflict,* edited by David Wippman, 296–325. Ithaca, N.Y.: Cornell University Press, 1998.

Pakenham, Thomas. *The Scramble for Africa.* New York: Avon, 1991.

Palestine Partition Commission Report. London: Colonial Office, October 1938.

Palestine Royal Commission Report. London: Secretary of State for the Colonies: His Majesty's Stationery Office, July 1937.

Pape, Robert. *Bombing to Win.* Ithaca, N.Y.: Cornell University Press, 1996.

Parsons, Talcott. "Racial and Religious Differences as Factors in Group Tensions." In *Approaches to National Unity,* edited by Lyman Bryson, Louis Finkelstein, and Robert M. MacIver, 182–99. New York: Harper, 1945.

Perkins, Kenneth J. *Qaids, Captains, and Colons: French Military Administration in the Colonial Maghrib, 1844–1934.* New York: Africana, 1981.

Posen, Barry R. "Military Responses to Refugee Disasters." *International Security* 21, no. 1 (Summer 1996): 72–111.

———. "The Security Dilemma and Ethnic Conflict." *Survival* 35, no. 1 (Spring 1993): 27–47.

Putnam, Robert. *Making Democracy Work: Civic Traditions in Modern Italy.* Princeton: Princeton University Press, 1993.

Pye, Lucian. *Guerrilla Communism in Malaya: Its Social and Political Meaning.* Princeton: Princeton University Press, 1956.

Quandt, William B. "Lebanon, 1958, and Jordan, 1970." In *Force without War,* edited by Barry M. Blechman and Stephen S. Kaplan. Washington, D.C.: The Brookings Institution, 1978.

Quinlivan, James T. "Force Requirements in Stability Operations." *Parameters* 24, no. 4 (Winter 1995–96): 59–69.

Rabinovich, Itamar. *The War for Lebanon, 1970–1985.* Ithaca, N.Y.: Cornell University Press, 1985.

Rabushka, Alvin, and Kenneth Shepsle. *Politics in Plural Societies.* Columbus, Ohio: Charles E. Merrill, 1972.

Rai, Satya M. *Partition of the Punjab.* New York: Asia Publishing House, 1965.

Rekhess, Elie. "Israeli Arab Intelligentsia." *The Jerusalem Quarterly* 11 (Spring 1979).

———. "Israel's Arab Citizens and the Peace Process." In *Israel under Rabin,* edited by Robert O. Freedman. Boulder, Colo.: Westview, 1995.

———. "Red Lines and Realities." *The Jerusalem Post,* February 3, 1993.

Ricciardone, Francis J. "An American Diplomat's Perspectives on Kurds in the Global Arena." Remarks made at American University, April 17, 2000.

Richards, Alan, and John Waterbury. *A Political Economy of the Middle East: State, Class, and Economic Development.* Boulder, Colo.: Westview, 1990.

Rose, Gideon. "The Exit Strategy Delusion." *Foreign Affairs* 77, no. 1 (January–February 1998): 56–67.

Rose, William. "The Security Dilemma and Ethnic Conflict: Some New Hypotheses." *Security Studies* 9, no. 4 (Summer 2000): 1–51.

Roy, Olivier. *The Civil War in Tajikistan: Causes and Implications.* Washington, D.C.: United States Institute of Peace, 1993.

———. *The Lessons of the Soviet-Afghan War.* Adelphi Papers 259. London: International Institute for Strategic Studies, 1991.

Rubin, Barnett. "The Fragmentation of Tajikistan." *Survival* 35, no. 4 (Winter 1993): 71–91.

Rudge, David. "Rabin Campaigns in Arab Village." *The Jerusalem Post,* May 27, 1992.

Sagarin, Edward, and James Moneymaker. "Language and Nationalist, Separatist, and Secessionist Movements." In *Ethnic Autonomy—Comparative Dynamics,* edited by Raymond Hall. New York: Pergamon, 1979.

Sambanis, Nicholas. "Partition as a Solution to Ethnic War: An Empirical Critique of the Theoretical Literature." *World Politics* 52 (July 2000): 437–83.

Schaeffer, Robert. *Warpaths: The Politics of Partition.* New York: Hill and Wang, 1990.

Scham, Alan. *Lyautey in Morocco: Protectorate Administration, 1912–1925.* Berkeley: University of California Press, 1970.

Schama, Simon. *Landscape and Memory.* New York: Alfred A. Knopf, 1995.

Schiff, Ze'ev, and Ehud Ya'ari. *Israel's Lebanon War,* translated by Ina Friedman. New York: Simon and Schuster, 1984.

Seale, Patrick. "Asad: Between Institutions and Autocracy." In *Syria: Society, Culture, and Polity,* edited by Richard T. Antoun and Donald Quataert. Albany: State University of New York Press, 1991.

Segev, Tom. *One Palestine, Complete: Jews and Arabs under the British Mandate.* New York: Metropolitan Books, 2000.

Shammas, Anton. "Diary." In *Every Sixth Israeli: Relations between the Jewish Majority and the Arab Minority in Israel,* edited by Alouph Hareven. Jerusalem: Daf-Chen, 1983.

Shimshoni, Jonathan. *Israel and Conventional Deterrence.* Ithaca, N.Y.: Cornell University Press, 1988.

Shlaim, Avi. *Collusion across the Jordan: King Abdullah, the Zionist Movement, and the Partition of Palestine.* Oxford: Clarendon, 1988.

Shulsky, Abram. *Silent Warfare: Understanding the World of Intelligence.* New York: Brassey's, 1991.

Smith, Anthony. *The Ethnic Origins of Nations.* Oxford: Blackwell, 1986.

Smith, M. G. *The Plural Society in the British West Indies.* Berkeley: University of California Press, 1965.

Smooha, Sammy. *Arabs and Jews in Israel: Change and Continuity in Mutual Intolerance.* Boulder, Colo.: Westview, 1992.

———. *Arabs and Jews in Israel: Conflicting and Shared Attitudes in a Divided Society.* Boulder, Colo.: Westview, 1989.

———. *The Orientation and Politicization of the Arab Minority in Israel.* Haifa, Israel: University of Haifa, 1984.

Smooha, Sammy, and Theodore Hanf. "The Diverse Modes of Conflict-Regulation in Deeply Divided Societies." *International Journal of Comparative Sociology* 33, nos. 1–2 (January 1992): 26–47.

Smooha, Sammy, and John E. Hofman. "Some Problems of Arab-Jewish Coexistence in Israel." *Middle East Review* 9, no. 2 (Winter 1976–77): 5–14.

Snyder, Jack. "Nationalism and the Crisis of the Post-Soviet State." *Survival* 35, no. 1 (1993): 5–26.

———. "The New Nationalism." In *The Domestic Bases of Grand Strategy,* edited by Richard Rosecrance and Arthur A. Stein, 200. Ithaca, N.Y.: Cornell University Press, 1993.

———. "Perceptions of the Security Dilemma in 1914." In *Psychology and Deterrence,* edited by Robert Jervis, Richard Ned Lebow, and Janice Gross Stein, 151–61. Baltimore: Johns Hopkins University Press, 1985.

———. *From Voting to Violence.* New York: W.W. Norton, 2000.

Snyder, Jack, and Robert Jervis. "Civil War and the Security Dilemma." In *Civil Wars, Insecurity, and Intervention,* edited by Barbara F. Walter and Jack Snyder, 15–37. New York: Columbia University Press, 1999.

Solonar, V. "Hatred and Fear on Both Banks of the Dniester." *New Times International,* April 14, 1992, 8–9.

State Failure Task Force Report: Phase II Findings. McLean, Va.: Science Applications International Corporation, July 31, 1998.

Statistical Abstract of Israel 1993. Jerusalem: Hemed, 1993.

Stedman, Stephen John. "Spoiler Problems in Peace Processes." *International Security* 22, no. 2 (Fall 1997): 5–53.

Stubbs, Richard. "Malaysia: Avoiding Ethnic Strife in Deeply Divided Societies." In *Conflict and Peacemaking in Multiethnic Societies,* edited by Joseph Montville. New York: Lexington, 1991.

Tadjbakhsh, Shahrbanou. "Tajikistan: From Freedom to War." *Current History* 93, no. 582 (1994): 173–77.

Taw, Jennifer M., and Alan Vick. "From Sideshow to Center Stage: The Role of the Army and Air Force in Military Operations other than War." In *Strategic Appraisal 1997,* edited by Zalmay M. Khalilzad. Santa Monica: RAND, 1997.

Teson, Fernando R. "Ethnicity, Human Rights, and Self-Determination." In *International Law and Ethnic Conflict,* edited by David Wippman, 86–111. Ithaca, N.Y.: Cornell University Press, 1998.

Tilly, Charles, ed. *The Formation of National States in Western Europe.* Princeton: Princeton University Press, 1975.

United Nations Human Rights Field Operation Report, cited in UN Department of Humanitarian Affairs Integrated Regional Information Network for the Great Lakes. "IRIN Weekly Roundup 24–97 of Main Events in the Great Lakes Region (26 Sept.–2 Oct. 1997)." Available at http://wwwnotes.reliefweb.int:81/. Accessed on February 4, 1999.

Upton, Joseph M. *The History of Modern Iran: An Interpretation.* Cambridge, Mass.: Harvard University Press, 1960.

Van Dam, Nikolaos. *The Struggle for Power in Syria: Politics and Society under Asad and the Ba'th Party.* New York: I. B. Tauris, 1996.

Van Evera, Stephen. *Causes of War: Power and the Root of Conflict.* Ithaca, N.Y.: Cornell University Press, 1999.

———. "The Cult of the Offensive and the Origins of the First World War." *International Security* 9, no. 1 (Summer 1984): 58–107.

———. *Guide to Methods for Students of Political Science.* Cambridge, Mass.: MIT Press, 1997.

———. "Hypotheses on Nationalism and War." *International Security* 18, no. 4 (Spring 1994): 5–39.

———. "Primed for Peace: Europe after the Cold War." *International Security* 15, no. 3 (Winter 1990–91): 7–57.

Volkan, Vamik D. "Psychoanalytic Aspects of Ethnic Conflicts." In *Conflict and Peacemaking in Multiethnic Societies,* edited by Joseph Montville. New York: Lexington, 1991.

Walter, Barbara F. "The Critical Barrier to Civil War Settlement." *International Organization* 51, no. 3 (Summer 1997): 335–64.

———. "Introduction." In *Civil Wars, Insecurity, and Intervention,* edited by Barbara F. Walter and Jack Snyder, 1–14. New York: Columbia University Press, 1999.

Waterbury, John. "Bargaining for Segmentarity." In *Tribe and State: Essays in Honor of David Montgomery Hart,* edited by David M. Hart, E. G. H. Joffe, and C. R. Pennell. Wisbech, England: Middle East and North African Studies Press, 1990.

———. *Commander of the Faithful.* New York: Columbia University Press, 1970.

———. "Tribalism, Trade, and Politics." In *Arabs and Berbers,* edited by E. Gellner and C. Micaud. London: Gerald Duckworth, 1972.

Weber, Eugen. *Peasants into Frenchmen: The Modernization of Rural France, 1870–1914.* Stanford, Calif.: Stanford University Press, 1976.

Weber, Max. *Economy and Society.* Berkeley: University of California Press, 1978.

Weiner, Myron. "Bad Neighbors, Bad Neighborhoods: An Inquiry into the Causes of Refugee Flows." *International Security* 21, no. 1 (Summer 1996): 5–42.

———. *Sons of the Soil.* Princeton: Princeton University Press, 1978.

Welsh, David. "Domestic Politics and Ethnic Conflict." In *Ethnic Conflict and International Security,* edited by Michael E. Brown. Princeton: Princeton University Press, 1993.

Wippman, David. "Introduction: Ethnic Claims and International Law." In *International Law and Ethnic Conflict,* edited by David Wippman, 1–25. Ithaca, N.Y.: Cornell University Press, 1998.

Wolf, Eric. *Peasant Wars of the Twentieth Century.* New York: Harper & Row, 1969.

Woodward, Susan L. *Balkan Tragedy: Chaos and Dissolution after the Cold War.* Washington, D.C.: The Brookings Institution, 1995.

Young, Crawford. *Ideology and Development in Africa.* New Haven: Yale University Press, 1982.

Zartman, I. W. *Ripe for Resolution: Conflict and Intervention in Africa.* New York: Oxford University Press, 1989.

Zisser, Eyal. "Hizballah: New Course or Continued Warfare?" *Middle East Review of International Affairs* 4, no. 3 (September 2000), electronic version.

Zonis, Martin. *The Political Elite of Iran.* Princeton: Princeton University Press, 1971.

Zureik, Elia T. *The Palestinians in Israel: A Study in Internal Colonialism.* London: Routledge & Kegan Paul, 1979.

INDEX